The Paint Diva
METHOD

A Practical guide to choosing paint colors for every room in your home.

Cindy Gelormini

Copyright © 2023 by Cynthia Gelormini

"The Paint Diva", "The Paint Diva Method", and all contents of this book are covered under copyright. All rights reserved solely by the author, including the right to reproduce this book or portions thereof in any form whatsoever. No part of this book may be reproduced in any form without the written permission of the author.

All opinions and thoughts expressed in this book are solely those of the author. Mention of specific companies or organizations does not imply that they endorse this book, its author, or the publisher.

All trademarks, logos and brand names are the property of their respective owners.

Photography: Joe DeVico, Christen Snyder, Cindy Gelormini
People in the Kids' Room Chapter: Christen Holly Photography
Cover Photos and Headshots: Carley Storm
Cartoons: Cindy Gelormini
Graphic Design: Joe DeVico, Jordan Detlet
Cover Design and Prepress: Transcend Studio

Paperback ISBN: 979-8-88955-406-6
Ebook ISBN: 979-8-88955-409-7

Dedication

This book took over seven years to write. It began in 2016 when I left the paint store and went out on my own as a Color Consultant, and I finally figured out how to actually write out the Method. Then I needed photos, so I looked up clients who would have the rooms for pictures that I needed and we went to their homes taking photos.

In 2017 as we were working on the editing process, my son Robbie, who was profoundly Autistic and had seizures, went to heaven unexpectedly. So, I stopped working on this book and began another project of a children's book series called "Robbie's World and His Spectrum of Adventures" about a little penguin with Autism. It's a series of 12 stories, and I also painted all of the illustrations. The books were released in April 2021 for Autism Awareness Month. It was followed by a whirlwind of podcasts and TV interviews, and I started the Robbie's World Foundation. (Learn more on my website RobbiesWorldBook.com)

Once that book project was over, I decided it was time once again to pick up this project. As I picked it back up and read through it, I realized that I was still missing photos. So, I went back to more clients' homes and took more photos. I got a new graphic designer, and we worked on weekends to pull it together. Now here it is 2023 and it's finally done!

I would like to thank my husband Robert for always supporting me in all of my projects and ventures and being my biggest cheerleader. He even had to take care of me for 6 weeks in the middle of it all when I fell off a ladder and broke my right wrist! He's the best and I could do none of the things I do without him.

Thank you to my sister Christen for jumping in and taking last minute photos and for always supporting me. Thank you to all of my clients who have trusted me with their homes over all these years, and especially to those who allowed us to come in to take photos and share their homes with the world.

Thank you to Jordan Detlet for helping me with all the graphic design, for being so patient and sweet, and never rolling her eyes at all of my changes!

I'd like to thank Scott McGrath, owner of McGrath's Paint and Hardware, for hiring me in 2005, for trusting me and giving me the freedom to develop the color area on my own while allowing the Paint Diva to be birthed!

Most importantly, I'd like to thank my Heavenly Father, for salvation and for giving me any gifts and talents that I may have. Thank you, Lord, for giving me eyes that see, ears that hear, a voice to speak, hands to do the work, and for guiding my steps throughout my life. I love you and look forward to seeing my son once again and spending eternity with you in heaven.

Part 1: The Basics

Introduction	1
Color Basics	9
Color Seasons	17
Fan Decks and Color Collections	36
Toning Down and Fixing Colors	47
My Favorite Colors	55
Paint Color Trends	59
The Paint Diva Method	63
The Rule Book	71

Part 2: Room by Room

Kitchens	75
Family Rooms	101
Living Rooms	115
Dining Rooms	123
Foyers and Hallways	143
Bathrooms	157
Master/Primary Bedrooms	197

Contents:

Page	Section
207	Guest Bedrooms
213	Kids' Bedrooms
229	Playrooms
235	Mud and Laundry Rooms
241	Offices
249	Sunrooms and Porches
255	Basements, Garages, & Bonus Rooms

Part 3: The Next Steps

Page	Section
267	Choosing Trim Colors
281	Ceilings
291	Sampling Paint Colors
294	Paint Basics
301	Mixing Custom Colors
305	Problem Solving
313	Communication and Mediation
319	Worksheet & Index

Introduction

Growing up I was always good at art and enjoyed it, but after graduation I got an office job. I used to sketch a lot during down time, and during the holidays I was asked to paint murals on the glass windows. I didn't even know what kind of paint to use and had to ask at the craft store! After the birth of my twins, I left that job and became an aerobics instructor at a women's health club where I was able to put my girls in the nursery while I taught my classes. One day a woman came to paint a mural in the nursery and I was blown away at the idea of painting murals. I went home and painted my first mural in my girls' Bedroom of Mickey & Minnie, Winnie the Pooh, and Snow White and the Seven Dwarfs. I began to learn how to use a paint brush and to work with paint. I painted the mirrors at the health club for the holidays, and I eventually began to paint clothing and sold it at the club.

We bought a new house where I practiced painting on every wall and floor in the house. I painted murals in the kids' rooms, I sponge painted and stenciled the Living Room and Dining Room, striped the Bathroom, and then learned the words "Trompe L'oeil" (fool the eye) and "faux" (fake). I painted faux area rugs, faux topiaries, painted my Kitchen cabinets to look like they had faux dishes and faux baskets of fruit, and the Basement had a faux barn door with a horse! It was a faux-pocalypse! Eventually the health club went out of business and I went to work at the YWCA where I painted murals in the nursery and an Interior Designer hired me to paint an Italian Restaurant. Both of these jobs led to a business painting murals and faux finishes for Designers and my own clients.

After 10 years of this, in 2005 I could see that the faux finish fad was coming to a close and I was going to have to reinvent myself. To be totally honest, I was really sick of rag rolling walls, and it seemed that everyone who wanted a faux finish lived in new construction homes with 20-foot ceilings and I was afraid of heights! I decided it was time to retire from painting.

I went to work in a paint store as their Interior Designer and Color Consultant. It turned out that I was pretty darned good at the job! There really was no such thing as a "Color Consultant" back then and most people were shocked that I was there to help them. They didn't know that someone like me even existed, but they were thrilled to have me there to help. After a while I began to create formulas that seemed to work for everyone. For a while Benjamin Moore had something called the "Expert's Exchange," which was sort of a "Dear Abby" page where people could write in looking for help choosing colors and I was one of their Color Experts who wrote in the answers. I did a couple of seminars for Benjamin Moore and later began to do my own seminars and public speaking engagements to talk to people about how to choose paint colors using the formulas I had created.

One thing I learned through my years of painting and working in the store is that most people really have a hard time visualizing how a room will look once it's painted. My job was to help people visualize their homes. I learned Benjamin Moore paint colors inside and out and knew which colors would work, or not work, and why. My years painting faux finishes helped to train my eyes to be able to see colors that other people typically couldn't. I went to hundreds and hundreds of homes to choose paint colors for clients, as well as helping thousands of customers in the store. As the years went on, I found myself repeating the same speeches to all of my clients and customers about colors, what will happen to them, and about which colors to use in which room.

One of my last murals was of mountains and vineyards outside of a local restaurant.

Here I am busy as the Paint Diva helping a store customer, a client at home, speaking at a seminar, and hosting a cable TV show.

So, you may be wondering how I got the name "The Paint Diva". Have you ever seen the Seinfeld episode of "The Soup Nazi"? Well, there was a person in another town that tended to get impatient with customers, so people nicknamed them "The Paint Nazi". When I went to work at the paint store I began to hear stories about them. Then one day, someone walked in and said to me "So you're the Paint Diva!" Oh no. I asked if they were confusing me with someone else. They said, "Oh no, that's the Paint Nazi. They are mean. You are the nice one. Don't worry, it's a compliment. It means you know your stuff." Whew! I decided to keep the name and use it for my website. Since then, I have earned many pseudonyms such as The Paint Guru, The Paint Doctor, The Paint Jeanie, and even The Paint Whisperer. I laughed every time they came up with a new one, but it just shows that they were amazed that I can see colors and visualize them in their rooms.

In 2016 I decided to go out on my own as an independent Color Consultant and Stager, and got my Real Estate License. I became very focused on adding to the resale value of a home and helping homeowners create homes that sell. I worked with hundreds of new home buyers and knew what they liked, so that made it easy for me to help sellers create that look that buyers want. Leaving the store also opened the door for me to use any brand of paint I wanted. I met some people from Sherwin Williams and learned about their paints. Now I can help my clients with color selection no matter which brand they choose.

Eventually I began getting calls and emails from people all over the country who needed help with choosing paint colors. They said there was no one in their area that could do what I do. Basically, what I have learned is that people need help with how to choose paint colors, and there doesn't seem to be very many color consultants like me out there to help them. It was then that I decided it was time to write the book. I tried to make it simple and easy to follow and to get right to the point without too much flowery language. When I choose paint colors for people, I'm very quick and decisive. I know which colors will work and know the 3,500 colors that will NOT work. I don't like to waste time. So, this book gets right to the point! I hope you find it helpful.

Find me on Facebook and Instragram
"THE PAINT DIVA"

Or visit my website
www.PaintDivaNJ.com

Cindy Gelormini

The Paint Diva

Preface

Have you ever been lost when you were driving and turned down the radio so you could concentrate better?

This book and the "rules" and guidelines outlined are here to help drown out that noise and make it easier to focus.

Eliminating Confusion.

My work differs from a typical Interior Designer because they usually focus on designing one or two rooms at a time and only work with a handful of clients each year. Occasionally they get to design a whole house, but it usually takes months, if not a year or two to finish the entire project.
I don't have the luxury of spending months to work on clients' homes, I have **one hour**. Yep, I'm not kidding. Most of my clients are painting the whole house, and *I need to choose colors for their entire house in an hour*.

These days I do about 400 in-home consultations per year and helped approximately 1,500 customers per year while working at the paint store. If you do the math, that's nearly 4,000 Paint Diva clients and over 16,000 store customers over 15 years. That's just the amount of *people*, not the amount of *rooms*. If I were to total the amount of *rooms* I've consulted on, it would be in the tens of thousands. Then, if you add the 20 years of painting murals and faux finishes, that's a lot of paint!

Most people, especially if they are renovating or just bought a new house, are completely overwhelmed at the task of deciding on paint color choices. They seem to dread choosing paint colors about as much as they dread having a root canal. My goal for this book is to make it as quick, easy, and painless as possible. When choosing colors in the paint store, most people are completely overwhelmed with too many colors to choose from. As a consultant, I would ask a series of questions about the room, and quickly eliminated 3,494 colors that would not work. Customers were always pleasantly surprised at how painless and easy I made the process of choosing paint colors for them. Often people would show me a dozen colors they were contemplating, and I would quickly begin to narrow the choices by pointing out; "This is too pink, this is too green, this doesn't match, but THIS one works." As I did this, I would pull away all of the chips that didn't work leaving them with 1-2 colors that WOULD work. Just as I pulled away chips from customers in the store, this book is designed to help you remove the colors that don't work and simply narrow it down to the few best paint colors for your space.

In working with clients over the years I found myself offering similar advice to multiple clients, and eventually came up with a system of "rules" and formulas that seemed to work for every room in the house. Now, rules are always meant to be broken, but I have used them thousands of times and they really seem to work. My "rules" or my "method" is simply guidelines to follow when choosing colors for each room.

My hope is that when you follow my guidelines in this book, choosing paint colors will no longer be a stressful or difficult process.

With that in mind, I can't stress enough...

This is not a book on Interior Design!

The photos featured in this book are

REAL HOMES owned by REAL PEOPLE.

This book is not written to provide you with decorating inspiration or design ideas. The photos featured in this book were taken in homes of my actual clients. None of them are staged in photo studios or mocked up to look pretty to be in a magazine. Some have hired Interior Designers but most of them decorate their homes themselves. You'll see all different styles and types of homes. It's reality. This book was written for people just like my clients, everyday people who are not necessarily good at Interior Design. They just need help choosing colors! So, it's not written to tell you how to decorate your rooms, it's written simply to provide you with all the tools you'll need to choose paint colors for your rooms in a very practical way.

*Note: I am an independent color consultant. I am not employed by Benjamin Moore or Sherwin Williams. Any opinions expressed in this book are my own.

Part 1

In this first section we will discuss colors, undertones, Color Seasons Palettes, Fan Decks, The Method and how to begin.

Color Basics

Read the Entire Book Before You Begin!

If you're like me, you'll probably want to skip all of the beginning chapters and just jump straight to the chapters on choosing colors for each room. That would be like trying to put something together without reading the directions first, and then when you're all done you have a couple pieces left over. I'm going to mention things like warm, muddy colors on your fan deck and if you don't read the beginning you'll have no idea what I'm talking about. This book is laid out in exactly the order that you will need to follow. Consider it "step one, step two, step three".

Understanding my Language.

When I was in pre-school I loved to play with a toy color wheel. Then as I got older art class was one of my favorite subjects. As an adult I had assumed everyone learned about art. After many years of choosing paint colors for clients I learned that most people have never held a paint brush, were never taught the basics about mixing colors together and have never even seen a color wheel! They don't even know which two colors you mix together to make green.

If I began choosing colors for clients by showing them the color wheel and talked about Secondary and Tertiary colors, Analogous or Triadic Color Schemes, hue, value and saturation, my clients would look at me like I had two heads. So I describe colors in very basic, easy to understand language. Sometimes I use correct terms, but other times I use my own made-up color language. It's sort of a Spanglish, but I try to use terms that make what I'm trying to say the easiest to understand by the average person.

In order to understand what I'm talking about when describing color, here are the definitions of a couple terms you will hear me use repeatedly in this book. It may all sound like Greek to you now, but as you work your way through the book eventually it will all begin to make sense.

Understanding Undertones

In order to begin to see and understand undertones let's take it step-by-step and begin with the basics of color.

Primary Colors

Red, Yellow and Blue are the primary colors.
All colors begin here.

Blue + Yellow = Green

Blue + Red = Violet

Yellow + Red = Orange

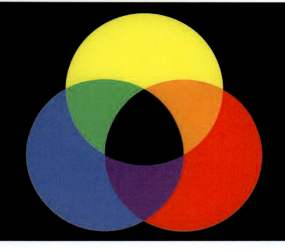

Variations

If you keep blending you can get variations of the Secondary colors. For instance, green is made by mixing blue and yellow. But you can create other variations of green. By adding more blue you can create a bluish green. Or you can add some yellow to make a yellowy green.

10

Warm Colors and Cool Colors

 Warm = The color of fire, as in yellow, orange and red. Warm colors have a drop of these colors in them.

 Cool = The color of water and ice, as in blue and silver. Cool colors will have some blue or gray in them.

Over the years I have found that most people tend to gravitate toward either warm or cool colors, and some like a little mix of both.

Warm

People who prefer warmer colors tend to like yellows, greens and warm beiges. They like feeling warm and cozy, dislike gray, and feel that blue is too cold.

Cool

People who like cooler colors like gray and blue tend to strongly dislike warm colors like yellow or peach. They like their home to be light and bright with lots of windows and light.

Mixed

Some people don't have very strong opinions about color and tend to like a little mix of both warm and cool.

Unsure

Many people just aren't really sure what they like! If you're not sure then take a look at things you buy like your furnishings and accessories, and even things like your clothing and jewelry. You'll start to notice a pattern of colors that you tend to prefer.

Warm Colors:

A warm beige has a yellow, gold or peach undertone.

A warm gray has beige in it.

A warm green is more yellow than blue.

A warm blue is a greenish blue because it has a drop of yellow in it.

A warm pink is slightly peach because it has a drop of yellow in it.

A warm red is more orangey than dark red.

A warm yellow has a hint of orange, like the color of a sunset.

A warm purple is more of a pinky purple than a blue purple.

A warm white is creamy and may have a drop of yellow.

Cool Colors:

A cool beige is taupe because it has gray in it.

A cool gray is silver and can tend to turn blue.

A cool green is more blue or gray. These are mint, teal green, aqua and sage greens.

A cool blue is a true blue, gray blue, purple blue.

A cool pink is slightly purple because it has a drop of blue.

A cool red is almost burgundy because it has a drop of blue.

A cool yellow can be slightly green, because it has a drop of blue.

A cool purple is more blue, like periwinkle.

A cool white is a stark white, almost blue.

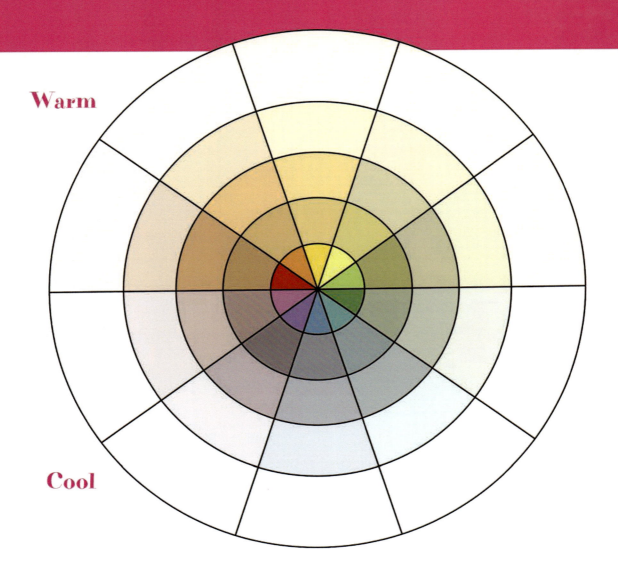

Warm

Cool

Neutrals

Now let's take the color wheel further and discuss neutrals. If we take yellowy green and add a touch of brown to it now you'll get a more olive green. Or make a bluer green a little more gray and then you'll have a sage green. Look at the beiges in the Neutral Color Wheel and you'll see some have a bit of yellow in them, some have a bit of peach in them, and some have a bit of red in them.

Practical Use: Imagine you have a tile floor that is beige. Most beige tiles look like the beige in the red section of this color wheel. Now imagine that you want to paint the walls in a beige color from the yellow section. They will clash! Even though both colors are "beige", when you put them together the floor will look pink and the walls will appear yellow.

Are you beginning to see the difference yet?

Undertones and Saturation

Undertones

In the following chapters when I say things like "Choose a color with yellow in it," that doesn't mean you can only use yellow. It means you can use a color with yellow **undertones**. An *undertone* is a color that isn't necessarily obvious until you compare your color to others in the same family. For example, these three blocks are all "beige," however, the one on the left has a yellow undertone, the one in the middle has a peach undertone and the one right has a green undertone.

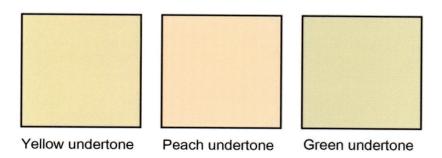

Yellow undertone   Peach undertone   Green undertone

Saturation

Being more "saturated" means there is more tint in the color, which makes the color stronger. That means it becomes either brighter or darker.

While working with clients I have noticed that most people are afraid of colors being too dark or intense and tend to prefer colors that are very light. If that's you, then you'll probably be choosing light and off-white colors and the undertones will be very subtle. Occasionally people prefer a mid-toned color that is a little deeper and with a bit more contrast. Deep colors are more saturated. I like to use deep colors in only one or two rooms for a little "Wow factor" or as an accent wall. Then I'll use plenty of neutrals to balance it out.

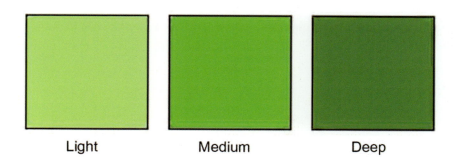

Light   Medium   Deep

"Clear Bright", "In-Between" and "Muddy" Colors.

Most people are afraid of color and worry that colors will be too bright, too dark, or too intense. I am forever trying to tone colors down. I break the colors down into three categories to help clients understand how bright or muted their colors will appear on the wall. Basically colors are either **Clear Bright Colors** or **Muddy Colors**, and then there is an **"In-Between"** category. I know "muddy" is not a pretty word, but it gets the point across in my explanations and when I show "clear bright" paint chips next to a "muddy" chip, people understand what I'm trying to say. In the chapter *Toning Down and Fixing Colors* we will discuss toning down colors, which occurs by adding a touch of beige or gray to a color. **In-between colors** are the ones that add beige or gray a little bit, and **muddy colors** add them a lot.

*Note: Since I rarely ever use clear bright colors you will not find any in the *Color Seasons* palettes.

Here is an Example:

When I choose a turquoise color, there are three different places to look for turquoise depending on how intense you want the color to be. First, there are colors that are clear bright turquoise . Then there are others that are definitely turquoise but have gray in them so they are not too bright. Then others are very gray with just a hint of a turquoise in them.

Clear Bright turquoise will appear very bright. Even the lightest version of this color will still look bright without some gray to tone it down.

In-Between adds some gray to tone it down a little bit. But it will still definitely appear turquoise on the wall.

Muddy is mostly gray with a touch of turquoise. This is the softest version of the color.

*Note: Whenever I mention to use a Muddy Color, this includes In-Between Colors as well.

Clear Bright Colors

These colors are bright and strong and look like a highlighter. Lemon yellows, lime greens, bright orange, really red and royal blue. The deepest hues are mixed into a clear base which we will discuss in the **Paint Basics** chapter. When they go up on the wall they will be very bright. Even the lightest colors on the strip will still appear bright. I rarely use clear brights. Kids love these colors, but they're usually too stimulating for their Bedrooms. They are good for fun rooms like Playrooms, Workout Rooms, Music Rooms, Laundry Rooms and work well as accent walls.

In-Between Colors

These are colors that have a muddy quality. They're not as dull as muddy colors and yet are not as bright as clear bright colors. If I definitely want a stronger color but don't want it to be too neon bright, I'll choose the in-between colors. A good example is if a young girl wants her room to be purple, she'll want a clear bright purple. But her mom will want to tone it down and choose a muddy gray purple. The compromise will be an in-between purple. It's enough color to satisfy the girl, and yet won't be too overwhelming for the mom.

Muddy Colors

These colors are more opaque and are beige and gray, or have beige or gray undertones. Yellows have beige in them to look more like soft gold. Greens are more olive, sage or khaki. Blues are gray-blues like denim and slate. Orange looks more like pumpkin or squash. Usually, I will choose a muddy color first. But if the lighting in the room is not very good and the color looks too washed out, I will move on to the "in-between" colors for a slightly brighter version of the color. They are still muddy, but yet not too intense.

Color Seasons

When choosing colors for the whole house, you'll want the colors on the first floor to "flow". That means you want them to look good together when you see the colors room-to-room and you'll want them to have **similar undertones**. For instance, if you want all gray undertones, then every color you choose should have some gray in it. That includes gray beiges, gray blues, gray greens etc. When I choose colors for my clients I tend to choose colors that have an overall calming effect. Most are soft and light and they have the same undertones so that the transition from room to room is easy on the eyes, and only one room is dark or bright.

To make the undertone and warm and cool concepts easier to grasp I have divided colors into seasons.

Winter colors are soft, subtle, cool grays and blues. They are clean and modern and create a very calming environment.

Spring colors are a warmer grays and taupes. A more feminine mix of warmer blush pinks and cool gray greens, they are soft and subtle, making a very calm and relaxing environment.

Summer colors are warm and vibrant, bolder and more fun. They fit traditional homes, as well as cottages and beach houses and are great for color lovers.

Autumn colors are warm, bold and earthy. They are more masculine and go great with natural wood and leather furniture.

Changing Seasons.

If you want to jump to another Season of color for a room then by all means, go ahead. I'm just trying to simplify the task for you. This is how I choose colors, but for you these are just gentle guidelines. All of the colors in each Season are just suggestions.

Trim Choices for Each Season.

We will discuss choosing colors for trim at length in the **Trim** chapter on page 267. In this chapter I am offering suggestions for trim colors that have similar undertones to the colors in each season. The trim color you choose should be consistent in each room of the main living area of the home. This is one of the main reasons to choose colors with similar undertones so that you can choose one trim color that will work with every room.

*Note: Due to printing, photography, and lighting, the color representations in this book will probably appear slightly different than the actual paint colors. I recommend you visit the paint store and obtain actual fan decks or paint chips to get a better representation of the actual colors.

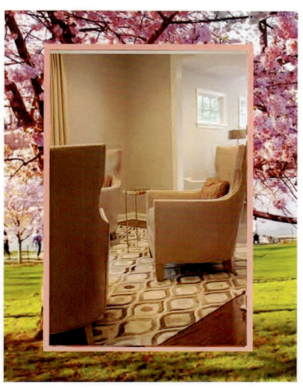

Winter

Winter has cool grays and blues. As the earth becomes quiet and peaceful during a snowfall, this collection contains off-whites and the colors are very soft, neutral, calming and spa-like. During the winter the trees have no leaves and flowers fade away, so this collection has greens that are very cool, gray sage greens. There is nothing in the warm family so there are no yellow, orange, or red undertones. Even the beiges are not beige but actually cooler taupes.

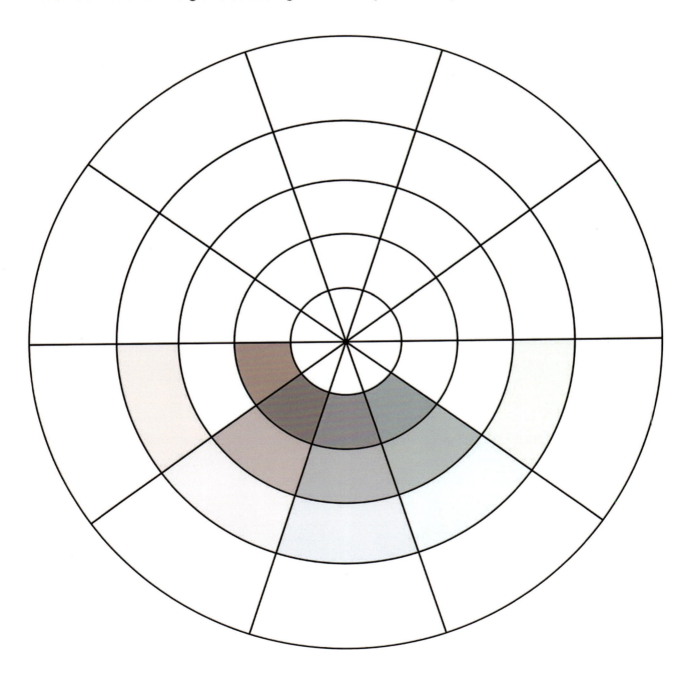

Sherwin Williams Winter Palette

SW 7006 **Extra White** 257-C1	SW 7005 **Pure White** 255-C1	SW 7757 **High Reflective White** 256-C1			
SW 6252 **Ice Cube** 257-C3	SW 6084 **Modest White** 267-C5	SW 7656 **Rhinestone** 257-C4	SW 6246 **North Star** 225-C1	SW 6224 **Mountain Air** 273-C1	SW 6525 **Rarified Air** 273-C4
SW 7666 **Fleur de Sel** 258-C3	SW 6071 **Popular Gray** 242-C1	SW 6254 **Lazy Gray** 234-C2	SW 6248 **Jubilee** 225-C3	SW 6218 **Tradewind** 219-C1	SW 9136 **Lullaby** 221-C1
SW 7064 **Passive** 236-C1	SW 6072 **Versatile Gray** 242-C2	SW 6255 **Morning Fog** 234-C3	SW 6243 **Distance** 224-C6	SW 6213 **Halcyon Green** 218-C3	SW 9138 **Stardew** 221-C3
SW 7658 **Gray Clouds** 238-C3	SW 6080 **Utterly Beige** 198-C3	SW 6256 **Serious Gray** 234-C5	SW 6249 **Storm Cloud** 225-C5	SW 6221 **Moody Blue** 219-C5	SW 7603 **Poolhouse** 280-C3
SW 7067 **Cityscape** 236-C5	SW 6075 **Garret Gray** 242-C6	SW 6257 **Gibraltar** 234-C6	SW 7602 **Indigo Batik** 224-C7	SW 6222 **Riverway** 219-C6	SW 9178 **In the Navy** 253-C3

Benjamin Moore Winter Palette

OC-149 Decorator's White	OC-65 Chantilly Lace	OC-152 Super White			
1478 Horizon	858 Athena	2124-50 Bunny Gray	2120-70 Stone White	2139-60 Green Tint	2129-70 Silver Cloud
HC-171 Wickham Gray	989 Alphano Beige	2133-60 Sidewalk Gray	2127-60 Feather Gray	HC-144 Palladian Blue	1633 Brittany Blue
HC-170 Stonington Gray	1541 London Fog	2133-50 Pigeon Gray	2130-50 New Hope Gray	704 Del Mar Blue	2129-50 Winter Lake
HC-169 Coventry Gray	991 Grége Avenue	2133-40 Charcoal Linen	2130-40 Black Pepper	2136-40 Aegean Teal	2129-40 Normandy
AF-705 Cinder	1462 Gray Mountain	1630 Ocean Floor	2128-30 Evening Dove	713 Polished Slate	HC-156 Van Deusen Blue

Spring

Spring is still cool but just a bit warmer than Winter. In this collection you'll find grays that are a touch warmer, and the beiges are cooler tones of greige and taupe. As green leaves begin to bud in in the Spring, you'll find that these greens are still very subtle, cool, blueish-gray-greens. Trees and flowers begin to bud with pink and purple flowers so you'll find a hint of blushy pinks and slightly lavender grays.

Both Winter and Spring colors can be intermingled.

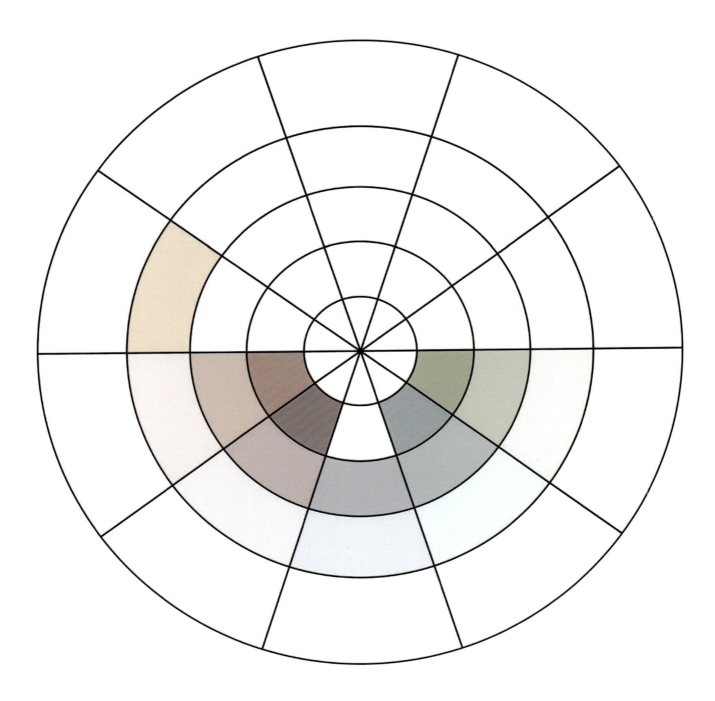

23

Sherwin Williams Spring Palette

SW 7004 Snowbound 256-C2	SW 7000 Ibis White 260-C2	SW 7100 Arcade White 260-C1			
SW 7028 Incredible White 256-C4	SW 7516 Kestrel White 266-C5	SW 6322 Intimate White 268-C6	SW 6008 Individual White 231-C1	SW 6168 Moderne White 258-C6	SW 6238 Icicle 273-C3
SW 7029 Agreeable Gray 243-C1	SW 7036 Accessible Beige 249-C1	SW 6057 Malted Milk 195-C1	SW 6009 Imagine 231-C2	SW 6190 Filmy Green 214-C1	SW 6239 Upward 224-C1
SW 7632 Modern Gray 283-C1	SW 7037 Balanced Beige 249-C2	SW 6323 Romance 114-C1	SW 6010 Flexible Gray 231-C3	SW 6177 Softened Green 213-C2	SW 9151 Daphne 224-C4
SW 7641 Colonnade Gray 283-C2	SW 7030 Anew Gray 243-C2	SW 6030 Artistic Taupe 192-C2	SW 9158 Coquina 230-C4	SW 9128 Green Onyx 213-C4	SW 6243 Distance 224-C6
SW 7643 Pussywillow 283-C4	SW 7031 Mega Greige 243-C3	SW 2704 Merlot 276-C7	SW 6272 Plum Brown 229-C7	SW 6187 Rosemary 215-C6	SW 6244 Naval 253-C6

Benjamin Moore Spring Palette

AF-15 Steam	OC-145 Atrium White	OC-151 White			
OC-26 Silver Satin	OC-23 Classic Gray	OC-72 Pink Damask	1458 Silver Bells	2141-60 Titanium	2127-70 Cascade White
OC-27 Balboa Mist	982 Cedar Key	1163 Tissue Pink	2109-60 Portland Gray	506 Silver Sage	2130-60 Iced Slate
OC-28 Collingwood	983 Smokey Taupe	AF-190 Boudoir	2109-50 Elephant Gray	508 Tree Moss	2128-40 Oxford Gray
1550 Cumulus Cloud	984 Stone Hearth	2110-40 Seaside Sand	2114-40 Wet Concrete	1496 Raintree Green	832 Blue Heron
1040 La Paloma Gray	HC-87 Ashley Gray	CW-355 Carter Plum	AF-645 Chambourd	1497 Rolling Hills	826 Stunning

Summer

Summer is warm weather and fun in the sun. In this collection you'll find a lot of sunny yellow undertones and citrusy colors. The beiges either have warm peach or yellow undertones or are sandy like the beach. The yellows and oranges glow like a sunrise, and the greens again are mostly yellow. Summers are spent by the water to cool off, so this collection includes blues to contrast with all of the yellow tones. However, they are still warm blues with the slightest hint of a greenish undertone (which is created with a drop of yellow), light blues that are soft and muted like the sky and deep blues like the ocean.

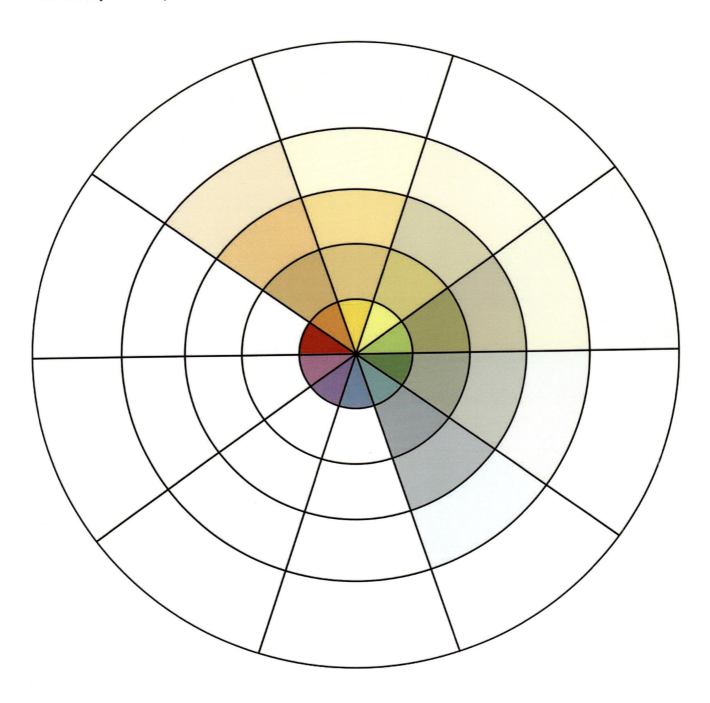

27

Sherwin Williams Summer Palette

SW 7103 Whitetail 261-C1	SW 6385 Dover White 261-C2	SW 7757 High Reflective White 256-C1			
SW 6140 Moderate White 266-C3	SW 6378 Crisp Linen 264-C3	SW 7561 Lemon Meringue 295-C1	SW 6476 Glimmer 271-C1	SW 6420 Queen Anne's Lace 270-C5	SW 6511 Snowdrop 272-C2
SW 7572 Lotus Pod 264-C6	SW 6386 Napery 139-C1	SW 6680 Friendly Yellow 135-C1	SW 6212 Quietude 218-C2	SW 6414 Rice Paddy 145-C1	SW 9056 French Moire 173-C3
SW 6106 Kilim Beige 204-C1	SW 7681 Tea Light 294-C2	SW 6638 Flattering Peach 121-C1	SW 6484 Meander Blue 171-C1	SW 6708 Springtime 148-C1	SW 9058 Secret Cove 173-C5
SW 6107 Nomadic Desert 204-C2	SW 7684 Concord Buff 294-C4	SW 6317 Gracious Rose 113-C2	SW 6485 Raindrop 171-C2	SW 9031 Primavera 148-C3	SW 7607 Santorini Blue 279-C6
SW 6108 Latte 204-C3	SW 9023 Dakota Wheat 139-C3	SW 6566 Framboise 103-C7	SW 6487 Cloudburst 171-C5	SW 9029 Cool Avocado 145-C3	SW 9185 Marea Baja 279-C7

Benjamin Moore Summer Palette

OC-85	Mayonnaise
2143-70	Simply White
OC-152	Super White
OC-5	Maritime White
OC-87	Capri Coast
OC-147	Cameo White
2123-60	Sea Foam
2145-50	Limesicle
1632	Glass Slipper
1037	Muslin
2153-60	Rich Cream
HC-5	Weston Flax
2123-50	Ocean Air
HC-1	Castleton Mist
HC-150	Yarmouth Blue
1038	Everlasting
OC-148	Montgomery White
HC-53	Hathaway Peach
2051-60	Bird's Egg
2028-50	Wales Green
HC-153	Marlboro Blue
1039	Stone House
192	Key West Ivory
2173-50	Coral Dust
2051-50	Tranquil Blue
2028-40	Pear Green
1665	Mozart Blue
1040	Spice Gold
2153-50	Desert Tan
1357	Bottle of Bordéaux
2051-40	Majestic Blue
2147-40	Dill Pickle
AF-530	Lucerne

Autumn

Autumn is warm in the beginning but then begins to cool off. In this collection you'll find golds, oranges and reds that add a pop of color like the leaves on the trees in the Fall. Imagine these trees against a blue sky and you'll realize that a warm greenish blue looks great against these colors, as well as khaki beiges and olive greens that have gold and green undertones.

Both Summer and Autumn colors can be intermingled.

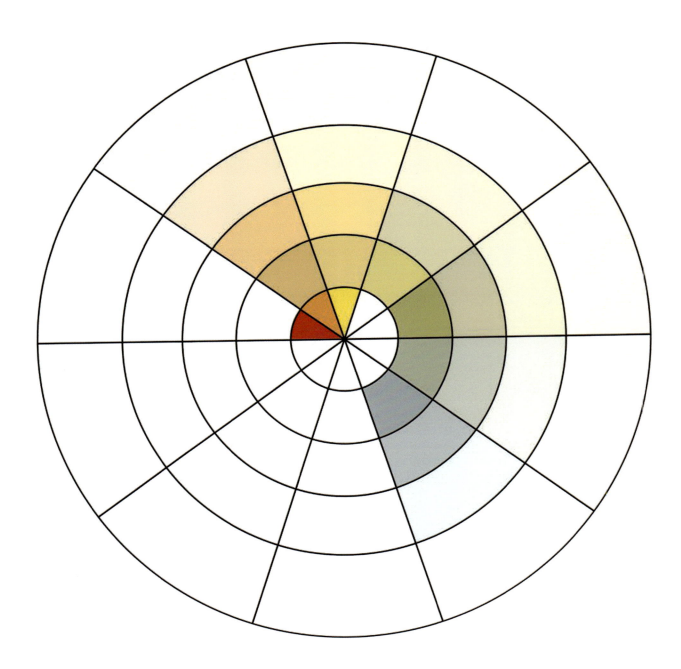

Sherwin Williams Autumn Palette

SW 7104 **Cotton White** 265-C1	SW 7001 **Marshmallow** 267-C1	SW 7008 **Alabaster** 255-C2			
SW 6147 **Panda White** 266-C2	SW 6126 **Navajo White** 264-C5	SW 7683 **Buff** 296-C1	SW 6372 **Inviting Ivory** 129-C1	SW 6155 **Rice Grain** 210-C1	SW 6204 **Sea Salt** 217-C1
SW 7015 **Repose Gray** 244-C1	SW 7569 **Stucco** 286-C2	SW 6120 **Believable Buff** 141-C1	SW 6373 **Harvester** 129-C2	SW 7736 **Garden Sage** 297-C2	SW 6219 **Rain** 219-C2
SW 7016 **Mindful Gray** 244-C2	SW 7542 **Naturel** 286-C3	SW 6121 **Whole Wheat** 141-C2	SW 6356 **Copper Mountain** 126-C7	SW 7727 **Koi Pond** 298-C2	SW 9051 **Aquaverde** 170-C3
SW 7017 **Dorian Gray** 244-C3	SW 6150 **Universal Khaki** 207-C3	SW 9127 **At Ease Soldier** 212-C4	SW 6335 **Fired Brick** 115-C7	SW 7734 **Olive Grove** 297-C5	SW 6228 **Refuge** 220-C5
SW 7046 **Anonymous** 245-C5	SW 6041 **Otter** 232-C7	SW 6480 **Lagoon** 170-C5	SW 6307 **Fine Wine** 111-C7	SW 6173 **Cocoon** 211-C6	SW 6230 **Rainstorm** 220-C7

Benjamin Moore Autumn Palette

OC-95 Navajo White	OC-146 Linen White	OC-17 White Dove			
OC-142 Sail Cloth	OC-10 White Sand	HC-32 Standish White	178 Golden Lab	521 Nantucket Breeze	1563 Quiet Moments
HC-173 Edgecomb Gray	HC-81 Manchester Tan	HC-26 Monroe Bisque	2160-40 Roasted Sesame Seed	515 Baby Turtle	HC-146 Wedgewood Gray
HC-172 Revere Pewter	HC-80 Bleeker Beige	HC-35 Powell Buff	AF-225 Firenze	494 Lewiville Green	710 Kensington Green
HC-105 Rockport Gray	HC-77 Alexandria Beige	2142-40 Dry Sage	HC-50 Georgian Brick	HC-110 Wethersfield Moss	720 Bella Blue
AF-720 Sparrow	HC-76 Davenport Tan	CW-570 Mayo Teal	AF-300 Dinner Party	1498 Forest Floor	1666 In the Midnight Hour

Fan Decks and Color Collections

In order to begin choosing paint colors for each room you will first need to obtain fan decks. But which fan deck should you get? It depends on which paint brand you will be using. Which paint brand should you use? Well, it depends on what paint store you have near you. **Benjamin Moore** stores are all individually owned, so each retailer will do things their own way as far as displays, product availability and pricing. **Sherwin Williams** directly owns their paint stores and they are pretty consistent. You will find their stores throughout the US. These are the two brands we will focus on in this chapter and throughout this book.

Other stores like hardware stores and boutique paint stores may carry several different brands. Big Box stores like **Home Depot** and **Lowes** carry brands like **Behr** and **Valspar** and usually they **do not have fan decks for their color collections.** You will need to create your own fan deck. (We will discuss this on page 64). Look through their brochures to get a feel for muddy colors, clear brights and neutrals. You can bring home their paper chips and create your own fan deck or cut the chips out of the brochures. They are capable of mixing Benjamin Moore colors, so another option is to order Benjamin Moore fan decks online, and then have them mix the color in their brand of paint. However, I don't personally recommend having colors mixed in other brands because in my experience the color tends to be a little off. As for all other brands, either obtain a fan deck or make your own color wheel.

Restoration Hardware

Restoration Hardware has a great color collection and all are made to go together room to room. Hopefully you can obtain a fan deck. If not, bring home each of their paper chips and create your own fan.

Farrow and Ball

Farrow and Ball paint comes from England and you'll have to search for a dealer, but they have a beautiful color palette that is made to go together, and their paint is highly regarded as being a superior product. Try to obtain a fan deck rather than just a paper brochure. You can order them on their website.

** For a crossover list between Benjamin Moore and Sherwin Williams Colors, see page 335.

Benjamin Moore

Benjamin Moore Color Collections

Benjamin Moore has over 3,500 colors and 8 color collections. Most customers usually walk into the store and quickly become overwhelmed with the amount of colors. Luckily, it's the brand I'm most familiar with. When customers go into the paint store and ask for a fan deck, they are usually not aware that there are a few different ones to choose from. Here is a breakdown so you know which ones to choose. The company updates every couple of years, so I will explain the old fan decks and newer ones. If you borrow one from a friend or contractor they may have one that is older than the ones available at the store, so I'll explain them all. I will break this all down by color collections. Over time the fan decks and and wall displays may change, but THE COLORS DO NOT CHANGE. So no matter which fan deck you have access to, they will still be able to mix any of the colors you choose.

Classics Collection

This is the original group of colors. This collection has mostly "muddy" colors and has a lot of beiges and green colors. If your store only has the old wall display you will not find chips available for every color. The new displays however have all of the color chips.

Color Preview Collection

In an effort to offer brighter colors, this collection was introduced around 2000 and includes lots of Clear Brights. The old fan deck included **off-white collection and the Historical Colors** but the new fan deck does not include these collections. Most of the grays in this collection are cool and look blueish. It also has a large collection of blush pinks. Color numbers begin with a 2000.

Historical Colors

This collection was developed as part of the bicentennial celebration in 1976 and these colors have been favorites for decades. The colors are all muddy and work very well together. If you're looking to make all your rooms flow together, this collection works. When choosing colors for the exterior this is the first place to look. Both the OLD Classics and Color Preview collections fan decks include the Historical Colors. In new fan decks they are found in the "Collections" fan deck. Color numbers begin with an "HC".

Color Collections

AC Colors

AC means "Americas Colors" and they can be found underneath the Historical Colors in the old wall display. They are similar to the Historical colors in their muddy tone and there are some good grays and taupes. These colors have two names and in the new displays the AC colors have disappeared. If you have an old fan deck you won't find the chips for these colors in a new display. See page 44 for new color numbers.

PM Colors

PM means "Premium Colors". These are your basic colors like Navajo White that are tried and true and you used to be able to buy them right off of the shelf. Many were previously called "EXT" colors that were pre-mixed for Exteriors. When choosing colors for the exterior there are some terrific colors here and the perfect place to start. They have since done away with pre-mixing these colors and now they need to be mixed in the store. In the new fan decks and displays these colors were given new numbers and are now OC and HC colors. See page 43 for the new numbers.

Off-White Collection

Off-whites are not really white, they are all either a little beige, a bit pink, slightly yellow, etc. Labeled as "OC" colors, most of these colors are found already in the Color Preview section or the Classics Colors as the lightest color on the strip. So some of these colors will have two numbers. For instance, Balboa Mist in the Off-Whites is numbered OC-27, but it's also found in the Classics Collection as number 1459. If you want to know what's really in an OC color, Google the name to see if it has another number. You can also look it up in the alphabetical index at the back of the Classics or Preview fan decks to see if it has two numbers. Then look up the color by the other number and view the other colors on the strip to get a good sense of the undertones.

Affinity Color Collection

When Aura paint was introduced around 2005, they also released the Affinity Color Collection. Aura was the original self-priming, low VOC paint. (Volatile Organic Compound=no odor). I found that when I was trying to match designer color palettes, like Ralph Lauren and Restoration Hardware colors, the Affinity colors came very close. The colors in this collection were all meant to go together, so if you're looking for a palette to work in each room that will flow together, this collection was meant to do that. There are no clear brights in this collection. Color numbers begin with an "AF".

Affinity Colors are now part of the "Collections" fan deck and are in the center of new store displays. But they used to have their own display with pull out drawers for small paint sample jars. They also had their own large fan deck. I really like this deck because the chips are much larger and sturdier. If you're lucky you may still be able to obtain one at your paint store.

Williamsburg Color Collection

Introduced in 2013, many of these colors are very similar to the Historical Colors. It turns out that when they did scientific research of the paint in Colonial Williamsburg, they found that the paint had faded over 250 years and that the colors were originally much more vibrant than we had originally thought. (Gee, I could have told them that! LOL). This collection has mostly muddy colors and neutrals, with a few more vibrant colors mixed in. This is a great collection for exteriors and the colors flow together nicely.

Color Stories

Introduced in 2011, this is another color collection created for Aura paint and is available in Aura, Regal and Ben paints for interior only. This collection is not displayed in every store. They may have the fan deck, and they can mix the colors, but you may not find a display of chips on the wall. Color Stories has a lovely collection of gray colors and Interior designers seem to love this collection. However, the selling point to this collection was that each color has about 5 different tints per color which make the colors change in different lighting. After dealing with thousands of clients who get frustrated with colors changing in different lighting, I don't see this as a positive selling point! I have also found that most colors tend to appear lighter once they go up on the wall. As pretty as these colors are, I just personally don't use them very often.

These three fan decks below are the ones I use daily. I almost never use Color Stories or Williamsburg Colors.

Fan Decks

Color Preview Collection: This fan deck no longer includes the Historical Colors or the Off-Whites. Depending on the year it was printed, the names of the colors may be on the back or on the front.

Benjamin Moore Collections: This fan deck combined all of the smaller collections together. It includes the **OC-Collection of Off Whites, the HC-Historical Colors, AF-Affinity Colors, the PM colors**, and yet even another collection not previously available in the United States, the **CC–Canadian Colors**. The Canadian Colors are much like the Classics Colors, muted muddy colors and in fact some of the colors actually repeat in the Classics Color Collection.

The Color Stories Collection will be added to the Collections Fan Deck in 2024.

Benjamin Moore Classics: This fan deck includes all the original **Classics Colors**. Depending on when it was printed, it may or may not include **AC Colors**. The number on the very bottom of the strip is the display number. These were needed to find colors in the old display. See page 41.

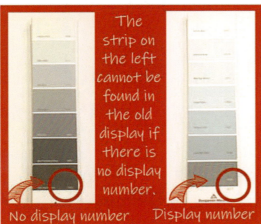

The strip on the left cannot be found in the old display if there is no display number.

No display number | Display number

Benjamin Moore

Old Display

Some stores have old displays that look like this: All of the color collections are divided up into their own separate displays. The Williamsburg Collection is in a separate display if they have it. Not all colors in the Classics Colors fan deck can be found in this old display.

New Display

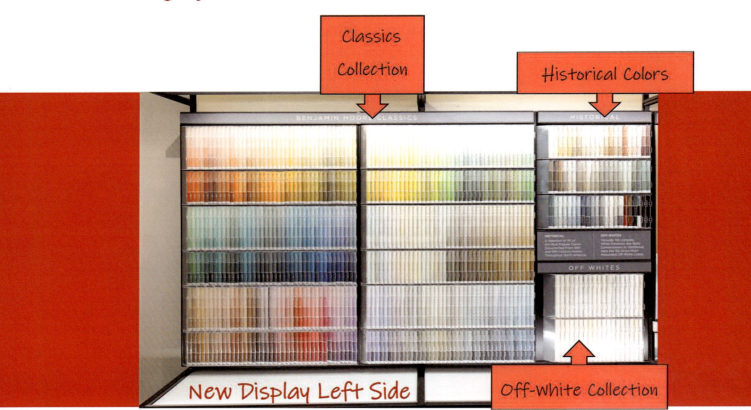

Color Displays

New Display

In the new displays all of the Classics Colors have paper chips. Plus, all of the colors are now simply in numerical order the same way they appear in the fan decks. So the chips are much easier to find now. The new displays are configured differently depending on the size of the store. Some are large enough to have the display all along one long wall, while other stores have the display turn a corner. These new displays include the Affinity Collections and Williamsburg Collections, which used to be in their own little displays. Some stores may not have the Color Stories Collection in their display. I rarely use these collections. **The most important collections are the main ones, which are the Classics Collection, The Color Preview Collection and the Historical Colors.** These collections you will find in every display in every store.

New Display Right Side

42

Premium Mix and America's Color Collection Crossover Reference List.

This page is for people who have painted in the past and now can't find that old color they were looking for. The one's who say, "What happened to that Pismo Dunes color?", or can't find the traditional colors that used to be in the same old place but now they say, "Where did White Dove go?"

In the new fan decks and displays, the Premium Mix Collection (PM colors have been folded into other color collections. The darker shades are now found in the Historical Colors (HC and the lighter shades can be found in the Off-White Colors (OC. These colors include the typical trim colors like Linen White and White Dove, and the others were made for Exteriors, previously marked with "EXT". If you're looking for good exterior paint colors by the way, refer to this chart below. All of the colors in the America's Colors (AC already existed in the Classics Collection, but sometimes were given a new name in the AC collection). In the new displays the AC colors have disappeared, but they still exist. Below are the new and old names and numbers.

Premium Mix Color Collection – PM Colors

Original PM #		New #	Original PM #		New #
PM-1	Super White	OC-152	PM-19	White Dove	OC-17
PM-2	White	OC-151	PM-20	China White	OC-141
PM-3	Decorator's White	OC-149	PM-21	Sail Cloth	OC-142
PM-4	Brilliant White	OC-150	PM-22	Antique White	OC-83
PM-5	Clifffside Gray	HC-180	PM-23	Charleston Brown	HC-186
PM-6	Hamilton Blue	HC-191	PM-24	Tudor Brown	HC-185
PM-7	Platinum Gray	HC-179	PM-25	Cameo White	OC-147
PM-8	Charcoal Slate	HC-178	PM-26	Montgomery White	OC-148
PM-9	Black	HC-190	PM-27	Richmond Bisque	HC-177
PM-10	Chrome Green	HC-189	PM-28	Linen White	OC-146
PM-11	Essex Green	HC-188	PM-29	Navajo White	OC-95
PM-12	Black Forest Green	HC-187	PM-30	Bone White	OC-143
PM-13	Atrium White	OC-145	PM-31	Lancaster White	OC-144
PM-14	Annapolis Gray	HC-176	PM-32	Briarwood	HC-175
PM-15	Cottage Red	HC-184	PM-17	Classic Burgundy	HC-182
PM-16	Country Redwood	HC-181	PM-18	Heritage Red	HC-181

America's Color Collection - AC Colors

AC Name and #		New Name and #	
AC-1	Coastal Fog	Coastal Fog	976
AC-2	Berkshire Beige	Brandon Beige	977
AC-3	Texas Leather	Stampede	979
AC-4	Yosemite Sand	Alpaca	1074
AC-5	Springfield Tan	Capilano Bridge	1076
AC-6	New Chestnut	Hillcrest Tan	1078
AC-7	Adobe Beige	Adobe Beige	1128
AC-8	Butte Rock	Hidden Oaks	1129
AC-9	Nugget	Autumn Leaf	1131
AC-10	San Clemente Rose	Clementine Rose	1219
AC-11	Sierra Ridge	Grazing Fawn	1220
AC-12	Copper Mountain	Lenape Trail	1222
AC-13	Mochachino	Crossroads	1226
AC-14	Pecos Spice	Nutmeg	1227
AC-15	Colorado Clay	Roman Shade	1228
AC-16	Kentucky Haze	Mount St. Anne	1565
AC-17	Sea Pine	Stonybrook	1566
AC-18	Smoky Mountain	Night Train	1567
AC-19	Homestead Green	Rhine River	689
AC-20	Mountain Laurel	Dartsmouth Green	691
AC-21	Silver Pine	Jack Pine	692
AC-22	Nantucket Fog	Santorini Blue	1634
AC-23	James River Gray	Water's Edge	1635
AC-24	Charlotte Slate	Providence Blue	1636
AC-25	Harbor Gray	Silver Chain	1472
AC-26	Ozark Shadows	Gray Huskie	1473
AC-27	Galveston Gray	Graystone	1475
AC-28	Smoke Embers	Smoke Embers	1466
AC-29	San Antonio Gray	Baltic Gray	1467
AC-30	Winter Gates	Willow Creek	1468
AC-31	Hot Spring Stones	Ashen Tan	996
AC-32	Pismo Dunes	Baja Dunes	997
AC-33	Mesa Verde Tan	Cabot Trail	998
AC-34	Cape Hatteras Sand	Himalayan Trek	1542
AC-35	Valley Forge Tan	Plymouth Rock	1543
AC-36	Shenandoah Taupe	Waynesboro Taupe	1544
AC-37	Big Bend Beige	Desert Light	1004
AC-38	North Hampton Beige	Hazelwood	1005
AC-39	Mt. Rushmore Rock	Creekbed	1006
AC-40	Glacier White	Dune White	968
AC-41	Acadia White	Ivory White	925
AC-42	Grand Teton White	White Swan	927

Sherwin Williams

If you find that the multiple color collections and fan decks by Benjamin Moore are too confusing and you'd rather have your choices narrowed down, then you'll be happy to know that Sherwin Williams has only one fan deck to choose from. They have recently redesigned their displays and the fan deck, and according to Sherwin Williams it was designed to make it faster and easier to use.

Old Fan Deck SHERWIN-WILLIAMS.

I personally love the older fan deck because it's divided exactly the way I explain colors in this book! It's divided up by muddy colors, clear brights and in-between colors. To the far right are neutrals called *Black, White, Gray Area* ". Then to the left of the neutrals are the muddy colors called "*Fundamentally Neutral*". To the far left are the clear bright colors called "*Energetic Bright*". Then to the right of the brights are the "in-between colors" called "*Color Options*".

New Fan Deck

In the new fan deck colors are now divided by color families and collections. To the far right you'll find the "**Color**" section divided up like a rainbow beginning with the red family all grouped together from the brightest red down to a muddy salmon color. To the left of that comes the orange family, then yellows, then greens, etc. The next section is the "**Neutrals**". These are muddy colors moving from pinky taupes, to beiges, to all shades of grays included gray greens and gray blues. To the left of that is their off-white collection called "**Whites and Pastels**", then the "*Timeless* " section which seems to be a mixture of tried and true colors that are a little bit of everything. Lastly to the far left you'll find the Historic Colors. If you visit their website, you'll find the colors listed under time period so if you have a Victorian home for instance, they'll tell you which colors best represent that time period.

The main display features color chips found in the Color, Neutral and White and Pastel sections of the new fan deck.

A fun feature of this display is that the sections spin around to feature a larger sample of a popular color in each color section.

The "Timeless" and "Historic" color collections found in the new fan deck can be found on their own display wall. The "Favorites" and "Trends" in this section are colors that are in the main color collections but reappear here just to let you know what are currently the most popular colors at the moment.

Where there once was the "HGTV" collection, there is now a section labeled the "Designer Inspired" collection. This area features brochures with ideas for different color palettes for the home, and all of the chips above each brochure are the colors featured in each collection.

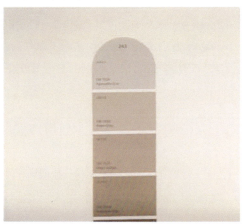

Finding chips on the display may seem difficult but you just need to know the system. Each color has a COLOR number which begins with a "SW" and a DISPLAY number. For instance, Agreeable Gray SW 7029 has a display number which is 243-C1. When searching for the chip in the display, look at the display number. So to find 243-C1 look for row 243, column 1. Of course, if you need help just ask someone who works in the store and they will help you.

Toning Down and Fixing Colors

Tell me if this sounds familiar: For months you have dog-eared pages in decorating magazines, pinned hundreds of pictures on Pinterest, followed influencers on Instagram and religiously watched HGTV. By now you think you're quite the expert on what decorating style you're going after. You find what you think will be the perfect color for your room because, after all, some big shot designer used it so it must be the perfect color. Right?

So you send your husband off to the paint store Saturday morning to buy the paint, then he begins painting while you take the kids to soccer practice.

When you come home in the afternoon you gasp! "Stop!" The color looks hideous! What could possibly have gone wrong? The first thing you need to understand when choosing colors is that **the color you think you want is not really the color you want!** I have heard many stories of people who think the paint store mixed the wrong color. The problem is not that they mixed the wrong color, it's that people are not choosing the correct color in the first place.

Most people tend to walk into a paint store and look at the wall of colors like it's a huge box of crayons. When they want the color blue, they choose a chip of a color that is clearly a very distinct blue. Then when they paint it on the wall they are stunned to find out how blue that blue really is! What they really needed was a cloudy, gray blue, not a clear bright blue.

Tone it Down!

One day when I was working in the paint store a woman came in and said "I wanted to paint a soft, butter yellow, but now it looks like someone threw up lemons all over my wall! What's the problem? What did I do wrong?" The problem is that the yellow tint that goes into the can is so bright that it can literally hurt your eyes. So even if you choose the lightest shade of yellow, it's still going to be too yellow. **Contrary to popular belief, adding white is NOT the way to tone down a color.** The way to truly tone down a color is usually to add either a little beige or gray into the color and make it "muddy".

Keeping it Simple.

Years ago, when I was painting murals, a woman hired me to paint a beach scene in her daughter's room where she decorated with fake palm trees, a fishing net hanging from the ceiling and all things beachy. In her son's room I painted a mountainous ski slope and she decorated with skis and flannel sheets and all things ski related. Her Kitchen had flowery wallpaper and her Foyer had lots of ivy and hanging bird cages, and every room had a kitschy theme. The house was so **BUSY** I couldn't wait to get out of there! My eyes had nowhere to REST.

When I worked for a male Interior Designer he used dark, masculine colors in all of the rooms he designed. But to me they felt **DREARY**, like a cold, rainy day. Living with dark colors everywhere can get depressing.

As a result of these types of experiences I try to bring a simple, clean, calming atmosphere, and will choose **no more** than two dark rooms per house. The rest of the rooms need to be light and bright.

Sometimes I feel more like a Psychologist than a Color Specialist. Most colors that I choose tend to have a calming, peaceful feel to them. Most of our lives are just too busy and hectic, and I believe our home should be a sanctuary from the world where you can rest, relax, and feel at peace. Too much color and stimulation everywhere can make the house feel manic. This is why I want rooms to flow and colors to be toned down.

Colors can affect your mood. I'm not talking about Feng Shui or the Psychology of color, but to put it simply, different people like different colors, and if you don't like the color in a room it can make you sad, uncomfortable or even grouchy. I believe you should use colors that make you happy! However, I think **too much of a good thing can become overstimulating.** This is why I am forever trying to tone down colors and even wrote a chapter on how to tone them down. Following the method will give you a calming environment where your eyes can rest and not get over stimulated.

Colors are Affected by Lighting

When choosing your paint colors for each room, keep in mind that lighting will affect the color. You could paint your whole house the same color and it would look different in every room. That's because one side gets morning light, the other gets afternoon light, another gets full sun while the other gets no sun at all. Your colors will look different in the daytime and in the nighttime, on sunny days and rainy days, near windows and away from windows.

Daylight is cool and blue. So, if you have a lot of sunlight in your room it will make cool gray walls appear to be blue. Since most of my clients want their main living areas to be neutral and not blue, I stay away from cool grays in those areas and use a warmer gray, greige or taupe. However, I do like the cooler grays in Bedrooms and Bathrooms because a soft blue is very calming and restful.

Light bulbs can give off a warm yellow light, or a soft pink glow, and fluorescent bulbs can give off a ghastly green undertone. Gray can turn blue; beige can turn peach and taupe can turn purple. So after you narrow down your color choices, put samples up and then look at them for a couple days so that you can see them in the daytime and the nighttime, on a sunny day and on a cloudy day.

If you don't get much natural light the colors may get washed out and a light color will look almost white. A color may look good in the paint store, but when you bring it home it may look very gray or washed out due to the lack of daylight. So you may need a shade brighter than you think you do. So bring home a few chips that are lighter, darker, brighter and more dull.

Important! Don't drive yourself crazy over this! Match the color to things in the room following the guidelines in this book. Then accept the fact that the color will look different at night in the lamp light than it does in the daytime. As long as the color matches your fabrics in the room it will be just fine. If the color matches your stuff then that's the right color to use. Don't over think it.

Daylight is cool and lamp light is warm.

So this yellow room appears cooler in the daytime and warmer at night.

Colors are Affected by Their Surroundings

When choosing colors, it depends on what the surroundings look like. Colors look different when they are next to other colors. As we learned in the chapter on **Color Basics**, if you look at a bunch of beige paint color chips all next to each other you'll notice the different undertones. Some are a little peach, a little pink, or a little yellow, and then some are either warm or cool. If you look at them individually you won't notice it until you look at them next to each other. The same thing will happen to paint on the wall. The color you choose will be affected by other colors.

Here are examples: If you have wood with a pinkish undertone and then paint a beige with a greenish undertone then your wood will look pink and the walls will look green and you'll hate them both. If you have **warm** gray cabinets and you put a **cool** gray on the walls, the cool color on the walls will look blue not gray. If you have **cool** gray and white marble and use a **warm** gray on the walls, the walls will look beige.

Before

After

Color Correction: The homeowner wanted beige walls. But this khaki beige looks green next to the pinkish cabinets. The fix is a cooler taupe with a slight pink undertone.

The same paint strip below looks totally different in three different rooms because:

A) It's held up against different colors

B) The lighting is different

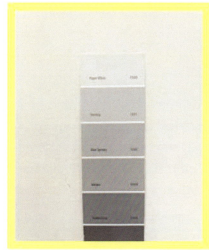

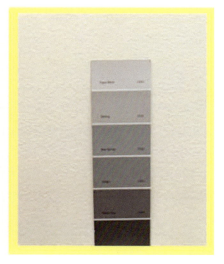

Toning it Down: Color by Color

Colors appearing too bright is a common problem that I need to teach people how to solve. Here is a list of colors and the typical problems that happen with each color and how to fix them including ways to tone down and soften colors to make sure they don't turn out too bright or intense.

Yellow

Even the lightest yellow can be too intense. To achieve a softer yellow choose one that is muddy, not clear. It should have some beige mixed in and look more like a soft gold. Even tan will sometimes read like a buttery yellow. Most colors called "bisque" or "buff" have yellow or gold undertones. For Benjamin Moore, look in their Historical Colors and their Off-White Collection. For Sherwin Williams, look in their White and Pastels, and the Timeless Atemporal Section. Also see **My Favorite Colors** for a list of my favorite yellows.

Blue

Add gray to tone down blue. Most silver grays tend to turn blue so when I want the softest blue I actually use a silver gray. For Benjamin Moore, look at the Color Preview Section from 2119-2136, and the Classics Color Collection from 1562-1635. For Sherwin Williams, look at the cool grays and blues in the Neutrals Section.

Red

Reds can turn either orange or hot pink and years ago it was very difficult to choose a good red. I would tend to choose either burgundy colors or reds that had a touch of brown in them to keep the light from brightening the red and turning it into an orange. When the Affinity Colors were introduced by Benjamin Moore the collection included three reds that work great and they became my "go-to" reds. Sherwin Williams has some nice dark reds and burgundy colors in display rows 275 and 276.

Green

Blue + Yellow = Green. Bluer greens can be minty, and yellow greens can be too lime. Remember yellow tint is intense and will look brighter on the wall. If you want an earthy green then look for colors that are more "muddy". I have found many times that what I really need is a khaki color with a slight green undertone. For Benjamin Moore, look at the Historical Colors. For Sherwin Williams, look in the Neutrals Section and the Timeless Atemporal Section. See **My Favorite Colors** for a list of my favorite greens.

Orange

It's hard to find good colors in the orange family. I have found a deep gold actually makes a nice warm orange similar to the color of orange juice. Most tend to be too dark, and the lighter colors are peach. Good terracotta colors or a salmon that's not pink just don't seem to exist. If you want a bright orange, then there are some good clear, bright oranges. But if you're looking for a nice muddy orange to go with neutral beige colors, look at Benjamin Moore's Affinity Color Collection. For Sherwin Williams, look at Row 290 in the Timeless Atemporal Section.

Pink

Sometimes the palest pink on a pink strip is still too pink. In order to tone it down you need to muddy the color. You will need a soft blush with gray or beige undertones. Some of these blush pinks can lean toward purple, so if you're not going for purple then look for one that's a little warmer, which is a pink with just the slightest hint of peach. For Benjamin Moore, look at the Color Preview Section from 2088-2096. For Sherwin Williams, look at Rows 113, 114, 115, 118, and 268.

Navy

There is a difference between navy blue and cobalt blue. When sunlight hits dark blue it can turn cobalt. So if you want a true navy you need to add some black to tone it down. Especially for exteriors, you may want to use a color that almost looks black inside, but outside it will look navy because the sunlight will draw out the blue. For interiors you may want to use a dark slate blue if there is not much light. I list my favorites in **My Favorite Colors**.

Beige

Many beige colors can turn peach. If the beige you choose looks too peach then find a taupe or a beige that has some gray or khaki undertones. Khaki beiges can turn a little green. So if your lighting turns colors pink or peach, use a color that looks more khaki. If you choose a beige to match other beiges in the room and you just want a softer, lighter version of that matching color then look for the lightest color on the strip. If it's not light enough then have them cut the formula for you. See the chapter on **Mixing Custom Colors** page 303. See **My Favorite Colors** for a list of good beiges.

Greige and Taupe

Greige is a trendy word for "gray/beige" and is another word for taupe. Most taupe colors have a slightly pink or purple undertone. If you are working with pink, like pink tile or pickled wood, then this is the color to use. When choosing a taupe first match any other taupes in the room. If you want the one that is the least pink, just lay all the chips out next to each other and try to find the one that is the most neutral. If lighting is turning the color too pink or purple then you'll need to choose a color that is more khaki with a greenish undertone. See **My Favorite Colors**.

Grays

By now you should certainly know that gray is the new beige. Ten years ago, beige was all the rage. Now it's gray all the way. For me as a color consultant, every house I choose colors for seems to be 50 Shades of Gray. All gray, every day. I have a love/hate relationship with gray. I love the color and how it looks, but it is by far the most difficult color to use. I have seen it do all kinds of unpredictable things so you really need to sample it following the guidelines in the chapter on **Sampling Paint Colors**. I have divided gray into two categories: Cool Gray and Warm Gray.

> **Cool grays** are silvery and can tend to turn blue or purple. If even the most neutral gray looks blue, then use a warm gray.
>
> **Warm grays** have a little beige and may turn greenish on a rainy day, but pinkish light from light bulbs may counteract that in the evening. If it's too green or yellow then try taupe or a cool gray instead.

Grays do not need to be toned down. They need to match whatever grays you have in the room, and then just use a lighter version if you want a lighter gray. However **light grays tend to reflect everything around them and they are the most unpredictable.** Medium to dark gray is easier to work with because they tend to stay more gray because they don't reflect other colors as much. If you choose a light gray make sure you sample it first. See **My Favorite Colors**.

Whites

My number one rule with whites is "Don't mix whites"! If you use different whites in the same room, one will look dirty and the other will look clean. For a description of different whites refer to the chapter on **Trim Colors**.

Off-Whites

Obviously you don't need to "tone down" off-whites, but you will need to figure out what the undertones are to be able to use them. All off-whites have a little bit of something in them, like a little pink, a little yellow, a little beige, or a little gray. To figure out what undertones are in the Benjamin Moore off-whites, look up the color in the index of the fan deck and see if it has two numbers. If so, then look it up to see all of the colors on the strip. For instance, "Simply White" by Benjamin Moore has two numbers "OC-117" and "2143-70". (OC=Off-White Color.) But if you look up Simply White as 2143-70 you'll see that the rest of the colors on the strip are greenish, so you'll know that Simply White may have a drop of green in it. You can also Google the color or ask the paint "Barista" at the paint store to check on their computer to see if the color has another name or number.

Creamy Off-White

When I worked at the paint store I had customers ask for a color that was "off-white, not a stark white, a color that's creamy but not yellow" and the description went on. What they usually end up selecting is **White Dove**, which is a color so common you used to be able to buy it pre-mixed right off the shelf. Most brands have a version of a very common off-white like this, like Sherwin Williams' Alabaster SW 7008.

My Favorite Colors

Here is a list of my favorite colors in each color family. My "go-to" colors are colors that I literally use EVERY DAY. That's because they tend to match current fabrics and tile and they are the colors my clients like the best too. I will pull these colors out FIRST, see if they work, and if not then I'll move on and tweak it. But it's a good place to start. I am an expert on Benjamin Moore colors, and use Sherwin Williams occasionally, so these are the brands you'll see here. If you shop at a store that carries other brands, they usually can mix these colors in their brand. **My GO-TO's are marked with an *.**

Benjamin Moore Colors:

Taupe– Winds Breath 981, *Cedar Key 982, Smokey Taupe 983, Stone Hearth 984, Ashley Gray HC-87

Greige that is more GRAY- Edgecomb Gray HC-171, Revere Pewter HC-172, Abalone 2108-60

Greige that is more BEIGE- Greige Avenue 991, Hampshire Taupe 990, Shabby Chic 1018, Baja Dunes 997

Warm Beige– Muslin 1037, Everlasting 1038, Carlisle Cream 1031, Bar Harbor Beige 1032, Cotswald AF-150, Shaker Beige HC-45

Khaki Beige– White Sand OC-10, Manchester Tan HC-81 (AKA Berber White 955) Bleeker Beige HC-80, Hush AF-95, Timson Sand CW-140

Cool Gray– *Stonington Gray HC-170, *Wickham Gray HC-171, *Alaskan Husky 1479, *Horizon 1478, Sidewalk Gray 2133-60, *Silver Chain 1472, *Shoreline 1471

Warm Gray– *Silver Satin OC-26, *Classic Gray 1548, *Balboa Mist 1549, Cumulus Cloud 1550, La Paloma Gray 1551, Gray Huskie 1473, *Light Pewter 1464, *Nimbus 1465, Smoke Embers 1466, Bruton White CS-710, Bone Black CW-715, Thunder AF-685

Dark Gray– *Cinder AF– 705, Delray Gray 1614, Kendall Charcoal HC-166, Chelsea Gray HC-168, Dior Gray 2133-40.

Gray Blue – Gray Tint 1611, Sterling 1591, Iced Slate 2130-60, Feather Gray 2127-60, Gray Cloud 2126-60

Soft Blue – Glass Slipper 1632, Brittany Blue 1633, Silver Mist 1619, Pale Smoke 1584, *Beacon Gray 2128-60, Silver Cloud 2129-70, Fantasy Blue 716

Benjamin Moore

Medium Blue– Woodlawn Blue HC-147, Wedgewood Gray HC-146, Silvery Blue 1647, Yarmouth Blue HC-150, Blue Springs 1592, , Northern Air 1676

Slate Blue– New Hope 2130-50, *Winter Lake 2129-60, Pikes Peak Gray 2127-50, Falls 1621, Mineral Alloy 1622, Bachelor Blue 1629

Deep Blue– Old Blue Jeans 839, Stratford Blue 831, *Philipsburg Blue HC-159, Blue Heron 832

Navy- Hale Navy HC-154, Newburyport Blue HC-155, Van Deusen Blue HC-156, Mysterious AF-565, Stunning 826

Blue/Green/Gray- Healing Aloe 1562, *Quiet Moments 1563, Gray Wisp 1570, Arctic Gray 1577, Tranquility AF-490

Soft Aqua Blue– Summer Shower 2135-60, Harbor Haze 2136-60, *Ocean Air 2123-50, Palladian Blue HC-144

Bright Aqua– Antiguan Sky 2040-60, Bird's Egg 2051-60, China Blue 2052-60, Barely Teal 2048-70, Arctic Blue 2050-60

Deep Teal- Santa Monica Blue 776, Calypso Blue 727, Aegean Teal 2136-40, Newburg Green HC-158

Lime Green– Pale Vista 2029-60, Potpourri Green 2029-50, Pale Avocado 2146-40, Folk Art 528

Sage Green– Vale Mist 1494, Silver Sage 506, Grecian Green 507, Thornton Sage 464, Wind Chime AF-465

Natural Green– Dune Grass 492, Guilford Green HC– 116, Harbour Town 493, Lapland AF-410, Dried Parsley 522

Khaki/Olive Green– Flowering Herbs 514, Sag Harbor Gray HC-95, Richmond Gray HC– 96, Clarksville Gray HC– 102, Meditation AF– 395

Pink– Elephant Pink 2087-70, Ribbon Pink 2087-60, Pink Cadillac 2002-70, Mellow Pink 2094-70, Beautiful In My Eyes 1170

Lavender– Lavender Ice 2069-60, Lavender Mist 2070-60, Iced Lavender 1410, Spring Iris 1402

Purple-Gray– Touch of Gray 2116-60, Hint of Violet 2114-60, Porcelain 2113-60, Portland Gray 2109-60

Red– Caliente AF-290, Pomegranate AF-295, Tucson Red 1300, Currant Red 1323

Burgundy– Dinner Party AF-300, Carter Plum CW-555. Classic Burgundy HC-182

Favorite Colors

Soft Gold– Harvest Time 186, Dijon 193, Safari AF-335, Desert Tan 2153-50

Yellow– Hawthorne Yellow HC-4, Weston Flax HC-5, Cornsilk 198, Goldtone 176

Soft Creamy Yellow– Simply Irresistible 205, Ivory Lustre 184, Windham Cream HC-6, Cameo White OC-147, Montgomery White HC-33, Linen White OC-146

Orange– August Morning 2156-40, Soft Pumpkin 2166-40, Buttered Yam AM-230, Firenze AF-225

Brown– Branchport Brown HC-72, Clinton Brown HC-7, French Press AF-170, Davenport Tan HC-76

Sherwin Williams Colors: Sherwin-Williams.

Taupe– Touch of Sand SW9085, Cool Beige SW9086, Smoky Beige SW9087, Bungalow Beige SW7511, Dhurrie Beige SW7524, Pavilion Beige SW7512

Greige that is more **GRAY**- Windfresh White SW7628, Worldly Gray SW7043, Amazing Gray SW7044

Greige that is more **BEIGE**- Natural Tan SW7567, Realist Beige SW6078, Diverse Beige SW6079, Angora SW6036, Accessible Beige SW7036

Warm Beige– Patience SW7555, Bauhaus Buff SW7552, Tres Naturale SW9101

Khaki Beige– Kestral White SW7516, Natural Linen SW9109, Kilim Beige SW6106, Urban Putty SW7532, Rice Grain SW6155, Stucco SW7569

Cool Gray– Ice Cube SW6252, Passive SW7064, Silverpointe SW7653, Lattice SW7654, Grayish SW6001, Essential Gray SW6002, Silverplate SW7649, Ellie Gray SW7650, Zircon SW76677, Knitting Needles SW7672, Light French Gray SW0055

Warm Gray– Drift of Mist SW9166, Simply White SW7021, Gossamer Veil SW9165, *Repose Gray SW7015, *Agreeable Gray SW7029, Mindful Gray SW 7016, Popular Gray SW6071, Modern Gray SW7632

Dark Gray– Dovetail SW7018, Gauntlet Gray SW7019, Cityscape SW7067, Pewter Cast SW7673

Gray Blue– Olympus White SW6253, Lazy Gray SW6254, Morning Fog SW6255, Reflection SW7661, Evening Shadow SW7662, Monorail Silver SW7663, Steely Gray SW7664

Soft Blue– Mild Blue SW6533, Misty SW6232, North Star SW6246, Krypton SW6247, Mountain Air SW6224

Medium Blue– Niebla Azul SW9137, Stardew SW9138, Sleepy Blue SW6225, Breezy SW7616, Windy Blue SW6240

Slate Blue– Poolhouse SW7603, Debonair SW9139, Let It Rain SW9152, Daphne SW9151, Distance 6243

Sherwin Williams

Deep Blue– Sporty Blue SW6522, Denim SW6523, Revel Blue SW6530, Frank Blue SW6967

Navy- Dress Blues SW9176, Salty Dog SW9177, In The Navy SW9178, Dignified SW6538, Commodore SW6524

Blue/Green/Gray– Frosty White SW6196, Opaline SW6189, Pearl Gray SW0052, *Sea Salt SW6204, Comfort Gray SW6205, Willow Tree SW7741

Soft Aqua Blue– Copen Blue SW0068, Window Pane SW62210, Tradewind SW6218, Rainwashed SW6211, Watery SW6478

Bright Aqua– Embellished Blue SW6749, Swimming SW6764, Spa SW6765, Tame Teal SW6757, Blue Sky SW0063, Holiday Turquoise SW0075

Deep Teal– Peacock Plume SW0020, Teal Stencil SW0018, Blue Peacock SW0064, Lakeshore SW6494, Loch Blue SW6502, Silken Peacock SW9059

Lime Green– Lime Granita SW6715, Dancing Green SW6716, Gleeful SW6709, Chartreuse SW0073

Sage Green– Filmy Green SW6190, Contended 6191, Liveable Green SW6176, Softened Green SW6177, Clary Sage SW6178, Cascade Green SW0066, Sage SW2860

Natural Green– Celery SW6421, Shagreen SW6422, Baby Bok Choy SW9037, Baize Green SW6429, Koi Pond SW7727, Rice Paddy SW6414, Hearts Of Palm SW6415,

Khaki/Olive Green– Cargo Pants SW7738, Portico SW7548, Ruskin Room Green SW0042, Lemon Grass SW7732, Garden Sage SW7736, Rye Grass SW6423

Pink– Intimate White SW6322, Comical Coral SW6876

Lavender– Elation SW6827, Potentially Purple SW6821,

Purple-Gray– Silver Peony SW6547, Grape Mist SW6548, Sensitive Tint SW6267, Studio Mauve SW0062, Individual White SW6008,

Red– Wild Currant SW7583, Sun Dried Tomato SW7585, Red Theater SW7584

Burgundy– Deep Maroon SW0072, Merlot SW2704, Blackberry SW7577

Soft Gold– Humble Gold SW6380, Inviting Ivory SW6372, Compatible Cream SW6387, Hubbard Squash SW0044

Yellow– Optimistic Yellow SW6900, Lemon Chiffon SW6686, They Call It Mellow SW9015

Soft Cream Yellow– Classic Ivory SW0051, Paper Lantern SW7676, Crisp Linen SW6378, Summer White SW7557

Orange– Osage Orange SW6890, Amber Wave SW6657, Determined Orange SW6635

Brown– Plantation Shutters SW7520, Homestead Brown SW7515, Turkish Coffee SW6076

Paint Color Trends

When I was in seventh grade, I moved from rural Pennsylvania to a New Jersey suburb about a half hour from New York City. It was the mid 1970's and I was wearing bell-bottoms, but all the kids at the new school were wearing straight legged jeans and corduroys. Apparently, Pennsylvania kids were behind the times with fashion. I had no idea until I showed up wearing bell bottoms to this town that was more "with it" and all the kids were staring at my very uncool wardrobe. I went home and cried to my parents that I needed to go shopping for new clothes.

Just as I was surprised to find out that bell bottoms were no longer in style, some people simply just have no idea what's in style or not. My theory is, if you love certain colors, then do what you want. But if you're trying to "update" your home, then you need to use updated colors, especially if you're planning to sell your house. Most buyers want "move in ready" which means they want it to look like new construction and as updated as possible.

Between being a paint color consultant, stager, and realtor, I have been to a LOT of houses. Just by looking at the paint colors and the décor, I can usually tell right away how old the people are who live there and when they painted the house last. The thing is, you really want to paint your house at the very least every 8-10 years, and styles change within that time period. So by the time the styles change, it's time to repaint anyway.

Many times I am asked, "Is this color too trendy? How long do you think this color will be in style? If I paint this color, is it going to go out of style in another year?". The truth is that just like clothing styles are ever changing, so are Interior Design styles. Take a look back at the pink tiled Bathrooms from the 1950's, the Mid-Century modern style of the 1960's, the Harvest Gold, Rust Orange and Avocado Green of the 1970's, the mint green and peach flowered wallpaper and balloon valances of the 1980's and you'll realize that every decade brings changes in style. It's inevitable.

Usually, people don't realize that so much time has actually gone by since the last time they have done any painting or updates to their home. I like to affectionately call 1995-2005 as "The Tuscan Era". It seems everyone wanted to live in Italy. This is the era that I was very busy painting faux finishes and grapevines. The Kitchens and Bathrooms had cherry cabinets, granite countertops and tumbled marble galore on the floors, on the backsplash and in the shower. I know to some people those Kitchens seem "updated", but in actuality that was 20 years ago already! If you still have glazed walls in your house, then all I have to say is, "The faux needs to go!" (That goes for your red Dining Room too!)

The faux needs to go!

This ship has sailed. It's time to come back to America!

I was still getting requests for red Dining Rooms in 2015 and I had to tell them "I'm sorry, but that ship has sailed. It went out of style about ten years ago." Of course, I will give them a red Dining Room if that's what they really want, but I also explain that it will look like it was painted fifteen years ago and it's time for a new paint job. That's when they realize that maybe it's not such a good idea.

Once the new Millennium was in full swing, we neutralized everything and every house became a sea of beige. Then gray became the new beige. Most people seem to need to see the new trends for about two years before they begin to follow suit. Even now as an adult I found myself once again in a fashion dilemma and resisted the skinny jeans trend for a couple years before I finally gave in! (I'm still waiting for Bell Bottoms to come back!) At the time I'm writing this book gray has been the in thing for a few years. The trend setters were probably using gray for a couple years before the rest of America jumped onto the gray train. So if trends last for a decade, then we are nearing the end of the trend. Over the past year whites and off-whites have become very popular. So I find I'm using a lot of pale grays that are found in the Off-White Collection. I'm still using neutrals, but just lighter versions.

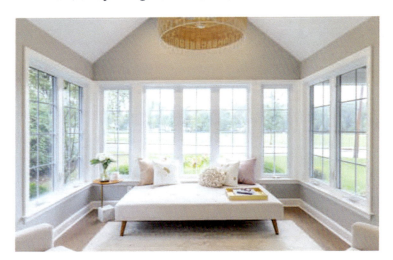

What's Coming Next?

I get asked this question a lot. "What's the next color trend coming?" What I have seen happening over the past few years is a move toward becoming more and more contemporary. But the problem is that most people are not ready for contemporary homes, so we are in what I call the "Transitional Phase". We have come out of a time period of very traditional homes that have formal Living and Dining Rooms with large, dramatic window treatments, oriental carpets, wallpaper, lots of pillows and a lot of fuss. But I believe that to jump from all of that pomp and circumstance straight over to mid-century modern, contemporary style is too much of a stretch for most people. First of all, it's so different from what they're used to that it feels uncomfortable. Secondly, all that "stuff" they own cost them a lot of money!

Thanks to decorating shows on TV, the farmhouse trend has been going strong for a while and people like all white walls. The updating being done in most homes right now consists of ripping out carpets and replacing with hardwood, neutralizing walls with gray and taupe paint colors, choosing furniture with cleaner lines, using window treatments that are less fussy, and remodeling Kitchens and Bathrooms in gray and white. So while we still have homes with traditional architectural elements like crown molding and wainscot, our eyes are gradually getting used to seeing less fuss.

The Gray Train: If you're just catching up and thinking about painting some gray walls, I would say that since gray goes really well with contemporary style, then it's pretty safe to paint gray walls and expect it to still be in style for a while. These colors are cool grays from the **Winter** palette. People are saying "Gray is out now", but they still want neutrals. They still want gray, but just a much lighter, off-white version of gray.

Since gray and white is essentially the complete absence of color, I predicted several years ago that the next trend would be color, and I was right! The next color trend coming is vibrant jewel toned colors like fuchsia pink, deep purple, chartreuse greens, royal blue, and teal. You'll see this more and more. As a color specialist, I'm excited because I have spent the past decade toning down color and riding the gray train with my clients, but now I will be able to finally have some fun!

It took me six years to finish this book and the hardest part about writing it was worrying about color trends changing. But the seasonal palettes I've created are the answer for that. When I first went to work in the paint store the **Autumn** palette colors of red, rust, gold, and olive green were in style. Then we moved into the cooler grays and blues from the **Winter** palette which have been in style for the past few years. Now I have heard that warmer colors are coming back in, like beige and green. But you'll find those colors in the **Spring** palette. As color styles and trends change they should still fall into one of the **Color Seasons** palettes and this book should stay pretty evergreen. As you'll learn in this book, the trick to choosing colors is to match your existing stuff in your home. Whether your stuff is brand new or old, just find colors that go best with your furniture and tile, and you should be just fine.

All aboard!

The Method

When I worked in a Benjamin Moore store for 11 years I found myself saying the same things over and over and over again. Eventually I began to start making up my own little rules for every room, and they always worked. So now I'm sharing my method with you. Here it is in a nutshell:

1. Choose a Color Season. To figure out what colors you like look at your furniture and your clothes to see what you tend to choose. Refer to the chapter on **Color Seasons** and decide which season seems to fit you best.

2. Get Fan Decks or Paint Chips. You can't do anything without them.

3. Match your Stuff. It's that simple. You will lay your fan deck or paper chips on your surfaces to see which colors match the stuff in your rooms. You'll match the tile, furniture etc. That will help you to eliminate thousands of colors that won't work and are a waste of time.

4. Go Room by Room. Follow the order of rooms laid out in the book. After doing these tens of thousands of times, I have found that this is the best order to follow. If you're doing every room in the house start in the Kitchen. If you're not painting the Kitchen then obviously you don't have to start in the Kitchen. However, as you begin to choose new colors for other rooms, you may discover that the Kitchen may look better with a new color too.

5. Take Notes. As you go room by room, you'll take notes. Then when you're done with the first floor, look at the colors you chose for each room. See which ones all fit into the same season of color. This will help you cross some choices off the list. Try to choose colors with similar undertones. Then the rooms will flow, but more importantly, the transition will be very easy on the eyes as you walk from room to room.

6. Follow the Rules. I have simple rules to follow to keep it, well… simple. The rules are outlined in the next chapter.

Fan Decks

Get Fan Decks.

You can't choose any colors without paper chips of the available paint colors. The first thing you will need is paper chips. Ideally you should get a fan deck. (This is a wheel of paint colors. Usually, you can buy them at the paint store depending on the brand of paint they sell. Sherwin Williams has one fan deck. Benjamin Moore has about 6, one for each different color collection, and you can either borrow them, rent them or buy them, depending on your retailer. If you hire a painter or have a contractor, they will usually have their own fan decks that they will let you borrow. For more, refer to the **Fan Decks and Color Collections** chapter.

Small designer collections like those by Restoration Hardware or Farrow and Ball don't have that many colors to choose from and they are all lovely. If you only have a brochure, then cut each color chip out carefully, and save them in an envelope or create a mini fan deck. If you can get chips, collect one of every chip. You can always make your own fan deck by bringing home one of every chip.

Creating Your Own Fan Deck

If you can't get fan decks then you'll have to go to the paint store and just start grabbing paint chips and bring them all home. If this is the case, then read through the chapter for the room you're painting first and get an idea of the type of color you should be using. Then go to the paint store and grab a bunch of chips in that color family. For instance, if you're painting a Dining Room and I tell you do NOT use beige, but do get blue or green, then you know that you won't need to get any beige chips, but DO get an assortment of blues and greens. Make sure to also read the chapter on **Toning Down and Fixing Colors** because you may also want to bring home an assortment of grays that look blue and khakis that look green.

Pick out chips that look good in the store, and then also get versions that look brighter, and more muted, because chances are the color will not look the same in your home as it does in the store. For instance, a yellow may get either much brighter or look too pale and white in your house. So get a few chips that may potentially solve the problem later. Refer to the chapter on **Toning Down and Fixing Colors**. Also look at **My Favorite Colors** and pick up some of those chips too.

Big box stores like Home Depot do not have fan decks. (I did see one once but they had it chained down and wouldn't let anyone touch it! LOL) They have free brochures but as you work your way through this book, I will tell you to lay the chips directly on surfaces to see if the colors match, and this is next to impossible to do using a brochure. You'll need to either cut the chips out of the brochure or get the paint chips from the wall display. Once you have all your chips, punch a hole in each of them and then use a string or chain to hold them all together to create your own fan.

How I Always Begin

The One Minute Color Lesson.

Every time I go to a client's home for a color consultation, I first ask them to give me a tour of their home. I take mental notes. Are they using warm colors and have warm colored furniture everywhere? Or do they have cool colors? Is their style very traditional and conservative? Is their style very monochromatic or do they like color? Do they like contrast, or a softer look? Have they just remodeled their Kitchen? If so, is it all white with cool gray and white marble? Or did they go with creamy colored cabinets and warmer colors? Are they buying new furniture? Is it beige or gray? I try to tap into my client and figure out what they're going to like. Next, I give them my one-minute color lesson before we begin choosing colors. Here it is:

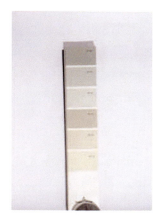

1) **Historical Grays:** First, I show them the strip of gray colors in the Historical Collection by Benjamin Moore. I point out that the top three colors are Covington Gray, Stonington Gray and Wickham Gray, and they are all "Cool Grays". They are silver and lean toward turning a little blue in certain light. Then I point out that the two colors below them, Revere Pewter and Edgecomb Gray are "Warm Grays". They have a bit of beige in them to warm them up. These two grays go well with beige and yellow. If they are still in the "Tuscan Era" then these colors will work well with their existing furniture and tile.

2) **Cool Grays:** Next, I show them these 5 gray strips in the Classic Collection. I show them that the one second from the top with Horizon Gray 1478 is a cool gray. Then I put Horizon next to Stonington Gray HC 170 to show them that it looks like those cool grays that I showed them first. Then I push it away. I point out that the strip all the way to the right has a little bit of a purple undertone. I usually only use it in Bathrooms because it tends to match some Bathroom tile. Then I push it away. If they like cooler grays then we may return to these strips later.

3) **Warm Grays:** Now we are down to 3 strips. I show them that these are "Warm Grays" but not as beige as Revere Pewter that we saw on the first strip. I show them that the strip on the left with Balboa Mist, and the one on the right with Nimbus are the two warmer ones, and the one in the middle with Shoreline is more of a straight gray.

4) **My Favorite Shades of Gray:** These last three remaining strips with Balboa Mist, Shoreline and Nimbus will probably be the ones we will be using. How do I know? Because after doing this thousands of times, these are the ones it always seems to come down to, and because I know that all of the other grays will turn blue, green or purple.

At this point they are beginning to see the difference between the colors. They are seeing the undertones, and they are seeing the difference between warm and cool colors. When I break it down like this, I am eliminating 3,400 colors that will not work and that we won't waste our time on! They're starting to relax and see that this won't be so difficult after all. (They also see that I know what I'm doing and begin to trust me.)

If I can tell that they will probably prefer warmer colors, or if after the tour I know that taupe will match their stuff better than gray, I will continue the color lesson and explain beiges and taupes.

5) **Beiges:** I fan out the Classic fan deck and show them the section of beiges showing them how yellowy and peachy they are. I used to use these colors a lot 12 years ago, but don't use them anymore. They don't go with new stuff anymore. The only strip I use occasionally is the one with **Muslin** and **Everlasting**. (Now I just eliminated all the beige strips except one.)

6) **Taupes:** Next, I fan out the taupe section and show them that they all look a little pinkish or purple. (They nod in agreement. They're getting it!) except for the one all the way on the right which has **Winds Breath**, **Cedar Key** and **Smokey Taupe**. These colors are the taupes that are the most neutral and are not pink. This is the strip I use every day. (Again, we narrowed it down to one taupe strip). The only time I will use one of the other taupes is if that's what matches the tile in a Bathroom.

7) **Off-Whites:** If I feel like they're going to prefer really light colors and off-whites, then I explain the off-whites. I open up to the Off-White Collection in the "Collections" fan deck, and show them that all of the colors are a little "something". They are all a little pink, yellow, green, beige, gray, something. Then I tell them that a lot of these colors have been taken from a section in the other fan decks, and they repeat.

8) **My Favorite Off-White:** To make my point about off-whites repeating, I show them an example. I open up to the strip with OC-22-OC-28. Then I bring back the warm gray strip with Classic Gray 1548 and Balboa Mist 1549 and show them that OC-23 is Classic Gray and OC-27 is Balboa Mist. (They are amazed!) Next, I'll tell them that **Silver Satin OC-26** is currently my favorite off-white color because it's not yellow, or pink, or peach, or green. It's just neutral. It's not even really gray because it's so light and it's warm. It's just a really great, barely there color that goes with everything.
*For a list of comparable colors in Sherwin Williams, see pages 335-336.

After the color lesson, we go room by room starting in the Kitchen.

How to Look At Color Chips

A. Hold It Perpendicular to the Surface.

First make sure the color works with your couch, tile, cabinets, etc. as outlined in the book for each room. Lay the chips right on the surface to find a color that matches. For instance, if you have beige tile and you're painting the room beige, lay the chip right on the tile to make sure you're choosing the correct beige.

B. Hold the Chip Up Vertically.

When you lay a chip on the horizontal floor or countertop the light will reflect onto the chip differently than it will on a vertical wall. To see how the color looks on a WALL you need to pick up the chip. You'll be amazed at how different the chip looks when held vertically after looking at it horizontally.

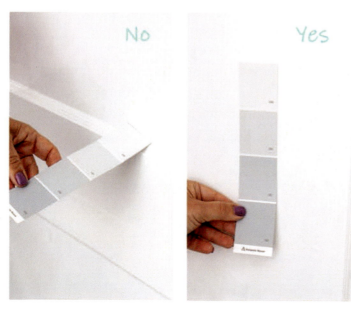

C. Hold It Against Something White.

You don't want to hold the chip up in the middle of the wall because holding it against the existing wall color will affect how the new color looks. Instead look at the chips against something white. I always hold chips up against a white door, or white window trim. If there's nothing white, then put a piece of paper behind the chip, because you need to see the color against a clean slate. If you like how the chip looks, then it's time to buy sample paint.

Take Notes.

When I choose colors for clients I immediately eliminate colors in my head and narrow it down to about 2 colors that will work in the room. I want you to do the same thing. For each room I will give you categories to look at to figure out what your possible color choices could be. Begin by taking out a sheet of paper and a pen. As you go through each category, write down what your possible color choices are, and then go back and compare notes. See which colors will work in every category and it should leave you with only a couple color choices for the room. Hopefully you'll narrow it down to about three colors.

Go Room by Room and Match Your Stuff.

When I am helping clients choose colors for the whole house I **start in the Kitchen.** We look at the quartz, granite, marble or tile and the cabinets, assessing the room and deciding which handful of colors may work. If the cabinets are white or off-white then that will determine the trim color for the entire first floor. Then, out of that Kitchen collection of color possibilities, if the Kitchen is open to the Family Room, I'll choose a color that works for both the Kitchen and Family Room. I think of the whole first floor or main living area as a whole. Living Room, Dining Room, Kitchen, Family Room. There are usually no doors closing these rooms off from each other and you can see one room from the next. I want these colors to flow and like to use the same trim color in all of these rooms.

After the Kitchen and Family Room, I'll look at the Living Room and then the Dining Room, and if it's a Center Hall Colonial, I will choose a Foyer color that works with both the Living Room and Dining Room. If there is a Laundry Room, Mud Room, Office, Sunroom, or other rooms on the first floor, they come next. They are usually behind closed doors so they don't necessarily have to flow with the other rooms. Next, I'll move onto the Bedrooms and Bathrooms, treating each room separately. The Basement usually comes last.

We will discuss matching your stuff in more detail in the chapters for each room.

Things That May Come Up

What If I Have Too Many Color Choices That will Work for a Room?

In most rooms you'll have several color choice possibilities. For instance, you may have a beige couch and blue in your pillows and rug. So you could potentially choose a warm beige, or cool blue. By starting to realize whether you prefer warm or cool colors it will help you to decide which color choices to make for your rooms.

If you're painting every room, and as you read through the guidelines for each room you find that you have too many color choices available for one or two of the rooms, then put that room on hold until you've chosen colors for other rooms first. If you're confused about which color to choose, then wait until you choose colors for other rooms because then you'll begin to get a clearer picture of what direction to go in for that room. For instance, in an all-white Kitchen pretty much any color will work, but in the adjoining Family Room there will only be a few colors that will work. So you'll paint the Kitchen a color that works for the Family Room. Or, if most of the other rooms have gray undertones for instance, then that will tell you that you'll want to choose a color that flows well with the other gray rooms. Even if you're only painting one room, if it's on the first floor (or part of the main living area, not a Bedroom or Bathroom then choose a color that coordinates with the other rooms.

What If I Have No Choices?

In rooms that have nothing in them to inspire a color choice like an all-white Kitchen, a Foyer, or a Dining Room with no fabrics or rugs, then you may have nowhere to start and have no idea which colors to choose from. If this is the case then the place to start is in a room that has something that you can match, like the Living Room that has a couch. Look at which colors will look good in that room. If you start to realize which palette of colors you like then it will help you to choose a color for these spaces. After you decide which season you like, then look within that palette to find color ideas for the other rooms that you weren't sure what to do with.

The Broken Rule.

Rooms behind closed doors, not open to other rooms, do NOT have to flow! If it's a room like a Bedroom or an Office upstairs and behind a closed door not seen from the rest of the house, then it does not need to flow with the rest of the house. Choose a color that makes you happy!

The Rule Book

My goal with the "rules" is to make sure you're not overstimulated with too much color and your eyes have somewhere to rest. Basically, what I'm trying to say is:

"Too much stuff, too much color and too much going on is just too much!"

Rule #1: Avoid the "Crayon Box".

Unless you live at the White House, you don't want a red room, blue room, green room, yellow room and orange room. This is the basis for all of the other rules.

Rule #2 "Have a Neutral Space".

You will want at least one main living area to be neutral so your eye has somewhere to rest. Usually that area will be the space that you spend the most time in.

Rule #3: "The Rule of Three".

Try to stick to no more than 3 main colors in your furniture and fabrics in a room. A fourth or fifth color should only be in small doses, like accent pillows or accessories. As far as painted walls, when you stand in one room and look into the other adjacent rooms, you should not see more than 3 paint colors from that space. Especially when using strong colors like red, green, blue or yellow, make sure one of the third colors is neutral.

Rule #4: "Less is More".

Keep strong colors and dark colors to a minimum of two. Don't paint more than two dark rooms and keep strong colors to a minimum. If you love red, you don't need to paint the walls red, or buy a red couch. Keep the walls and couch neutral and get some red pillows and accessories instead. You'll find that the red has more impact and your eye will go right to that red accessory. Then if you get tired of the red, it's much easier to buy new pillows than to repaint the whole room or buy a new couch. I can't tell you how many times I have heard "I don't know what I was thinking

when I bought that...". Simply put, don't over decorate. Rooms don't need a "theme" and everything in them doesn't need to match. If you're a collector, keep your collections to one room. When I'm staging homes, I tell homeowners to put half of their stuff into storage. After a while they realize they don't need half of the things they own. If you were moving tomorrow, would you take everything with you or get rid of a bunch of things? Similarly, when choosing paint colors, try to keep it simple. By using this book you'll be able to eliminate some of the "clutter" and narrow down your choices to only a few simple choices.

Rule #5: Go with the Flow.

Treat the whole main living area of the house as a whole, rather than each room individually. You'll want all the rooms on the first floor to have the same undertone, whether it's beige, gray or yellow, you want the rooms to FLOW. It should be easy on the eyes as you look from one room to the other, and you should be able to take a chair from one room and place it in the other room and it still works. This will make it easy to choose one trim color that will work in every room.

Rule #6: Don't Mix Whites.

If you use different shades of white in a room one will look clean and the other will look dingy and dirty. If you have white in the room, like white cabinetry, then match that white and have it become your trim color. Likewise, if you have off-white cabinets, white trim will make the cabinets look dirty.

Rule #7: Don't Ask for Everyone Else's Opinion.

You could love green and want to paint your room green, and then your best friend who HATES green will walk in and see your sample and say, "You're not going to paint it THAT color are you?!". Trust me...**too many cooks in the Kitchen spoil the soup!** The guidelines in this book are very simple. You will be choosing colors that go with YOUR stuff, not theirs.

> Just because a color looks good in your friend's house, doesn't mean it will look good in yours.

You may see a color you really like at your friend's house, or even at a Designer Show House, but if you don't have the same furniture and lighting that they have their color will not work in your house.

Rule #8: "Keep Calm and Carry On".

DON'T OVER THINK IT! Everyone gets way too stressed out over choosing the perfect color. Remember, IT'S ONLY PAINT. It's not set in stone, like choosing tile where once it's up its permanent. Paint is not permanent. If you don't like it, you can change it. In the scheme of life, there are much more important things to worry about, like your health and your family. So try and relax and don't sweat the small stuff. **Try NOT to be a perfectionist.** Don't obsess over it because if you do you will drive yourself crazy.

Part 2

In this second section we will discuss how to choose colors going room by room.

The Heart of the Home

Kitchens

Checklist

 Cabinets

 Counters

 Backsplash

 Flooring

If you're choosing colors for the whole house then the Kitchen will be the first room to start in because everything in this room is already set in stone, literally.

The first step to choosing colors for the Kitchen is to look at your **cabinets**. It will give you an idea of the general direction in where to go. Can you use a clear bright color? Or should you use a muddy color? Can you use warm or cool tones? Write down what your options are and take notes. Next look at your countertop and your backsplash, then go back and compare notes. See which color choices will work in each category. As you work your way through your choices should get narrowed down to only a couple color choices for the room.

Cabinets

Since the cabinets take up a lot of space in the Kitchen, and the wall color will be right next to the cabinets, the first step for choosing color for the Kitchen is to look at your cabinets and see what colors will look good with them.

White Cabinets

If you have white cabinets then the first thing to do is try to match the white. Is it really white? Or is it off-white? Start by putting a white chip on one of the cabinets to see if it's really white or not. When you find the white that matches the best that will become your trim color. Don't drive yourself crazy over this. There are some pretty standard whites in each paint brand, so see if the cabinet color comes pretty close to one of those whites. Read the chapter on **Trim Colors** for more about whites.

Super White PM-1

If they are truly white then you can choose just about any color you want for the walls. You can use clear bright colors, muddy, in-between, warm, or cool colors. The sky is the limit. The next step will be to look at your countertop and backsplash for wall color ideas and choose a color that goes with them. If the cabinets are not a true white, then refer to "off-whites".

Tip! Most new white cabinets match Super White by Benjamin Moore.

Off-White Cabinets

If you have off-white cabinets then try to match the cabinets to see what the undertones are. They may have a touch of peach, yellow, pink, or beige in them. You may notice that when you lay beige paint chips next to the cabinet that suddenly the cabinet looks peach and the paint chip looks green. If you have trouble seeing the undertones it may help to put a **gray paint chip** next to the cabinets to draw out the undertone color a bit more. If they have a **peach** undertone then choose a warm color for the walls like a beige that has a slightly peachy undertone, or a chocolate brown or orange. A muddy greenish blue actually compliments peach nicely. If they have some **pink**, then refer to "pink, pickled cabinets." If they have some **yellow,** then refer to "blonde wood" cabinets. Most off-white cabinets have one of these warm tones, so **Summer** and **Autumn** palettes will work best.

Off-whites need a "**muddy**" color on the walls. Clear bright colors will make the cabinets look dingy and dirty. Once you figure out which color the cabinets are use that color for your **trim** color, or a slightly lighter version of that color.

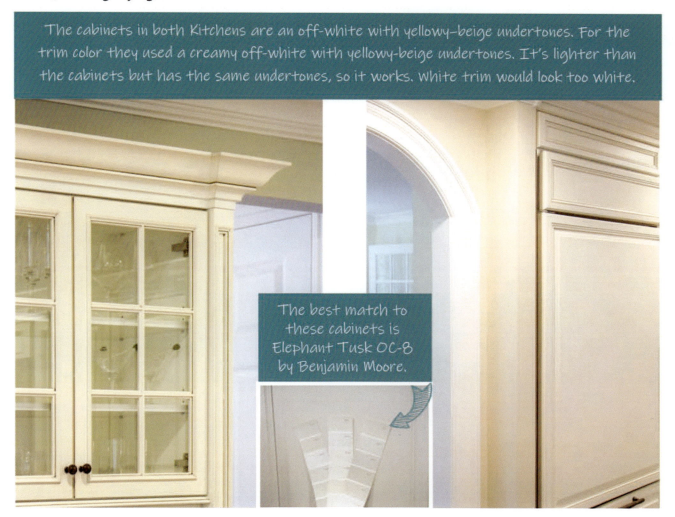

The cabinets in both kitchens are an off-white with yellowy-beige undertones. For the trim color they used a creamy off-white with yellowy-beige undertones. It's lighter than the cabinets but has the same undertones, so it works. White trim would look too white.

The best match to these cabinets is Elephant Tusk OC-8 by Benjamin Moore.

In this kitchen there is a soffit above the cabinets. So in order to make the cabinets appear taller, they went with a light neutral that would blend with the cabinets rather than contrast.

Creamy, Yellowy, and Beige Cabinets

The first step in these Kitchens is to match the color of the cabinets. It will probably become your trim color. Then when you determine that the cabinets are warm and yellowy, then look at warm colors from the **Autumn** and **Summer** palettes that will go well with the cabinets. A cool color will contrast too much making the walls appear blueish and the cabinets will appear even more yellow.

In this Kitchen the owner had chosen a cool gray and white trim which really shows how beige the cabinets really are. That's fine if you want the cabinets to look beige. But this homeowner really wanted a whiter Kitchen. We held up chips and found that the cabinets match Navajo White. In order to tone down the beige and make the cabinets appear whiter, there needed to be less contrast. So we chose a warm gray for the walls and painted the trim Navajo White.

Colored Cabinets

If your cabinets are painted a color like a gray then try to match the color the best you can. Then choose a color that is lighter or darker than the cabinets. If the Kitchen is very small then you may want to blend the walls in with the cabinets. If you would like to do another color then figure out if the color is **warm** or **cool**. If the cabinets are a cool gray, then do a cool color from the **Winter** palette. If they're a taupe use a color from the **Spring** palette. If they're a warm beigey gray then use a warm color from the **Autumn** palette.

If your cabinets are painted a color like blue or green, then it's probably best to paint the walls neutral so that you don't have too much color going on. Follow the same rules. Use a warm neutral for a warm color, and a cool neutral for a cool color. Look at the countertop, tile, and floor for ideas for the right neutral.

Black or Dark Stained Cabinets

These cabinets are as neutral as white so anything goes. Consider your countertop and backsplash for a color choice.

80

"The Tuscan Era"

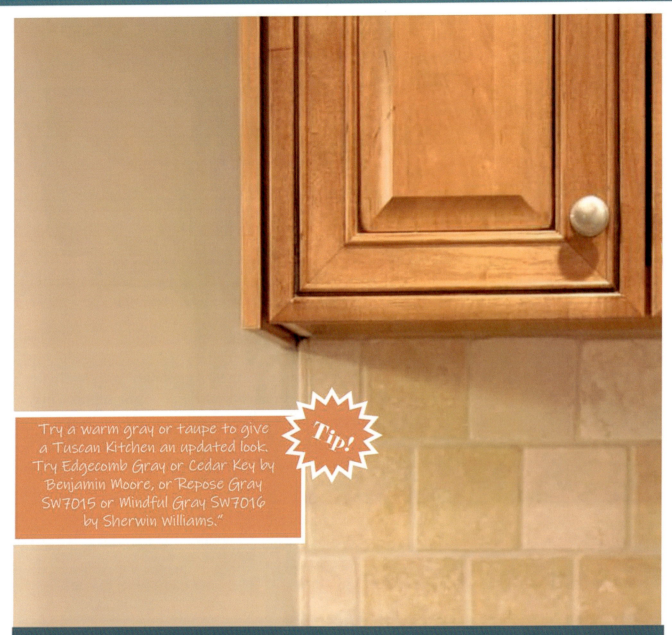

Tip! "Try a warm gray or taupe to give a Tuscan Kitchen an updated look. Try Edgecomb Gray or Cedar Key by Benjamin Moore, or Repose Gray SW7015 or Mindful Gray SW7016 by Sherwin Williams."

1995-2005 is the time period that I like to affectionately call "The Tuscan Era", when everyone wanted to live in Tuscany! Kitchens had stained wood cabinets, tumbled marble backsplashes and granite countertops. Walls were typically painted in olive greens or golds and Dining Rooms were red. These colors from the **Autumn** palette compliment-stained wood cabinets nicely, but they can also date your Kitchen. If you're looking for a more updated look, or you're planning to sell your house, then steer clear of the red-gold-green combo. As one client said to me who was sick of her Tuscan Kitchen, "It's time to leave Italy now and come back to America!" A warm gray is the perfect "transition color" for these Kitchens. For a fresher look, choose neutrals from the **Autumn** and **Spring** palettes to help these Kitchens look more updated.

Stained Wood Cabinets

Gold, Orange, Red, and Cherry Stains

These cabinets are very warm so warm colors from the **Summer** and **Autumn** palette work well. (But try to stay out of Tuscany.) For a neutral choose a taupe, warm beigey gray, or a beige with peach or gold undertones. If you hate the orange tone of the cabinets then avoid colors with green undertones because they will make the cabinets appear even more orange.

Look at the countertop and tile for color ideas. If you have granite and tumbled marble, then there is probably beige and gray, warm and cool tones to choose from. If you have some gray in the granite, or stainless-steel appliances, or if you just prefer cooler colors, then you can use colors from the **Winter** and **Spring** palettes like sage green, slate blue or taupe.

Use only muddy colors with these cabinets.

Neutral Stains

If the cabinets are a neutral stain color and more in the brown family and not too orange, then most colors will be fine, so look at your counter and tile for color ideas. If the floor, counter and tile are all beige and brown, then beige walls will simply create a boring sea of beige, so try to use something different.
Cool colors in the **Winter** and **Spring** palettes like blue, green and gray will contrast with the wood yet compliment it nicely. Warm colors in the **Summer** palette like a soft gold will brighten up a darker Kitchen and give it a nice glow.

Blonde Wood

Light colored cabinets and floors tend to have a warm yellow undertone, so colors in the **Summer** and **Autumn** palettes will work best. For a neutral, either choose creamy off-white or a beige with golden undertones. If you want to paint the walls gray, then go with a warm, beigey gray. Do not use a cool taupe because it has a hint of pink and the walls will look pink next to yellow cabinets. Green has yellow in it so it works, and if you like blue, choose a slightly greenish-blue. Obviously you can use yellow, but use a muddy version like a soft gold or a color with gold undertones. Do not use a clear lemon yellow because it will make the cabinets look dirty. Use muddy or in-between colors, not clear brights.

Pickled Cabinets

Pickled cabinets have pink undertones but do not try to fight against the pink. Painting the walls a color with yellow or green undertones will only make the cabinets look more pink. You need to use a cool color or a color with a hint of pink, which will actually tone down the pink. The best neutral to use is a taupe with a slightly pink undertone in these Kitchens because it tones down the pink and neutralizes the space. Anything in the red family will work. Cool, muddy colors in the **Winter** and **Spring** palettes work best.

Countertops

After narrowing down colors that work with the cabinets, then consider the countertop. Lay paint chips on the counter and try to match the colors that are in it. They will help you to make a good choice for your wall color.

Granite

Most granite and natural stone tend to have warm and cool tones. In other words, they have beige and gray. So that helps knowing you can choose either warm or cool tones for the walls. If you have mostly beige or brown granite, brown stained cabinets, beige floor, and a beige backsplash, then it's probably too much beige. Brown is warm, so you can use a warm color from the **Summer** or **Autumn** palette. If there is cool gray in the granite then consider cooler colors from the **Winter** or **Spring** palette like a muddy gray-blue or a gray-green color.

Here is an example of two kitchens with stained wood cabinets and granite that has both warm and cool tones. Neither kitchen has a tile backsplash. One chose a warm beigey gray to compliment the granite, the other chose a cool gray-green to compliment the cabinets. Both work. It's just a matter of personal preference.

Some granite has a bit of gold, and some are dark green. But there are always neutral beiges, creams, and grays within the granite to give you color choices. Find some paint colors that match sections of the granite, and then see if your choices look good with the cabinets.

Marble, Quartz, and Quartzite

Lay paint chips on the marble and see if you can match colors in the marble. Then hold the chip up to the wall and see if you like it with your cabinets and backsplash.

Carrera Marble is a cool white with gray veins. Look at the veining for an idea for a wall color. It goes really well with the **Winter** palette which includes cool grays, gray blues and gray greens. If you prefer colors slightly warmer look at the **Spring** palette. If the marble or quartz is primarily white, then it's essentially as neutral as black and white, so you can use any color you wish. Look to the backsplash for more ideas.

These slabs of marble have cooler gray tones, so they went with cool grays on the walls that match the marble.

Some marble has a bit of gold which opens the door for warmer colors especially if it's more creamy. Look at the **Autumn** palette for ideas.

Quartz comes in many colors. Take notice if it's warm or cool. Match the color and decide what looks good with it. If its cool quartz look at **Winter** and **Spring** palettes. If it's warm look at **Autumn** and **Summer** palettes.

These slabs of marble have cool gray veins and also have hints of warm gold and green. So either a warm color or a cool color would work with this kitchen.

Formica and Other Countertop Materials

If the overall color of the countertop is white then anything will work. If the countertop is primarily off-white, then follow the same rules for off-white cabinets and figure out what the undertones are. If they're neutral then try to match the neutral to find out what the undertones are. If they're a warm color then use a color from the **Summer** or **Autumn** palette. If they're cool, use **Winter** or **Spring** palette colors. If they're a strong color then it's probably best to use a neutral color on the walls.

Agreeable Gray
SW 7029

Tip!

If you have an older kitchen with a soffit above the cabinets, then paint the soffit in a color similar to the cabinets to make them appear taller!

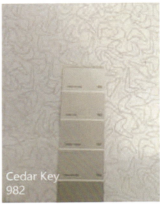

Cedar Key
982

If it's a color from the '50's, '60's, 70's, or '80's, then refer to the chapter on Bathrooms for color problem solving ideas.

Backsplashes

Your paint color will most likely be next to the backsplash tile so make sure the paint looks good with the backsplash. You can either match the tile, or let the tile stand alone as an accent color in the room. Just make sure the paint color does not clash with the backsplash.

White Tile or Stainless Steel

For both of these tiles you can do any color. Take clues from the countertop to decide what color to do. With Stainless anything in the gray family will work especially well. Look at the **Winter** palette for ideas.

Gray Marble and Tile

With gray tile try to match the color the best you can and use that on the walls. Don't venture off into a gray green, or gray blue, because it will look like you were trying to match the gray tile but you're off. You can go lighter or darker but stay in the same color family.

Beige Ceramic Tile

Lay beige paint chips on the beige tile and choose colors that match. Sometimes there are beige and gray tones, both warm and cool. Next, hold the chips up to the cabinets to see which of those chips look best with the cabinets. If the cabinets are white, you can use a cooler beige or taupe. If the cabinets are creamy, then use a warmer neutral.

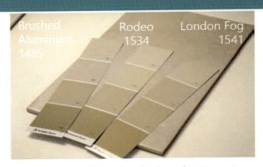

If the cabinets are stained wood, and the countertop and backsplash are all in the beige/brown family, then consider using a color. To choose a color, try to figure out what the undertones are. Then choose a color that compliments it. For instance, if there is yellow in it, make sure to choose a warm color that works with the yellow undertones. Be sure to use a **muddy color** or else the beige tile will look dirty and dingy.

If there is an accent color in the tile, then you can match the accent color instead.

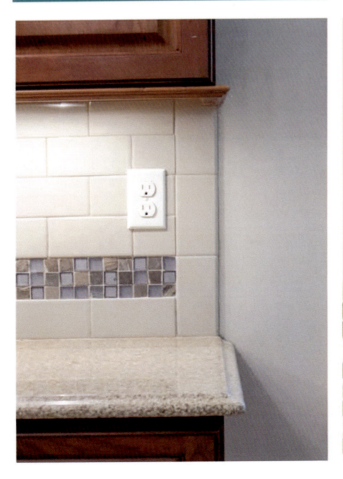

Tumbled Marble

One way to find a color is to hold paint chips up to the tile and match the neutral tones of the tile. If you prefer to paint the walls beige, then match the beige in the tile. If you want to use gray, you'll probably find a hint of a warm gray in the tile, so a warm gray will work very well. You could also contrast with the tile by using a deep warm gray or try a cool color like a gray blue or green which look great against natural stone. Use only muddy colors with this tile.

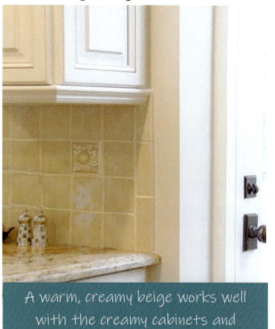

A warm, creamy beige works well with the creamy cabinets and matches the tile.

Mocha Cream 995   Alphano Beige 989   Cedar Key 982

A warm gray found in the granite breaks up all the beige and brown tones in this kitchen in a subtle way.

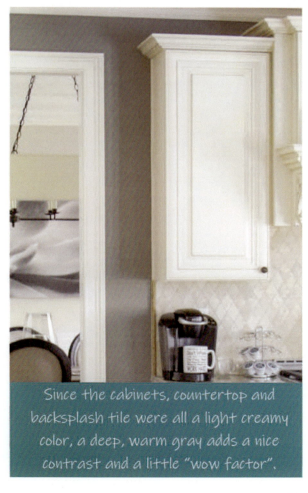

Since the cabinets, countertop and backsplash tile were all a light creamy color, a deep, warm gray adds a nice contrast and a little "wow factor".

Colored Ceramic and Glass Tile

If the tile is colored, then hold paint chips up next to the tile and find colors that match. You can use a lighter or darker version of the tile color if you wish. If you want the backsplash to stand out on its own as an accent color, then paint the walls neutral. If you have white cabinets then you can really have some fun with color!

Mix and Match

Here they ignored the cool gray granite and matched the warm, beige backsplash instead.

When trying to match a color to each surface, you may find that they are all slightly different neutral colors and each paint color that you try just won't work with everything in the Kitchen. In this case you'll just have to flip a coin and decide which one is more important to match. If the paint will be right next to the backsplash then it's probably best to choose a color that looks best with the backsplash. Another option is to paint the walls a color instead of a neutral. But you run the risk of too many colors going on in the room, so make sure the color is subtle and has beige or gray undertones.

A grayer version of the blue color in the flowered tile helped to modernize the space.

Old Tile

Sometimes the Kitchen is just old and it's primarily some color you don't like, but if you fight the colors, it will only get worse. Other times you may want some color that you have in mind but in reality, it just won't work with the materials in your Kitchen. Look at your tile and just try to find the most neutral version of the colors in the tile and use that. Don't stress over it. Sometimes you just have to say, "It is what it is" and let it go.

Flooring

The floor is the last thing to consider. If it's tile, then you may want to pull a color from that tile while looking for a color idea. For instance, if the cabinets, countertop, and backsplash are all white, but you have a gray floor, then match the floor. But sometimes the color you choose will match everything BUT the floor. In this case, the majority wins. Simply choose a color that goes with everything else and ignore the floor.

Wood Floors

If you have hardwood floors with gold, orange or red tones like golden oak or cherry then refer to cabinet colors with gold, orange, or red tones.

Dark and Neutral Stained Wood Floors

These floors are neutral as they have no gold or red undertones, so any color will work.

Gray, Greige, and Beige Floors

Laminate and Tile

You will probably find both warm and cool tones in these floors. Both grays and beiges. You can either match a color that's in the floor, or contrast with it to make the floor stand out. A color with gray undertones will work well with this floor. Look at the **Winter** and **Spring** palette for color ideas.

In the Kitchen below, there are beige chairs and tile, but blue fabric and island. They can either choose a warm neutral or a cool, muddy blue/gray. Both work. When working with beige colors always choose a muddy color so the floors don't look dirty!

Vinyl, Linoleum, and Other Floor Materials

Start by laying chips on the floor to see what the undertones are. Take notice if the overall background is white, gray, beige, or yellow. You don't want these floors to look old and dirty (even if they are!) so choose a muddy color with the same undertones. If there is blue, green, or yellow you may want to use a color with those undertones on the walls. If it's a strong orange or red, think of it as an accent color and follow rules for orange or red cabinets. If the floor is brown then just pretend its hardwood and try to ignore it.

Kitchens Attached to Family Rooms

When a Family Room is attached to the Kitchen I always paint them the same color because
A) There is barely any wall space in the Kitchen, so it doesn't make sense to use a different color.
B) It creates a more "open layout" feel. Sometimes you'll have a few choices for the Kitchen, both warm and cool neutrals, and you may not be able to decide which color to use.
So the next step is to look at the Family Room and decide which color will look best with the Family Room furniture. Take the color of the couch into consideration. Look at the pillows and the area rug too for color ideas. We will talk more about this in the **Family Rooms** chapter.

Smoke Embers 1466

Painted Kitchen Cabinets

If you really hate your Kitchen then consider painting your cabinets. It's cheaper than ripping out the whole Kitchen and at least you'll get a few more years out of it. You can hire a painter to do the job or you can do it yourself.

If you prefer more color, or are concerned about white cabinets getting dirty, then consider painting them gray or a color like teal, navy blue or sage green. If you choose a color, then consider the countertop, backsplash, and floor to decide on the best color. For more on choosing the right color to go with the countertop, see the section on painting Bathroom vanities in the **Bathrooms** chapter, pages 192-195. Because of wet and greasy fingers in the Kitchen you should probably opt for a muddy color with a gray undertone. Another option is to do white cabinets above, and a darker color below.

These homeowners changed the countertops and backsplash to be white so they were able to paint the cabinets a cool white.

Before

Option A: Paint the top cabinets white and the bottom cabinets blue.

Option B: Paint all of the cabinets white. The gray island matches the veins in the countertop.

Make sure you consider your countertop. If it's granite or marble that is really white, then you can paint the cabinets white. If the majority of it is off-white, then paint them off-white. If the countertop is creamy with a little yellow, then use a color that's creamy with a little yellow, or a light, warm, beigey gray.

Before

White cabinets would not have worked with a beige backsplash and orange/brown granite. A warm gray on the cabinets toned down the orange tone of the granite, and a very soft beige on the walls made the backsplash tile still work. New paint and floor stains made this look like a new kitchen!

After

97

Before

If you're keeping the old granite countertops then take it into consideration when choosing colors for the cabinets and the walls. White cabinets work with white marble or quartz, but not so much with warm, orangey granite. Choose a creamy white for the cabinets. I like to put color on the island. Choose a warm color to go with the warm granite. Either a warm gray, warm greenish blue, or a warm green will work.

A cool white would not work in this kitchen because there is no white in the granite. A warm creamy white and a warm greenish-blue is a better choice with the warm orange tone of the granite.

After

Before

After

Before

After

Steps to Painting Cabinets

1. **Sanding:** If you have built up grease and grime, ask the paint store if they recommend using a specific cleaner to use first. Next, sand the cabinets. The purpose of sanding is to give the cabinets some "tooth", which means to sand them a little to rough up the shine, enough so that the paint sticks. You don't need to sand them down to raw wood. DO NOT try and skip this step. I have seen multiple jobs in which the cabinets were not sanded and each time the paint chipped.

2. **Priming:** Primer helps the paint stick better so it won't chip later. Ask your paint store which primer they recommend.

3. **Painting:** Years ago, painters used "Alkyd", (oil-based paint) but no longer due to environmental reasons. Painters preferred oil because it floated out and you couldn't see the brush strokes. This gave it a nice smooth finish. There are several paints that have replaced oil-based paints. Benjamin Moore has one called "Advance" which floats out like an oil, but has soap and water cleanup. The other is called "Cabinet Coat" which is made specifically for painting cabinets and they say it won't chip. Sherwin Williams has "Emerald Urethane Trim Enamel" and "ProClassic Waterborne Interior Acrylic Enamel". If you're using a spray application they recommend using the Gallery Series. When choosing the type of paint, you can also choose the sheen, which means you can choose how shiny you want them to be. Most new cabinets look like a Pearl or Satin finish, so that's usually what I recommend. However, if you heavily use your Kitchen and want the cabinets more washable, then use Semi-Gloss. If you don't have a Benjamin Moore or Sherwin Williams dealer then ask your local paint store which paint they recommend.

4. **Clear Coat:** If you use regular paint and not the ones made for cabinets, then I recommend a few top coats of Polycrylic by Minwax. Not to be confused with Polyurethane which is oil-based and will turn yellow over time, Polycrylic is water-based. It's very thin, like water. Apply several very thin coats. When I was painting furniture, I was lazy and didn't want to do three thin coats and just did a thick coat, which dripped and looked terrible in the end. I learned the hard way. Don't be like me. Follow the directions on the can.

The Cozy Refuge

Family Rooms

Checklist

- ✓ Couches
- ✓ Fireplace
- ✓ Window Treatments
- ✓ Flooring
- ✓ Rugs

The Family Room is a place where you want to get cozy and lay down on the couch and chill out. It typically has a TV and if you're lucky it also has a fireplace. Since it's a room that you'll spend a lot of time in do NOT use a clear bright color in this space because it's too stimulating. You should use a color that's more neutral and relaxing. The couch is a large piece in the room so look at that first for color ideas. Next, look at the fireplace because it takes up a lot of wall space. Then consider the window treatments and lastly look at the floor.

Couches

Almost always I tend to paint Family Rooms neutral and rely on the pillows, area rugs and accessories for pops of color. If you can see the Family Room from the Living Room or Kitchen, make sure the rooms flow together and the paint colors look good next to each other. Read each category and create a checklist. Then go back and see which colors fall into each category and you should have your colors narrowed down.

Beige, Gray, or Taupe Couches

If you have a neutral-colored couch and want neutral walls then the easiest way to choose a color is to match the color of the couch. Simply lay a fan deck on the couch and try to match the color. Use a slightly lighter or darker version of the couch color on the walls because you don't want the couch to blend in with the walls. However, if it's a really small space, then it's okay for the couch to blend with the walls because it will help to make the space appear larger. If the couch is a darker beige, then follow the guidelines for brown leather.

Mixing Neutrals

You may have a situation where gray is the best color for your Kitchen, but your couch in the adjoining room is beige. That's OK! Beige and gray look great together, so you CAN paint gray walls with a beige couch. Preferably a warm gray would look best with beige. For more on this see the chapter on **Living Rooms**.

This room has a mix of neutrals to choose from. They were just sick of warm beige and wanted a change, so this time they went with gray. How do you make it work? New pillows!

103

Leather Couches

Brown Leather

Beige and taupe paint colors work with leather because they have brown in them. Brown is warm, so warm green-blues, khaki, olive greens, and gold tones from the **Summer** and **Autumn** palettes all work with brown leather. If it's a cooler taupe, then use cooler toned colors from the **Spring** palette.

Dark Leather

These couches are very heavy and masculine. Don't use soft, light, off-white colors though because they are too light and feminine and there will be too stark of a contrast between the walls and the couch. It will feel too black and white, and the room will feel cold and unfinished. Use colors that are a medium to deep tone.

Black Leather

Black is very neutral and pretty much anything goes with black. Look at an area rug or pillows for other color ideas. As with dark leather, off-whites can feel too stark. Go for a more medium toned color.

Colored Couches

A colored couch is a pretty strong statement, so it's better to keep the walls neutral. If the couch is a cool color like blue, then a cool gray would work. If it's red a taupe works best. If it's a warm olive green, then a beige would be best. Check out the **Color Seasons** to see which season of color the couch fits into to find good neutrals that will work. Then take into consideration the floor, fireplace and window treatments.

Go Darker

If you have a light-colored couch then you can go darker on the walls because it will help to make the room feel warmer and cozier. Look at the stone in the fireplace, area rugs, or pillows for color ideas.

Abalone 2108-60

Non-Neutral Walls

You don't have to paint the walls neutral. You can look at the pillows or the area rug for other color ideas for the room. Lay your paint chips on the rug or the pillows and try to match a color that's in them. Unless you have a black or white couch, muddy colors will probably look best. A clear bright color will make a beige couch or beige floor tile look dirty.

Fireplaces

If there is a fireplace then consider the color of the stone, brick, or tile. If It's stone then place color chips on the stone and try to match some of the colors to come up with a color for the room. Hopefully some of the colors that go well with the couch also go well with the fireplace.

Brick

Khaki beiges, olive greens, and taupes all look great with brick. You do not need to use red or orange just because the brick is that color. Gray-blue also compliments brick well. Look at your furniture and area rug to figure out which direction to go in. If you hate the brick, paint it!

Before

After

Painting this bump-out dark makes the fireplace appear larger and more grand!

Tip!

Old brick fireplaces can date your home. Consider painting over the brick to give it a fresh, new look!

Tile or Marble

If the stone or tile is only a small area within the mantle, then think of it as just an accent color. You don't have to match it if you don't want to. If you just don't have any idea of what color to use because you don't even have furniture yet, then you could pull a color from the fireplace. You can match the overall color, but also look at the veining because it may give you more options. Like natural stone, marble may be beige but have gray veins.

This Family Room is attached to a newly remodeled Kitchen. They wanted a darker gray to make the white cabinets stand out. It also makes the warm stone stand out too. If you love the fireplace then that's a good thing.

Natural Stone

Most natural stone has warm and cool tones like beige and gray. This opens the door to choose colors in either color family. First look at the couch and then see if you find the couch color in the stone. Try to find something that compliments them both.

Mid-Century Stone

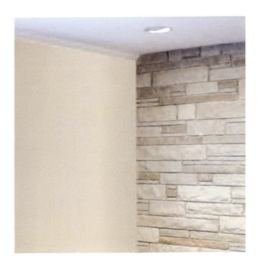

Some Mid-Century stone is taupe with a hint of pink undertones. Some are gray. First try to match the stone colors. A Khaki beige with a green undertone would not look good next to a stone with a pink undertone. This is why you should match the stone, especially if it takes up an entire wall in the room. Once you match a few stone colors, then figure out which one goes best with your carpet and couch, then use that one.

Love it or Hate it?

The question to ask about your fireplace is, "Do you love it or hate it?" If you love it you can make it stand out. If you hate it, then you'll need to blend it in with the walls. In this house, the homeowner really hated the peach tones of the stone. She wanted gray walls to match the gray couch. But a cool gray would have contrasted with the warm peach of the stone and exaggerated it. So the problem solver was to do a warm taupe on the walls to tone down the peach. It's still neutral enough to work with the couch and go well with the fireplace too. Another option is to paint the stone white!

These homeowners had their fireplace professionally limewashed to give it a cleaner, cooler palette.

Rugs and Flooring

Don't forget to think about the floor. If you have carpet or tile then you may need to match that color. Place the chips on the floor and try to match it. Hardwood floors are not that important to match.

Carpet

If you have wall-to-wall carpet, take it into consideration. If it's neutral, then match the carpet. You don't want the carpet to look dirty, so choose a muddy color. Sometimes you'll find that the carpet is a totally different beige than the couch. If so, then you'll have to make a judgment call. Which one is more important? Match the couch or the floor. See the **Living Rooms** chapter for more on carpets.

Hardwood Floor

Any color will work with most wood tones. But if it's golden colored wood try to avoid taupes and colors with a pinkish undertone.

Tile Floor

If you're going to paint neutral walls then consider matching the tile. If it's taupe, then avoid anything with yellow or green undertones because the taupe will look pink. Many beige tiles also have some gray in them, so match either the beige color or the gray color. You can always paint a muddy color besides a neutral. Look at pillows and an area rug for color ideas and make sure it looks good with the tile.

Nimbus 1465

Other Things to Consider

Window Treatments

Many Family Rooms don't have curtains, they have blinds, so it's not first on the list. But if you do have curtains, your paint color will be right next to them, so you DO want to make sure your color looks good next to them. Sometimes the fabric can be considered an accent color against neutral walls and you don't have to worry about them very much. But if you want beige walls and your curtains are beige, then make sure the color you choose looks good next to those curtains. If they are patterned and there is a neutral color in them, try to match that color.

Accent Walls

TV's look great on a dark colored wall. If you have an open layout, then consider a dark accent wall to separate the space. A fireplace wall looks good accented in a darker color. Look at your rug and pillows for a color idea. You can also look within the **Color Seasons** palettes for ideas, too.

High and Low Ceilings

Low Ceilings

In some homes, like Split Levels and Bi-Levels, the Family Room is on a lower level than the rest of the house. The ceilings are not very high and there are smaller windows and less light. In these rooms keep the color light for several reasons. First, to make the room feel like it gets some sunlight. Secondly, a strong, dark color will exaggerate the low ceiling. A light color will blend into the ceiling better and it won't be so noticeable that the ceiling is low.

High Ceilings

If you have very tall walls then a light color can make the room feel very empty and unfinished, and the artwork will look lonely floating on a large wall. A medium to dark color will fill up the space. Or consider an accent wall. For more on accent walls, see page 308 in the chapter **Problem Solving**.

Kitchen/Family Room Combo

If the Family Room is open to the Kitchen, then paint both rooms the same color. The point of an open layout is to have a large, open space. If you paint the rooms separate colors, then you are breaking up the space into smaller spaces. So, start with the Kitchen and consider the Kitchen cabinets, backsplash and countertop first. Then look at the couch in the Family Room and see if any of those colors will work. Try and find a color that works in the whole space overall.

If everything is very neutral and boring, then you may want to paint this space a color. But remember, it's the main living space of the house and you'll spend the most time here, so if you use a strong color, you may get sick of it very quickly. Consider an accent wall for a punch of color.

Smoke Embers 1466

This gray strip matches the couch and the granite.

Before

After

If you're selling your home be sure to freshen it up with an updated color palette. This house was not selling due to its outdated Tuscan gold color. After painting it a warm gray it had a fresh, new look and the house sold.

Tip!

Warm grays from the **Autumn** palette work well with orange/brown wood cabinets, leather, and counter tops, giving it a fresh updated look.

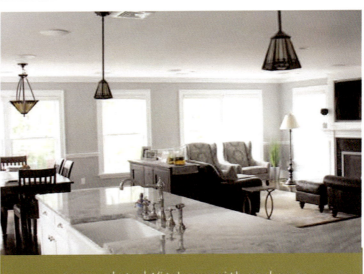

New updated kitchens with cool gray countertops look great with **Winter** colors.

Checklist

- ✓ Couches
- ✓ Pillows
- ✓ Window Treatments
- ✓ Rugs and Flooring
- ✓ Fireplace

Years ago, Living Rooms were so formal that no one ever went in them except for a holiday or when company came over. Usually, you were afraid to go in there for fear of possibly getting the couch dirty. Some people even had plastic on their couches to protect them, to make them even *MORE uninviting!* Today we live a more casual lifestyle and more often people are opting for more casual, comfortable furniture in their Living Rooms. The goal for Living Rooms is to create a warm and inviting environment.

Neutral Rules the Roost

In the chapter on **The Rules** we talked about the "Crayon Box" and how we need neutral spaces. You will need to decide which space is going to be the neutral one for your eyes to relax. Usually, it's going to be the Living Room. Why? Because between the couch, chairs, pillows, area rug, artwork and window treatments, there is enough going on and there is already plenty of color, pattern, and texture in the room. So you don't need to overdo it by loading the room with color on the walls too.

Occasionally using color makes more sense. If the Living Room furnishings are all neutral or white, then consider using either a darker, more dramatic neutral or a color. Or if most of the other rooms in the house are neutral, then this can be the room for color. Sometimes I may encourage clients to paint the Living Room a soft yellow, blue or green because either the homeowner has old furniture and I'm trying to make the color work with the furniture, or the room is too blah and needs a boost. If I do use colors then I will use the most neutral version of them possible. For instance, a soft gold is mostly beige, and a green or blue are mostly gray.

Trendy Colors

As of the time I'm writing this book, light neutral gray, taupe, and off-whites are hot. They work with anything, whether your furniture is old or new. When you venture from there though, be careful. Soft blushy pinks are in, but they only work with really hip, new, contemporary furniture. Don't try to use them with your 40-year-old sofa because it will look like you haven't painted the room in forty years! If you want to use a trendy color, like a deep teal for instance, then you had better have really cool, modern furniture. In my experience though, most people tend to play it pretty safe and have a basic neutral couch and furniture, and only want neutral walls. Look to your couch to figure out which neutral works.

The Couch

Old Couches

If you have older furniture, using a neutral will help to give the room a more updated look. Avoid dated colors like pink, yellow, peach, or a strong green. Look for any sign of beige or taupe in your couch or chairs and then match it.

A warm gray with a drop of yellow in it (like Edgecombe Gray by Benjamin Moore) works well with anything with yellow or gold undertones. It also works with hardwood floors that are gold, orange, or red.

If there is blue in the couch, like tiny blue flowers, you can use a silver gray that turns slightly blue. Avoid pink! Do not paint your walls pink. If there is pink in the couch then use taupe. You don't want an old couch to look dirty, so make sure you use a muddy color. No clear brights.

New Couches

If you have newer furniture that is gray or taupe, then match the overall color of the couch. You don't want the couch to disappear, so use a shade lighter or darker but in the same family. Beige and gray actually look great together so you can do gray walls with a beige couch. Color is always an option. Refer to the **Family Rooms** chapter for more on this.

White or Off-White Couches

If the couch is creamy then use a muddy color. Look at the colors in the rest of the furniture to determine if you should choose a warm or cool neutral. If most of the furniture is white and you have plenty of windows and sunlight, then consider either a color or a darker neutral on the walls like a charcoal gray. If most of the furniture is very neutral then consider a color. Remember the "Rule of 3". Since this is usually a neutral space, you'll need to make sure if you paint the Living Room a color, then make sure other rooms are neutral.

Colored Couch

If the couch is a soft color, then you can match it. But if it's a strong color then consider it to be an accent color in the room. Look at other things in the room to find out what neutral would be best. If the chairs and rug all have a creamy background, then it's best to put a creamy color on the wall. Is there a fireplace? Look at that for a color idea. If you're not sure, look at the other rooms nearby and see what direction you're heading as far as a **Color Seasons** palette. Choose a neutral color from that palette.

Colored Walls

Some people just love color and don't want neutral walls. If you want color in your Living Room them pull the color from fabrics in the room. Try to find something that unifies everything in the space. Green is a second cousin in the neutral family. Just remember the "Rule of 3's". Don't overwhelm the space with too much going on, and when you look room to room, you don't want to see too many different colors. Try to reign it in. Look at the **Color Seasons** palettes for ideas.

Windows and Pillows

If you have fabric panels on the windows then the paint color will be right next to them, so take them into consideration. If they are a neutral color, then match that neutral color. If the fabric is a strong color, then think of it as your accent color, and then keep the walls neutral. If they're a soft color then you can match them. If all of your furniture is beige and you don't want beige walls, then look at the window treatments, pillows and area rug for color ideas. If you don't have either, then look to the **Color Seasons** palettes for ideas.

Rugs and Flooring

Hardwood

If your hardwood floors are neutral, then you can use any color. For floors that are yellow, consider using a warmer color. If they're red, like cherry, then think of the red as an accent color. You don't have to match it, but taupe goes well with red tones.

Area Rugs

If the rug has a lot of color, then think of it as an accent and just match the couch. But if you want to paint the room a color, then use the area rug for inspiration. Sit on the floor with your paint chips or fan deck and match the colors in the area rug. You may need to use a toned-down version of the rug color. See the chapter on **Toning Down and Fixing Colors**.

Oriental Style Rugs

Most Orientals have really strong, primary colors. Consider them to be accent colors. Look for the neutral colors in the rug. Most have background colors in some sort of beige, taupe or gray. The color that matches the couch will probably look good with the rug. If the colors are more muted then you may be able to use one.

120

Wall-To-Wall Carpet

Not everyone has the luxury of hardwood floors. If you have wall-to-wall carpet, take the color into consideration. Beige and gray look great together, so you can mix your neutrals. If you don't like the color of your carpet, don't fight it. You'll only make it worse.

If you have OLD carpet with hardwood floors underneath, then rip out those old carpets! If that's not an option, then follow these guidelines. Remember, you don't want the carpet to look dirty so make sure you use a muddy color.

- If it's beige, taupe or gray, match it or paint the walls a color that matches other fabrics in the room.
- If it's blue, use a cool gray. (Don't use blue, it's overkill.)
- If it's pink, use a taupe.
- If it's in the yellow family, use a cream, beige or a beigey gray.
- If it's dark green, use a beige, cool gray or light sage green.

Ashen Tan 996

Other Things to Consider

Fireplace

If it's a traditional fireplace with a marble surround, you can ignore the marble and think of it as an accent. But if you're at a loss for a color idea, and it's a light neutral, then you may want to match it. Refer to the **Family Rooms** chapter for more detailed information on what works well.

Vaulted Ceilings

Rooms with very high ceilings can feel very empty if the wall color is too light. This is a room to go a shade darker than the other rooms to fill up the wall space.

Pulling it All Together

Now that you have matched paint chips to everything in the room, you're probably scratching your head trying to decide which color to choose! Hopefully when you bought your furniture, rugs, and window treatments you tried to pull it all together with colors that work together. But maybe not. I usually match the couch and then just do a quick check to make sure the color goes with everything else. If it goes well with MOST of the stuff in the room, then I'm done.

If, after matching all the stuff in the room, you have a mix of a bunch of different neutrals, then you will need to make a judgment call here and decide which is more important to match. What is your eye going to see first? What's up at eye level? The couch and fireplace are pretty big so they're kind of important. The window treatments are next to the walls. You can contrast with them, as long as the color doesn't make them look old, faded and dirty! The floor is the least important because it's mostly covered by furniture and the last thing you will look at. If everything in the Living Room is the SAME neutral color, then painting the walls that same neutral may be too boring for you. You may want to paint the room a non-neutral color. That's when you'll look at the area rug or pillows for ideas. Just make sure it flows with your other rooms.

Cedar Key is a color that goes with the couch, area rug and the window treatments. It's the winner!

My Philosophy

The room below shows you a perfect example of why I keep Family Rooms and Living Rooms neutral. If you paint the walls a color then you're locked into that color. But if you match the wall color to the couch and keep the walls neutral then you can change the whole look of the room easily. Simply by changing out the area rug and accessories it gave the room a quick, easy update on a small budget!

The Holiday Gathering Place

Dining Rooms

Checklist

 Type of Furniture

 Window Treatments

 Fabric

 Area Rugs

In the previous chapters we talked a lot about using neutrals. But the Dining Room is the one room you can throw caution to the wind and take a risk! Since formal Dining Rooms are usually not used on a daily basis and are mostly used on holidays and for candlelit dinners with guests, this room can handle some drama. In this chapter we will talk about all of your different color choices.
Have some fun with color!

Style of Furniture

People look at several sources for decorating ideas. They watch decorating shows on TV, look online, read blogs and visit designer show houses. They may even see a color they liked at a friend's house. But they never take into consideration that the furniture in that space looks nothing like their own furniture! Modern colors don't always work with traditional furniture.

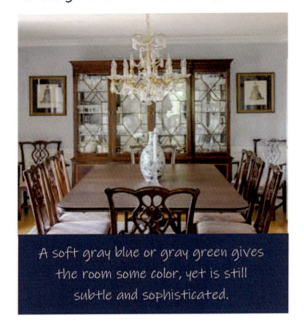

A soft gray blue or gray green gives the room some color, yet is still subtle and sophisticated.

Traditional Furniture

If you have traditional furniture, antiques, or your grandmother's old Dining Room set, then your Dining Room is basically what I call "**A Sea of Wood**". Wood table, wood chairs, wood hutch, wood china cabinet, wood floors, wood, wood, wood. That means the whole room is brown, brown, brown and more brown.

This means the LAST color I'm going to use in a formal Dining Room is anything in the brown family! No beige here folks. Beige or plain vanilla off-white colors will just be too bland. This is the room where you can have a little fun. Colors like blues and greens will draw out the natural beauty of the wood.

Yawn! This plain-Jane linen white is too safe. Don't be afraid to spice it up a little!

Before

After

125

Modern Furniture

Gray, greige and whites work best with new furniture. If you have newer, more modern Dining Room furniture then you can paint the walls neutral, or pretty much any color you wish. Even clear bright colors will work with modern furniture.

Mixing It Up

If you love neutral walls in gray, greige or off-white, but you have really traditional furniture, then it may look like you're just trying to force a color to work. If you really want that neutral to work then freshen it up with a new rug and change out the chairs at the head and foot of the table to fabric covered chairs. Then you'll have a good eclectic mix to work with, and a springboard to work off of. Choose a wall color that goes with your new rug or chairs.

The walls in this Dining Room above used to be green. They painted a warm gray, then made it work by adding fabric chairs in a warm gray, a new area rug and a mirror.

Other Things to Consider

Window Treatments

Since the wall color will be next to the window treatments, you'll want to think about how the paint color will look next to the fabric. If it's a strong color, then think of it as an accent color. If the window treatments are neutral, you may want to match them. If all of the furniture is wood and you're looking for an idea for a color for the room, then think about matching a color you see in the fabric.

Area Rugs

When looking for an idea for a color for the Dining Room an area rug is a good place to start! Place paint chips on the rug and try to match a few colors. Then think about the other rooms and decide which of those colors will flow the best with the other rooms.

Artwork

If there are no rug and no fabrics in the room then the last place to find inspiration is the artwork!

Sometimes everything in a client's house is gray and white, but they want something different in the Dining Room. I will look at their art for inspiration. They chose that art for some reason! There is something they like about it. So I'll try to match colors in the art to come up with a color for the walls.

Color Possibilities

Beige

If you have new furniture and chairs with pretty fabrics, then choose a beige that works with your fabrics. Take clues from the chairs, rug, and window treatments.

Gray

If you have chairs, window treatments or an area rug with gray in any of them, then try to match that. If you only have wood furniture then you can use any shade of gray, just make sure it's a shade of gray that looks good with the other rooms in the house.

Taupe and Greige

If your furniture is dark or white, then taupe is fine. But if the furniture has strong orange or red tones in it, then taupe will look almost purple next to it. I have seen people try to force this color to work, and it just doesn't work. Again, if you have new furniture and taupe fabrics, then match the fabric.

Off-Black and Black

Black or off-black will NOT make the room look smaller, but it will make it look dramatic and stunning! These colors are great with light, white or gray furniture, and goes well with Contemporary styled furniture.

Blues and Greens

Slate blue, gray-blue, and gray-green are all colors that look great in a Dining Room. In a formal Dining Room these colors look great against all of that wood. Take your clues from nature and think of the wood as the bark of a tree with green leaves set off by a blue sky. If you have an Oriental carpet, pull a color from there. Make sure you consider the window treatments. If there is blue or green in them, then match it. Try to avoid baby blue. If the furniture has a strong red or orange tone, then a greenish blue looks best.

Dark Blue and Navy

Dark blue looks great with all wood tones. Navy blue looks great with light furniture. The way to make a dark color work is to use a lot of white in the room. White ceiling, white trim, white window treatments, and even white wainscoting. We will talk about wainscot later in this chapter.

130

Turquoise, Teal, and Blue/Green

Since light blues tend to look like they belong in a little boy's nursery, I have found that a greenish blue looks more like a "grown up blue". Greenish blues also look great with wood tones. If you have traditional furniture, then use a muddy or in-between color, or go for a darker teal. A deep, clear bright turquoise or teal will go better with Contemporary furniture. If you go for a strong statement with a clear bright then make sure your other rooms are very neutral, even white or off-white to avoid the "Crayon Box".

*Remember to refer to the **Color Seasons** palettes for color recommendations!*

Tip!

131

Red NO!

We have already discussed this in the chapter on **Paint Color Trends**, and again in the **Kitchen** chapter. Back in 2000 everyone wanted their house to be Tuscan or Country French and every house had a red Dining Room. I never use red because it's out of style and as dated looking as a shag rug. The paint color won't look new, it will just look like you haven't painted the place in 15 years.

If you already have red walls, then you're used to seeing a dark color, so try something dark or bold. If you have Tuscan Era fabrics in red, gold, and green, check the rug or artwork for clues to see if there is any blue and match it, because a gray blue will look great. If blue won't work, then use a deep warm gray or earthy green.

If you're trying to sell your house, red Dining Rooms look dated and do NOT sell the house. Paint it neutral. A warm greige works best.

Tip!

Orange and Rust

Orange toned colors are the same color as wood, so if you have orange toned wood, don't use it because your furniture will just disappear. Fifteen years ago, I used orange as an alternative to red, so for me, it's outdated. But I do see it making a comeback in the future. Forget going lighter because peach and salmon went out in the 1980's. If you love the color, then use a bright, citrusy clear bright version for a Contemporary look, or use a nice pumpkin orange as an accent wall. Try it with a dark charcoal gray in a contemporary Dining Room for a fresher color combination.

Gold

Gold, just like red, is pretty dated and I rarely use it. But if you want it, choose a warm gold with a slightly orange undertone to compliment the orange tone of the wood in the furniture. Avoid gold with a greenish undertone.

Before

After

This room was given a fresher look by eliminating the darker "Tuscan Style" gold below the chair rail. Now it appears like a soft yellow and the bottom is ready to have wainscoting put up.

Yellow

Yellow is a color that can really brighten up a dark room. If you have stained wood trim then this color works well to brighten the room. If you live in a Tudor style home with stucco walls and dark stained trim, then a soft, muddy yellow is probably the way to go. I tend to use creamy yellows because a bright yellow will look like it belongs in a Nursery School. Yellow and gray is a great color combination, and a muddy, beigey yellow looks great with a warm gray.

Pink and Purple

In all of the tens of thousands of Dining Rooms I have done, I have only used each of these colors once. Raspberry and dark purple were in, sort of, when Faux Finishes and ivy wallpaper borders were in style in the mid 1990's. People who didn't like warm reds preferred these cooler versions of red. But color is coming back! The trick to using these colors is to make sure they don't look like they belong in a six-year-old girl's Bedroom.

If you like **purple,** try either a dark plum, or a "grown up" gray version of purple, which looks good with modern gray furniture.

This homeowner mixed traditional and modern pieces for an eclectic look. The deep plum color also adds a modern twist.

Location, Location, Location

In a **Center Hall Colonial** style home, there is a Living Room on one side of the Foyer, and a Dining Room on the opposite side, like two bookends. I like to balance the two. If I do a dark Dining Room, then I'll probably go darker in the Living Room. Or I'll use the light neutral color that was used in the Living Room again under the chair rail in the Dining Room. To create a flow, I always say you should be able to take a pillow from the Living Room and put it in the Dining Room and they should all work together.

Some Dining Rooms are located **in the middle** of two rooms or in the back of the house where they don't get any natural light. You'll want to keep the color light. Turn on the lights when you look at color choices to see how the color looks with that lighting.

In homes with an **open floor plan,** I tend to do most of the rooms the same color because if you paint each room a different color you'll be chopping them up into smaller spaces. The whole point of an open layout is to make the space feel larger and, well, open. Don't close the spaces off by choosing new colors in each room. If the Dining Room is small, then by painting it the same color as the adjoining space will help it feel larger. To break up the sea of gray though I still like color in the Dining Room. I'll put it above the chair rail if there is one or do an accent wall.

134

L-Shaped Living/Dining Rooms

Many **Split-Levels**, **Bi-Levels** and **Ranch** style homes have a Dining Room next to the Living Room in an L-shape. If there is a large doorway that separates the space, then you can paint the rooms two different colors. You'll want the two rooms to flow together. So, for instance, if you paint the Dining Room an aqua blue, then use that same aqua blue in the Living Room in accent pillows or accessories. You should be able to use the same window treatments in both rooms.

This Living Room color was based on the large fireplace. The color had to look good with all of that stone. The Dining Room is essentially part of the Living Room in this Split Level.

If there are no fabrics or window treatments in the Dining Room, then there is nothing to match a color to. So look at the Living Room and choose a color that goes well with the Living Room. If everything in the Living Room is neutral and you want to paint the Dining Room a color, look at the **Color Seasons** palettes for color ideas.

If there is a chair rail in the Dining Room only, then the top color will continue into the Living Room, so follow the rules for Living Rooms. For the bottom half, read the part of this chapter on chair rails.

Painting the Dining Room and Living Room the same color helps the space to look more like an open layout. But another option would have been to paint the Dining Room a blue that matches the accessories for a punch of color.

Dipsy-Doodle Split Level

A Dipsy-Doodle is a house where you walk up a few stairs to get to the Living Room, then go back downstairs to get to the Dining Room. These Dining Rooms have very high ceilings because they are one and a half stories high, and many times have a chair rail. The only separation between Living Room and Dining Room is a railing. In these homes the top half of the Dining Room wall is also the Living Room wall and will have to be the same color. With any rooms that have high ceilings, don't use a color that's too light or the walls will feel too empty.

If there is a chair rail, one option is to use a darker color below the chair rail just to add some interest if there is no wainscoting. If there is no chair rail then you can paint an accent wall on one wall to visually separate the Dining Room. This can either be the window wall, or the wall to the Kitchen.

Accent Wall DON'TS

If you have a chair rail, do not paint the top one color, the bottom another, and then create an accent wall too. It will just look goofy. Do one or the other and stick to two colors. If you really want an accent wall then have the colors run from floor to ceiling. Either remove the chair rail, or paint over the chair rail with the wall color to make it disappear.

Different Types of Trim

Wainscoting & Picture Frame Molding

In my opinion, painting a color inside the boxes is dated. Wainscot should be painted all the same color from the chair rail down to the floor. A traditional look is to paint it all white (whichever white is your trim color) in a semi-gloss or satin finish.

If you want a more contemporary look and wainscot is too traditional for you, then paint the wainscot either the same color as the walls in a glossier finish, or a shade darker than the walls for a tone-on-tone look. You can also paint it a neutral like gray, taupe or black. If you do, it usually feels more natural to have the crown molding and all the trim match the wainscot. So whatever color you choose then paint all the windows, doors and trim the same color. We will discuss this more in the chapter about **Trim Colors**.

Board and Batten

I love Board and Batten Wainscoting! Keeping it white helps the room stay light and bright, and then you can use a dark color or even a clear bright on the walls above because there is not a lot of wall space. Another look would be to do tone-on-tone neutrals.
PS: Don't be afraid to paint over stained wood!

Shiplap

The same rules apply with Shiplap. Usually, most people like it to be all white. Remember, "Don't mix your whites". Make sure all the windows, doors and trim are all the same white. Another alternative would be tone on tone neutrals.

137

Chair Rails

Chair rails were meant to keep chairs from scuffing up the walls. But they are rarely used that way so it seems now they serve no real purpose except to be decorative.

In the 1980's we went wallpaper crazy and Interior Designers made a lot of money back then selling wallpaper and big, poufy window treatments! We put flowered wallpaper on the top half of the wall, and striped wallpaper on the bottom.

In the 1990's people began removing the wallpaper, but sometimes they only took off either the top or the bottom half, painted it, and left the other half of the paper up. This is why I don't like to paint two separate colors on the walls like green on the top and yellow on the bottom, because it reminds me of the '90's. I prefer a neutral, tone-on-tone type of look. Here are some ways to tackle walls with a chair rail.

Tone-on-Tone

Paint a color on the top and a darker version of the same color on the bottom. (Choose colors from the same paint strip to keep it simple.) Painting the darker color on the bottom will "weigh it down", and it also helps to hide dirt and scuff marks on the bottom half.

Same Color Above and Below

Another choice is to paint the same color on both the top and bottom halves. If you want a more contemporary look then remove the chair rail. It's only held in place by tiny nails and maybe some glue so it can be torn off easily with a crowbar. Then simply spackle the holes, sand, cover with some primer, and paint.

Light Above, Dark Below

White and off-white walls are pretty popular now but I only use them with newer furniture. Off-white is just too bland with traditional wood furniture. When the whole house is off-white, then a way to add a little punch is to add a dark neutral below the chair rail. I have seen bright colors below, but I'm just not a fan. In my opinion, neutrals are more sophisticated.

White or Off-White Below

Over the years many clients have been adding wainscoting to the bottom half of the wall, which is an "upgrade" from just a chair rail. If they don't have it yet, I will create the illusion of wainscoting by painting the bottom half white, off-white, or a light neutral. One reason I like to do this is because I want to use a darker color on the top for more drama, but don't want the room to get too dark overall. I can get away with it if the bottom half is white. The other reason is to create colors that flow room-to-room.

Creating Colors that Flow

Many times, I will carry the color from the Living Room or Foyer (if it's neutral) and use it on the bottom half of the wall so that the rooms all flow together nicely. I want the color to look off-white, so if the color in the adjoining space is dark, I will use a lighter version of the color, or cut the color in half. (See page 303.)

Before

After

Colors That Sell a Home

I work for a lot of clients who are either getting ready to sell their homes, or they just bought a new house and want to paint the entire house before they move in. All of the new homeowners want the same thing. Basically, they want their whole house to be neutral, and more specifically, they all want gray. So when I work for clients who are getting ready to sell their homes, I try to make their homes look like the homes that buyers like. That means, we "gray it up".

I know from my experience as The Paint Diva, and a few years as a Realtor, that the most updated you can make a house look the better. That means, say goodbye to Tuscany! Buyers shop online first. If they don't like the photos, they won't come look at the house. And if they see gold rooms and a red Dining Room, they will swipe on to the next house! Several of the homes in this chapter sat on the market for a few months before they finally gave in and had the place painted. Then when they got rid of the red walls and took new photos, they all sold.

After

Before

Butler's Pantry

A Butler's Pantry is a small room off the Dining Room that is usually connected to the Kitchen. Since it passes between both rooms it can **either match the Kitchen** color or the **Dining Room** color. Since it's so tiny it really doesn't make sense to paint it a different color. This is considered a workspace so it shouldn't stick out visually, unless of course you have something amazing in there like a copper ceiling or amazing backsplash tile.

Usually, the Butler's Pantry has the same cabinets and counter top as the Kitchen, and if so, paint it the same color as the Kitchen because you've already chosen a color to match those cabinets and counter top. If it's around the corner from the Kitchen and you see it more from the Dining Room than the Kitchen, then you may want to match the Dining Room color so that it just flows with the Dining Room. You don't want your eye to be particularly drawn to the Pantry, where it would be if it was painted a new color. Another way to decide whether to match the Kitchen or the Dining Room color is to look at the floor.

If the Kitchen and Pantry both have the same tile floor, match the Kitchen. If the Kitchen has tile and the Pantry switches to wood like the Dining Room, and it has different cabinets than the Kitchen, then you can match the Dining Room.

The top Butler's Pantry matches the Dining Room and the bottom one matches the Kitchen.

In this Butler's Pantry, the cabinets are different from the cabinets in the Kitchen. They decided to paint the Pantry in the same color as the Kitchen. In the Dining Room, they decided to go with a greenish-blue that coordinates with the backsplash tile in the Pantry. In the Kitchen, the blue is also picked up in the fabric in the window treatment above the sink. Now the color flows through all three spaces.

The First Impression

Foyers & Hallways

Checklist

- ✓ Marry the Living & Dining Room Colors
- ✓ The Rooms Connected to the Foyer
- ✓ The Floor
- ✓ The Stairs
- ✓ The Ceiling Height
- ✓ Making a Statement

If you have an entry Foyer then it's the first thing guests see when they arrive in your home and it sets the tone for the whole house. Try to think of the first floor of your house as a whole, not as individual spaces. The Foyer and Hallway lead to all of the other rooms. So that color needs to compliment and "marry" the other rooms that you can see from the Foyer. To create "flow" from room to room, the transition from color to color should be easy on the eyes. The Foyer is the space that creates that flow by bridging the gap between rooms. Because of this, choosing a neutral color for this space may be your best option.

"Marry" Your Colors Together

Almost always I use a neutral color in the Foyer. That makes it easier to choose colors in the other adjoining rooms, and the Foyer will be a place where your eyes can rest from color. Choose a neutral that goes with the other rooms. If you stick within the **Color Seasons** palettes this should not be very difficult. If you like **Winter** colors and most of your rooms are cool grays and blues, then your Foyer will also be a cool gray. If you choose warmer colors in the other rooms, then you'll choose a warmer taupe or beige for the Foyer, unless your floor dictates otherwise. For instance, if you have a cool marble floor then beige won't work. You'll have to choose a cool color for the Foyer, and that's OK. Sometimes you'll have a mix of warm and cool colors in the other rooms. Your Living Room may be warm beige, and the Dining Room is a cool gray blue. Then you can paint the Foyer in a color that is either warm or cool.

The inspiration for the Dining Room color came from the dark green marble floor in the Foyer

The Foyer color coordinates with the Dining Room wallpaper. The same grayish blue is picked up in the chair and lamp in the Living Room.

The Living Room color is also below the chair rail in this Foyer. The pops of orange in the accessories help to further marry the spaces together.

145

Marrying the Living Room and the Dining Room

Look at the Dining Room

In the chapter on **Dining Rooms** we discussed chair rails and using the Foyer color under the chair rail. So consider using a color in the Foyer that will work in the Dining Room as well. Even if you have no chair rail think about using a color in the Foyer that coordinates the Living and Dining Room.

Look at the Living Room

You can probably see the Living Room from the Foyer, so you want them to go together. A simple trick is to paint the Foyer either the same color as the Living Room, or a lighter or darker version of the Living Room color.

Flooring

Look at the Foyer Floor

Lay paint chips on the floor and find colors that match the floor. Then see if any of those colors coordinate with the color you'd like to do in the Living and Dining Rooms. You can refer to the **Color Seasons** palettes for other ideas.

Hardwood

If the floor is hardwood, then you can pretty much do any color. If there is a carpet runner, look at that instead for color ideas.

Cedar Key 982

Ceramic Tile, Vinyl and Laminate

Most tile is beige or taupe. Some have a touch of gray. Laminate can be a mix of neutrals. Lay paint chips on the tile and see which color looks best. The goal is to make sure the tile doesn't look dirty. Cool gray will do that so avoid cool gray with warm neutral tile. If the tile is a color, try to find a neutral within it. If it's a cool color use a cool neutral. If it's a warm color use a warm neutral.

Marble Tile

Lay paint chips on the floor and try to match the color of the tile and the veins. If the tile is cool then use a cool color. If the tiles are warm, use a warm color. If the tile is dark green, use a cool gray. If the tile is beige but you want gray walls, use a warm gray. Sometimes tile is beige with gray veins. If so, you can use either warm or cool colors.

147

Look at the Stair Runner

If you have a carpet stair runner, then you may want to pull a color from there. If it's a solid color then try to match the color the best you can. If it's patterned or an Oriental, look for the background color. There is usually some beige or taupe in an Oriental. If it's a strong color, then think of the colors as accent colors and just ignore the runner and use a neutral that goes best with the other rooms. A cool gray will make beige look dirty, so if the runner is beige and the other rooms are cool, then use beige or greige, or a warm gray.

Carpet

If there is carpet on the stairs you don't want it to look dirty. So you should choose a muddy color that matches the carpet. If there is carpet and some sort of tile, then try to find something that works with both. Usually, your choice is between beige or gray. Remember, they both look good together. It's OK to do gray walls with beige tile, or vice versa. A warm gray looks best with beige carpet.

Center Hall Colonial

If you have a Center Hall Colonial (Living Room on one side, Dining Room on the other side, and the Foyer/hall in the center) then the center hall/Foyer leads to all of the other rooms and connects all of the spaces together. Since the center hall is exactly that, central, it is surrounded by all of the other colors in the house. The job of the Foyer is to connect all the colors together in unison.

Older Colonials

If you have low eight-foot ceilings and your upstairs Hallway has no windows and gets dark, then use a lighter color in the Foyer and Hallway. If you have a three-story house, and the stairs keep going up with no door to close off the third floor, then continue the same color all the way up to the third floor. Continue the same trim color all the way up the stairs too.

This hundred year old home has a window on the landing upstairs so they were able to use a darker color that makes the window trim pop!

2-Story Foyers

If you have a newer construction home built in the past 25 years then you probably have a dramatic entry Foyer with a large window. There is so much wall space that you need to fill it with color. Don't use a color that's too light because the walls will feel too empty. Use a shade darker than you think you need. Especially if the Foyer is flooded with sunlight, don't wimp out on the shade. If the walls run all the way to the Family Room, then you'll need to paint it the same color as the Family Room. See the **Family Room** chapter.

Small Entry Off the Foyer

Many older homes have a small entry, then a second door leading into the Foyer. You could paint it a bold color if you want to for a statement but remember that you'll be chopping up the entry and Foyer into two smaller spaces and the entry will feel even smaller. If it's tiny then it's probably smart to just paint it the same color as the Foyer. A large entry however is different and it's a space to have some fun. Think about colors you've used in the house, even just accent pillows, and recreate that color in this small entry to "wow" your guests.

Open Entry

If your front door leads into your Living Room then it will be your Living Room color, and/or your Hallway color too. If you have a nice, symmetrically shaped wall you could always do an accent wall for a pop of color.

Split-Levels and Bi-Levels

Many times these Foyers are open to the Living Room with no partition. One option is to paint the Foyer the same color as the Living Room color to make it feel like a nice, open floor plan. If you paint the Foyer a different color from the Living Room, then choose a color that will complement the Living Room, yet still work with the floor. If you have a tile floor, pull a color from the floor. Sometimes the Living Room color has to extend up into the second-floor Hallway as well as the Foyer, so you may feel like the whole house is the same color. That's OK. If you want color, you can do an accent wall for a little pop of color in either the Foyer or Living Room.

150

Making a Statement

Some people like to make an initial bold statement. You can always greet your guests with a bold color. The way to make statement colors work is to surround them with neutrals. This is how you will avoid the "Crayon Box". In this house the Living Room, Dining Room, and Kitchen are all seen from the Foyer, but they are all neutral. The teal they chose for the Foyer is repeated on the bookcase and in the pillows in the Living Room. This creates a flow and the color "makes sense". The white shiplap also helps the space to stay light and bright. An accent wall is another good way to make a bold statement that won't affect colors in other rooms, and when you're tired of it, just paint over it.

Front Doors

Typically, the inside of the front door is always painted the same color as the trim in the house, which is usually white. You can certainly get creative and paint it black, or an accent color. 99.99% of the time people paint it white, but I do like the idea of a pop of color or a black interior door. Occasionally I have been asked by a client about matching the exterior door color to the interior of the house because they leave the door open a lot, but honestly that's just over thinking it. The inside is the inside, the outside is the outside. It's more important that the outside of the door matches the exterior color scheme, not the interior colors. Think about it, a LOT more people are going to see the outside of your house than will see the inside!

Before

After

Notice that they also painted the trim around the door black too. If they didn't, the door would have appeared smaller than it used to look when it was all white.

Hallways

Hallways do not need to be their own, new, individual color. Keep it simple and just paint the hall in the color of whatever space the Hallway is connected to, whether it's a Foyer or a room. If it's a narrow Hallway, remember the fingerprint factor. Anything in the yellow family will show fingerprints. If the Hallway is dark, keep the color light. If there is no natural light, then the color will look washed out. This is not a space to really worry about choosing the perfect color. Don't over think it.

Front Hallway

In a front Hallway that is connected to the Foyer, you will paint the Foyer and the front Hallway the same color.

Back Hallway

If the back hall is mostly seen from the Kitchen, then just use the Kitchen color. If there is a Mud Room entry then you may want to use the Mud Room color in the hall. If so, then make sure that the Mud Room color looks good with the Kitchen color if the hall is seen from the Kitchen.

Tip! An easy trick that I do is simply painting the Foyer a lighter version of the Living Room color. Then I repeat that color under the chair rail in the Dining Room. It pulls everything together.

Upstairs Hallways

If the Foyer walls are connected to the walls running up the stairs and continue to the upstairs Hallway, then the Foyer and upstairs Hallway will all be the same color. If the upstairs gets dark, you'll want to consider doing a light color. Either do the Foyer and Hallway all a light color, or you could change to a lighter version of the same color upstairs.

Hallways Leading to Bedrooms

You do NOT have to worry about matching the Hallway color to the Bedrooms because they're behind closed doors. If the hall is connected to the Living Room or any other space then use the same color.

Painting the Staircase

I can always tell how old a house is by the staircase. When you enter a home and step into the Foyer, the first thing people look at is the staircase. Homes built in the '80's and '90's had a lot of stained wood. The entire staircase in these homes have stained wood on the handrails, ballusters and risers, and these types of staircases are usually found in houses that also have stained wood doors and trim in every room. The whole house is just a menagerie of wood! Unfortunately, I'm sorry to tell you that this look is outdated!

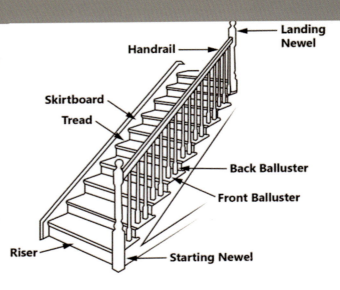

Ballusters

Paint the ballusters white like the trim. Use the same color and finish.

Back Risers

Dark stained risers create a "black hole" effect. The way to freshen it up is to paint the risers and skirt boards white. Use the same paint that you use on all of your trim.

Stain or Paint the Handrail?

Any section where hands or feet touch will get dirty so don't paint them white. The treads and the handrail should either be stained wood or painted a dark neutral color, like black or charcoal. The stain color does not need to match the hardwood floors, and the handrail doesn't have to match the treads. This mix and match look works best only if the colors are very neutral.

Newel Posts

The newel can either be stained or painted white, or both. You can paint the newel post white and stain the cap on top. It really just depends on the style of the stairs and personal preference.

Before

After

Wainscoting and Picture Frame Molding

As discussed in the chapter on **Dining Rooms**, paint the wainscot all one color. It's usually painted in the same paint as your trim, which is typically satin or semi-gloss in a shade of white.

Pulling it Together

Why Do I Like Gray?

Besides the fact that gray has been the go-to, in-style color for a few years and it's all my clients ever want, my reason is simple. It's very practical! Fingerprints and scuff marks are gray, so gray paint hides a multitude of sins. Every time I go to a house and I see yellow walls going up the stairs, I have always seen fingerprints on the walls. After having four kids, I think like a Mom. I don't want to be constantly washing the walls. If you have hands touching your walls as they go up the stairs, then gray (or a color with a gray undertone) is the way to go. You just have to decide which gray, warm or cool?

Making a Decision

Let's say you chose a blue gray in the Dining Room, and a neutral taupe in the Living Room. Then there will be a cool gray on one side, and a warm gray on the other. The Foyer is in the middle, so now you could use either a warm or cool gray in the Foyer. How do you decide which one? First consider the stair runner and the floor. If the floor is hardwood, then either one will work. If it has beige tile, then use a warm color. If it's cool marble, then use a cool color. If the rug is warm gray, then use warm. If the runner is blue or a cool color, then use cool.

The last decision maker is if you want to repeat the color under the chair rail in the Dining Room or not, which we discussed in the chapter on **Dining Rooms**. If you used a cool blue/gray in the Dining Room above the chair rail, then use a light, cool gray in the Foyer and repeat it below the chair rail in the Dining Room. Usually, it just comes down to personal preference. People who love blue will opt for cool gray, and people who prefer warmer colors will opt for warm gray.

Clean and Simple

Bathrooms

The trick to choosing color for Bathrooms is simply finding a color that works with the tile.

Most likely, the era that the Bathroom was built in determines the color and type of tile, as different decades had different styles.

Your goal will be to make your Bathroom look as fresh and updated as possible.

Choosing Colors for Bathrooms.

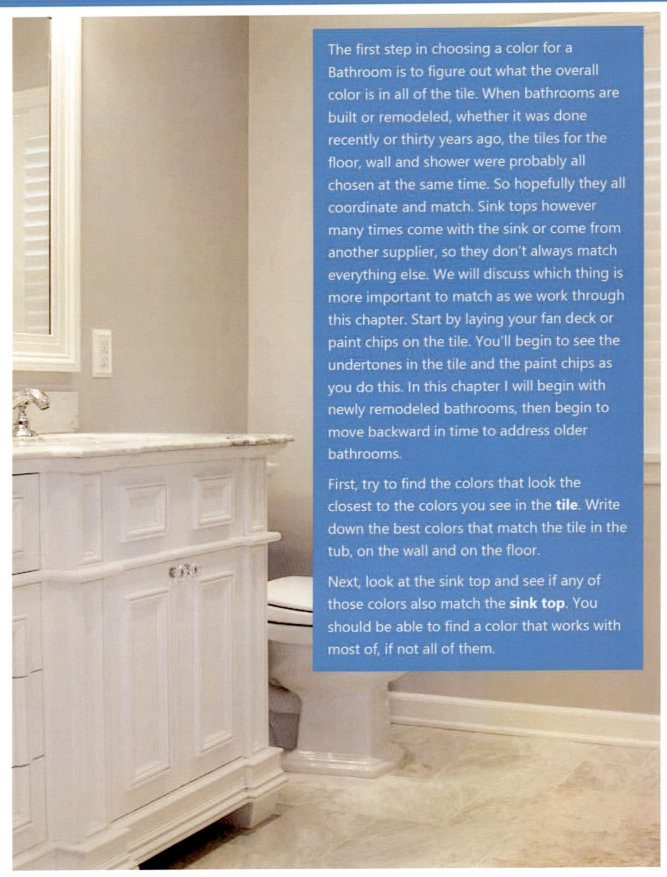

The first step in choosing a color for a Bathroom is to figure out what the overall color is in all of the tile. When bathrooms are built or remodeled, whether it was done recently or thirty years ago, the tiles for the floor, wall and shower were probably all chosen at the same time. So hopefully they all coordinate and match. Sink tops however many times come with the sink or come from another supplier, so they don't always match everything else. We will discuss which thing is more important to match as we work through this chapter. Start by laying your fan deck or paint chips on the tile. You'll begin to see the undertones in the tile and the paint chips as you do this. In this chapter I will begin with newly remodeled bathrooms, then begin to move backward in time to address older bathrooms.

First, try to find the colors that look the closest to the colors you see in the **tile**. Write down the best colors that match the tile in the tub, on the wall and on the floor.

Next, look at the sink top and see if any of those colors also match the **sink top**. You should be able to find a color that works with most of, if not all of them.

Brand New Bathrooms

The Star of the Show

When remodeling a Bathroom, ask yourself, "What's the star of the show?" Usually, it's your "big ticket item" or your favorite thing in the room. If you have a really cool sink cabinet, great mirror, fabulous tub, an incredible walk in shower or amazing tile that you fell in love with, then ask yourself if the color you choose will steal the limelight. Sometimes a strong color will enhance it, and other times it may distract from it. The Bathroom below has an entire feature wall with shiplap on the wall and a stylish mirror and hardware. This feature wall is the star of the show. Below are several different color options. Every color works in its own way. But ask yourself what you want to be the star. The walls? Or the feature wall?

White walls don't show off the shiplap, but they do make the mirror and floor stand out.

Light gray walls have just enough color to make the shiplap stand out, yet does not take over the room.

A darker gray wall contrasts even more against the shiplap making it stand out even more.

This green color is fabulous, but it steals all of the attention in the room. The walls will be the first thing you notice in the room.

Gray and White Bathrooms

Most newly remodeled Bathrooms tend to have a lot of gray and white tile and marble. The gray in the tile and countertops is usually a **cool gray**, so the colors that look best in these rooms are cool colors from the **Winter** and **Spring** palettes like cool grays, blues and greens. Lay paint chips on the tile and try to find the colors that best match the tile. I have seen people make mistakes choosing warm gray to go with cool gray tile. Then after they painted the walls looked green and the tile looked purple! It's very simple. Match the tile.

No!

If your tile has a slightly purple undertone, try Metro Gray 1459 by Benjamin Moore

Tip!

Sterling 1591

Yes!

Gray

A light cool gray is a perfect compliment to this tile.

Yes!

Cool Colors

For a softer look that will give you more of a relaxed, spa-like feeling, use a gray with a hint of an undertone of blue, green or blue-green.

Clear Bright or Muddy?
If you want the room to be bright and fun you can use clear bright colors as long as the tile is very white, otherwise the tile will look dirty. The best choices are always muddy and in-between colors.

Warm or Cool?
Do NOT use warm muddy yellows or beige colors with yellow or peach undertones because the warm tone won't look that great with cool tile. I have also found that a lot of this tile has slightly purple undertones, and yellow will make the tile look purple. The other reason is simply that these colors are dated and just don't look right with brand new tile and fixtures.

Light or Dark?
If everything in the room is predominantly white, and there's a window, then don't be afraid to go dark and add some drama. A darker color will make a feature like a standing tub pop! Also, Bathrooms with a lot of marble can feel cold, so a darker color will warm up the room. Try to match the veining in the marble for the right shade of gray, or try a deep teal, green, blue, or navy.

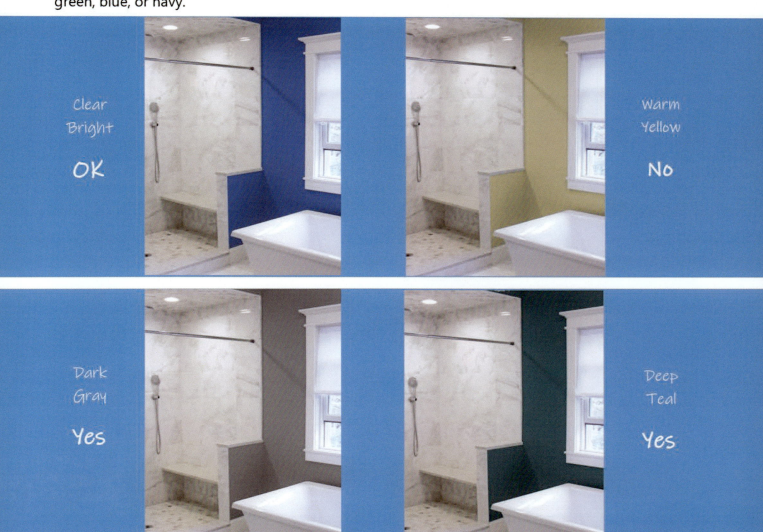

Match the Sink Top, the Wall Tiles, or the Floor?

If you want to paint the walls gray then you should either match the color of your sink top or your tile. In a perfect world your sink top and your tile will all match, but that's not always the case. Sometimes you'll have to make a decision which thing you're going to match. Visually the sink is closer to your eye than the floor, so if you must choose between matching either the floor or the sink, you may want to match the sink. But if it's a long or large Bathroom and you see a lot of the floor tile, then you may want to match the floor. If you really hate the color of the sink top, then match the floor. Another option is painting the room a different color besides gray so that your eye looks at the wall color first and the mismatch won't be so noticeable.

This sink top is right against the wall so they matched a color in the marble so that it would blend with the walls.

When the floor, sink and tile are all different, choosing a pretty color instead of a neutral is always a great option because it can help pull everything together.

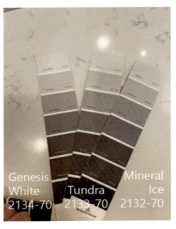

Genesis White 2134-70, Tundra 2133-70, Mineral Ice 2132-70

Light Pewter 1464

Genesis White 2134-70, Tundra 2133-70, Mineral Ice 2132-70

Shower Tile

If the shower is predominant, then choose a color that coordinates well with the shower tile because you will see a lot of the paint color next to the shower.

Wall Tile

If you have tile that goes halfway up the walls all the way around the room, then the paint color will be right next to the wall tile, so choose a color that looks good with the tile. The paint will not be next to the sink top, so it does not have to coordinate with the sink top.

Accent Tile

Accent tiles are a great place to look for color inspiration! Simply hold up paint chips to see which paint colors match the colors in the tile.

In this Bathroom the wall tile is white so any color would work. They chose to match one of the accent tiles for a wall color.

Wainscoting and Beadboard

Wainscoting (with square panels) and beadboard (with vertical lines) are usually painted in white semi-gloss for a Traditional, Beachy or Cottagey look. Look at the floor and tub tile and decide if white will look good next to your tile. If you have a white sink vanity then white will look fine. But if the sink vanity is stained wood and all the tile is beige, then white will look out of place. Sometimes white wainscoting or beadboard can make a beige floor look dirty. Consider painting the wainscot a color. You can do a tone-on-tone look, by painting the wainscot a lighter or darker version of the wall color, or paint them the same color, but paint the top in a matte or eggshell finish and paint the beadboard in a satin or semi-gloss finish. See the **Dining Room** chapter for more on wainscoting.

Tip! Darker colors do NOT make a room look smaller! They DO make the walls look warm and dramatic.

No

If the Bathroom is predominantly white, with white tile or wainscot halfway up the wall, then you can use a darker color. Especially if the tile is not marble, but it's just plain and there's nothing special about it, adding a dramatic color on the walls can give the room a little "Wow factor".

Yes

Sometimes white can make the floors look dirty. Painting the beadboard a light neutral color is the solution.

Patterned Floor Tile

Winter Orchard
1555

Shoreline
1471

In this Bathroom the floor tile is the star of the show. Since there is white tile going around the room that separates the wall from the floors, there are several options. Light neutral walls disappear and make the floor take center stage. Blue is the more fun option and still works because your eye goes up and down from the wall to the tile. Since this Bathroom is for young boys, they opted for the blue. When the boys get older, they'll switch to the more mature neutral.

Off-White Tile

In this Bathroom the floor is slightly grayish off-white. White walls or a clear bright color will make the floor look dingy and dirty. Not a good look for a Bathroom! The best choices are cool gray, or colors with gray undertones. If your floor is off-white, then lay paint chips on the floor to try and match the tile to see what the undertones are, then either use that color on the walls, or one with the same undertones.

Even though the toilet is white, the floor is noticeably not white. A color works better than white walls so the floor doesn't look dirty.

Clear Bright colors make the floor look dirty, plus putting a warm yellow with a cool off-white looks even worse.

A clear bright blue would make the floor look dirty, but a muddy blue works great with this tile.

A deep, cool gray that's even darker than the tile makes the tile look lighter, brighter and cleaner. Good choice!

Vanities

Dark Colored Vanity

If the vanity is dark and there is no window then you will want to use a lighter color so that the room doesn't get too dark, unless you want a really artistic, dark, dramatic Bath. Dark wood is neutral like black so you can use any color that goes well with the countertop or tile.

White Vanity or Stained Wood Vanity

When choosing a color for the walls, if the vanity is white or stained wood, just ignore it and find a color that goes well with the countertop and tile. If the vanity is white, then you may want to match the white to make it your trim color.

Gray Vanity

If you have a gray vanity and want gray walls, and there is NO tile on the walls, then it's important to choose the correct shade of gray since the two grays will be right next to each other. Place paint chips next to the vanity and then do your best to match the gray color of the vanity. Then choose a color for the walls that is either a shade lighter or darker than the vanity. If you choose the exact same color then the vanity will visually disappear against the walls.

Of course you can always use a different color than gray, but muddy colors will probably work best. Just make sure the color you choose doesn't affect the gray vanity and make it look purple or some color you don't want. You'll be able to tell when you hold paint chips up against the vanity. If there IS tile or wainscoting on the walls then the wall's paint color will not be next to the vanity, so you don't have to match the vanity color. You should choose a color that matches the wall tile.

Colored or Unique Vanity

If you have a vanity that is a really fun color, or it looks like weathered barn wood or a piece of furniture that's been made into a vanity, then it's the star of the show. You should choose either a neutral color, or a softer, lighter color for the walls so that the wall color doesn't steal the limelight. Look to your tile for the right neutral shade. If the vanity is very light then you may want to choose a darker color to make the vanity stand out.

When remodeling a Bathroom and you order a vanity online, it's important to get the vanity before you buy tile! When it arrives it may not be the shade of gray that you expected!

Tip!

Warm Gray and Taupe

Many taupe tiles have a slightly pink or purple undertone. The trick to choosing color for Bathrooms with this tile is to match the tile. You need to pay attention to the undertones. The **Spring** palette works best with this tile. Avoid **Summer** and **Autumn's** yellow and green palettes because they will clash with these tiles.

Paper White 1590
Winds Breath 981

This Bath has a taupe countertop and gray tile in the shower. Since the shower tile covers more square footage in the room, the decision was made to match the tile rather than the countertop.

Gray and Taupe Mixed

Sometimes if you look at the tile and the sink top, you'll find many variations of warm and cool tones. First lay paint chips on top of the tile and see how many colors you can find. Then look at the sink and the sink top to decide which color will look best overall. If both warm and cool neutrals will work with everything, then it just comes down to a matter of personal preference. Decide if you're more drawn to either a **Winter** or a **Spring** palette. Do you prefer warm colors or cool colors?

Since this is a very large Bath and you see a lot of floor tile, they decided to match the taupe color found in the floor tile.

In this Bathroom they opted to contrast with the sink cabinet so that it would stand out as the focal point. The walls match the taupe sink top.

Here the client prefers cooler gray tones, so they matched the cooler gray in the floor tile.

Sometimes you need to take a clue from the hardware. Is it a cool silver color? Or a warmer tone? This Bathroom is black and white so any color would work, so they looked at the hardware to decide on a neutral color that would work.

Large Master/Primary Bathrooms

In the 1990's almost all new construction had a huge whirlpool tub in the Master/Primary Bath. They were loaded with cold, hard materials like granite, stone, and porcelain. My goal in these Bathrooms was to warm it up, so I always used darker colors in there to make it feel cozier. Light colors tend to wash out these Bathrooms, so don't be afraid to use more color than an off-white. In a new gray and white Bath use a cool color from the **Winter** or **Spring** palette but try to go a shade darker than you normally would. (For more, see the **Master/Primary Bedrooms** chapter on page 204).

Creamy, Warm Colored Tile, Countertops, and Vanities

Neutrals

Most creamy tile and countertops are a little yellowy or beigey, and some marble has a warm, creamy background and warm gray veining that appears almost beige, gold or green. When choosing a neutral, warmer taupes and beigey-grays look better with this tile. A cool gray will appear blue and it will make the tile appear yellow.

Warm Colors

You'll want to use a warm color in these Bathrooms. **Autumn** is a good palette for these Bathrooms with colors like warm beigey grays, beiges, soft yellows, golds, olive greens and reds.

Clear Bright or Muddy?

Because the tile is not white but rather a creamy color then be sure to use muddy or in-between colors. Clear bright colors will make this tile look dingy and dirty.

Trim

Either match the overall creamy color of the tile for your trim, or if all your fixtures like the tub and toilet are white, then you can use white trim.

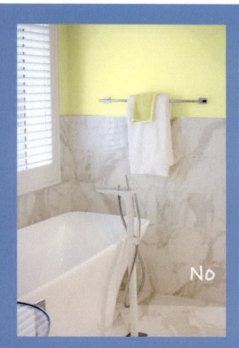

The clear bright color makes the tile look dingy and dirty.

The cool gray makes the walls look blue and the tile too yellow.

This warm gray with a slightly green undertone is a great match.

This homeowner wanted gray walls because there was a bit of gray in the countertop. But a cool gray would have made this warm, creamy sink vanity look too yellow. So a warm taupe is the better choice.

This countertop is taupe with pinkish undertones, but the rest of the tile has creamy yellow undertones. Since the paint will not be next to the vanity, it was best to ignore the countertop and choose a warm green to match the tile.

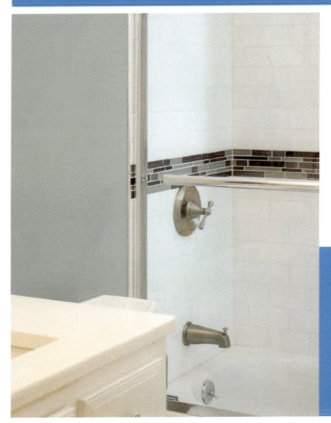

When things don't match in the Bathroom, like having white tile in the tub and a cream-colored sink and vanity, then the best way to distract away from it is to put a strong color on the walls. Then the paint color becomes the star of the show.

Choosing Colors for Beige Bathrooms

The safe thing to do in a beige tiled Bath is to paint the room a light beige color that matches the tile, and most people take this safe route. If you're going to paint the walls beige, first lay your fan deck or paint chips on the tile and find the closest color beige that you can find to match the tile. Then, after matching the tile you can choose to use a color that is a shade lighter or darker, but just make sure it's the same color family or else the color will clash. If you can't find the exact color then find the closest beige you can and use the lightest version of the color available.

But what if you can't find a color that matches everything? What if you don't like your floor tile? What if you'd rather paint a color other than beige? We will discuss all of this as we go on in this section.

Figure Out the Undertones.

Keep in mind that most beige tiles have a *slightly pinkish undertone*. Make sure to paint the walls the same tone of beige as the tile. If your tile is peachy or pink, don't fight it. For instance, if you use a khaki beige with a green undertone, it will make the walls look green and the tile pink.

This tile has a slightly pinking undertone. The color on the left is a khaki beige with green undertones that does not go well with the tile.

Wall Tile

When tile goes halfway up the wall all the way around the room, the paint will be right next to the wall tile. So it's really important to choose a color that matches the wall tile. It doesn't matter what color your floor tile or your countertop is, it's most important to match the wall tile.

Match the Sink Top, the Wall Tiles, or the Floor?

If you have beige tile in the shower with a glass enclosure then you'll see the paint color next to the shower. Make sure the paint color looks good next to the shower tile.

However, if you have a shower curtain that covers the tile, or the shower tile is not that noticeable and you see the floor more, then match the floor and the sink.

After trying to match the undertones in your tile, take a look at your floor and sink top. Hopefully all of the tile and the sink top in your Bathroom all match and have the same undertones. If not, then you'll need to make a decision. What's more important? Matching the tile, or matching the sink top? The sink is closer to eye level, so that may be more important to match the sink top. But if there is a lot of floor tile to be seen, then you may feel the floor is more important. You'll have to decide which one will bother you more, not matching the floor, or not matching the sink.

If your sink top touches the wall, then you WILL notice the paint next to the countertop. You can match it, or contrast with it. Many countertops of granite or stone have warm and cool tones, beige and gray. If this is the case then you can either use a warm color or a cooler color.

Tip! Cedar Key 982 by Benjamin Moore is the color I use the most often with beige tile. It is not peachy or pink. It's a neutral taupe that seems to go with beige tile 90% of the time.

175

Vanities

Stained Wood, Black and White

After matching colors in the floor and wall tile and the sink top, the last step is looking at the sink cabinet. Most vanities in Bathrooms of this style have stained wood vanities, which are warm wood tones very similar to the color of the tile. If you have a stained wood vanity, then it doesn't really come into play here. Ignore it and just match the tile. If you have tile going around the whole room then the paint color will not be near the vanity anyway, so again, don't consider the vanity. Black and White vanities are colorless. You can do any color with them.

Creamy Colored Vanity

If you have a vanity that is painted a creamy color, just make sure the wall color you choose compliments the vanity. Because the vanity in this Bathroom is a creamy color with warm yellowy-beige undertones a warm beige worked best. A cooler color would contrast too much and make the vanity look too yellow.

Tall Cabinetry

If you have a lot of wood cabinetry that is pretty dominant in the room then choose a color that compliments the wood. Beige is fine, but there are a lot of brown tones in the room. Blues and greens compliment wood tones, so you may want to consider doing a color on the walls besides beige.

Floor Tile

Sometimes the floor tile matches everything else perfectly, and sometimes is does not. If you're lucky you'll be able to find a color that matches your shower tile, sink top and the floor perfectly. If the floor is different then you'll need to decide if you should consider the floor or not.

If you have a really pretty floor tile that you like, or if it's a large Bathroom and you see a lot of the floor tile, then choose a color that compliments the floor tile.

Sometimes you can just ignore the floor. If you don't like the floor color, or if you found a color that you love that goes with everything BUT the floor, then just think of the floor tile as being like hard wood floors that are brown. You don't usually choose brown walls just because your floors are brown. Go with the color that you like on the walls, then maybe throw a rug on the floor and say, "It is what it is."

Here they opted to ignore the floor and chose a taupe that matches the countertop.

Cedar Key
982

This tile has warm beiges and cool taupes. They chose to use a cooler taupe to give it a more updated look.

Beige and Gray Combo

Many times if you look close enough at your granite or tile you'll notice that there are flecks of gray or taupe. If your Bathroom is over fifteen years old, keep in mind that warm beiges are older colors, and grays and taupes are more updated colors. So try gray or taupe walls to give the Bathroom a more updated look.

Lay a fan deck down on the granite or the tile and see if a gray or taupe will work. If you have a stained wood vanity, then you'll find that a cooler color like gray will contrast with the vanity and compliment it nicely, especially if it has off-black glazing.

> If you have busy tile then stick to a neutral color to calm it down. A color on the walls will look too busy.

Tip!

178

Beyond Beige

Warm Colors

After trying to match colors in the floor, tile, and countertop, if you find that nothing really matches all of the materials, then consider using a muddy color on the walls instead of beige. Sometimes this is the best option because your eye will be drawn more to the color on the walls rather than the color of the tile and countertops.

Another reason to use color is simply to break up the sea of beige! If everything in the Bathroom is beige then painting another beige on the walls is, well, just too beige! Since beige is warm you can use warm colors from the **Summer** and **Autumn** palette like red, terracotta or gold. Keep in mind however that these colors were in style 15 years ago and can date the room. If you love those colors, then go for it. But if you're planning to sell your house and are looking to make the room look as updated as possible, then either use a cooler color or keep it neutral.

When choosing a color to go with beige tile be sure to use a muddy or in-between color. Do **NOT** use a clear bright color. Clear colors look terrible because it makes beige tile look dingy and dirty.

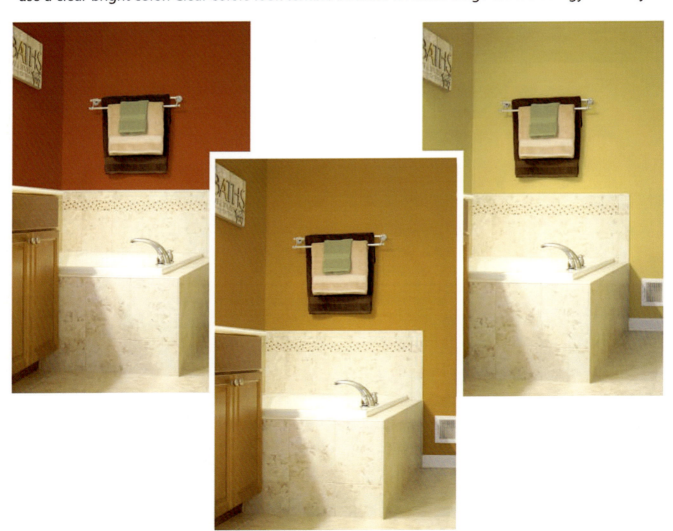

179

Cool Colors

If your tile is warm and has yellowish undertones, then greenish colors may work because they have a little yellow in them too and will go well with tile and countertops with yellowy undertones. However, if your tile is peachy or pink, green will make the tile look even pinker. If the tile is not yellow or peach, and has some cooler taupe tones, then try a cooler gray-green or sage green.

Blue is considered a calming, relaxing color, and it always looks good with beige. For a calm, restful, spa-like feel, try a gray blue, or muddy greenish blue.

180

More Things to Consider

Orange Tones

You may have a Bathroom with stained wood and tile that has very strong orange tones. You don't have to paint the walls peach just because of the orange tones. You can find the neutral beige or taupe in the tile for something neutral, or I have found that a turquoise color goes very well with orange. I like to use either an "in-between" version of turquoise or a "muddy" gray/blue/green like Beach Glass 1564 or Quiet Moments 1563 by Benjamin Moore, or Sea Salt SW 6204 by Sherwin Williams.

Matching the Accent Tile.

If you have an accent tile like glass tile, then you can match that tile. You can also do a shade lighter or darker. Match the tile first and then either follow the paint strip up or down for lighter or darker versions. Be sure to use a muddy or in-between color though. Clear bright colors don't look good with beige tile.

1980's and 1990's Bathrooms

These Bathrooms typically had shiny white or sponge painted looking tile with accents of flowers or Aztec patterns. They typically come in shades of blue, mint green or mauve pink, and back in the day the room probably had wallpaper. When choosing a color try to choose a neutral color to calm down the tile. If it has pink tones use taupe. If it has gray, match the gray. If it has blue or green, it's usually a gray blue or a gray green, so match the color. If you want to tone it down then match the lightest color you see in the tile or use a silver gray with a slight blue undertone.

Peach and Pink

The more you fight pink, the pinker it gets. Pink is warm, so use a warm color. Either use a soft, blushy pink on the walls or a neutral. Lay your paint chips on the tile and see if there is any taupe or warm gray in the tile. If so, then try to match it. By going a little deeper in color, it will tone down the pink.

This gray is OK, but you'll notice the pink is toned down more with a taupe color on the walls.

Hunter Green

A cool gray with a slight blue/green undertone goes well with this color. If there is a lot of dark green marble in the Bathroom, then don't use a color that's too light or off-white because the contrast will be too stark. Go a little deeper in color to match the heaviness of the dark marble.

1960's and 70's Bathrooms

Some bathrooms from this era had a shiny, taupe colored tile. For these bathrooms the color is actually a quite pleasing neutral, so just match the tile and then paint it a shade lighter. You can rely on towels and accessories for punches of color.

Other colors from this era were Harvest Gold, Rust, and Avocado Green. These colors are **Autumn** colors. I haven't seen any of these bathrooms personally in quite a while. The best thing to do with these bathrooms is to find a neutral cream or beige that works best.

Early Sunset
2096-70

Malted Milk
SW 6057

1950's Bathrooms

These Bathrooms were solidly built and many are still in good shape today, so they still exist in many homes. They came in a variety of colors like pink, blue, yellow, and green. Most people who own these Bathrooms complain about the color of the tiles and try to change the overall look. But the trick to choosing a color for these Bathrooms' is **don't fight the color**! If you paint the walls a contrasting color it will only intensify the color of the tile!

Some of these Bathrooms also have a contrasting border along the top in combinations like mint green tile on the walls and an accent of a burgundy border. At one time that Bathroom probably had wallpaper with little pink flowers and mint green leaves. If this is the case then it's probably best to match the overall color and ignore the accent color, unless the accent is gray or black, then you can paint the walls gray. Here are the colors I use with these tiles. I never use white because I feel a soft color gives it a softer look. A little bit of color will help tone down the tile color.

Pink and Burgundy Tile

An off-white with a pink undertone like Atrium White OC-145 by Benjamin Moore will work with pink. But if you would prefer a neutral, either gray or taupe is the best choice. Most taupes have a slightly pinkish undertone. It won't fight the pink and will actually tone it down a little bit. Using any other color will exaggerate the pink and make it pinker.

1/2 Remodel

A lot of homes replace the floor and the sink but leave the wall tile. Take a look at the sink top and the floor and see if any gray or taupe colors work with them.

Blue, Turquoise, and Mint Green Tile

Match the color of the tile as best you can and then use a softer, paler version. This will actually tone down the color and make it more pleasant. Don't try to fight it. You will only make it worse.

Another option besides painting the walls a lighter version of the wall color is to paint a cool gray. A deep, strong, neutral gray can hold its own against an intense color and actually tones it down a bit. This especially works with a black border.

Gray Tile

Hooray! You got lucky! Match the gray and do a softer, lighter version.

Black and White

You got REALLY lucky! Anything goes.

Yellow Tile

I have had trouble trying to find the right paint color to match yellow tile. The best thing to do is use a really light yellow or cream color that looks like a much lighter version of the color of the tile. Then it won't be so noticeable that it's not exactly the right color. Another option is to do a light, warm gray color or a warm white.

Paint the Tile! — Tip!

This is another option that people don't know exists. I don't suggest it for a long-term solution, but it's great for short term. If you're staging the house to sell, or you just want the Bathroom to look better for a couple years until you're ready to remodel, then you can paint the tile. (I suggest black and white). Use a good quality primer and ask the local paint store which product they recommend. There are people who you can hire also. Look for someone who can reglaze your tub and paint tile.

Powder Rooms

Follow the basic Bathroom rules for the Powder Room. Consider the tile, sink, vanity, and the floor. Usually there is no tile on the walls in a Powder Room so DO consider the vanity because the paint color will be next to it. Look at the sink top first to see what colors match the sink top or will look good. Next, see if you like the colors next to the vanity. Lastly, consider the floor. If you have a beige floor, use a muddy color. If you have a hardwood floor, or gray, black or white tile, then you can use any color including a clear bright color.

Location, Location, Location

Depending on where the Powder Room is located in the house will determine whether you can go crazy and have fun with a daring color that you're afraid to use anywhere else, or if you should keep it calm and subdued.

Off the Foyer

If the Powder Room is off of the Foyer and can be easily seen from the Living Room and Dining Room, then use colors that are calming and subtle so that you don't draw attention to the room. You may even want to use the Foyer color so as not to draw attention to the toilet.

Off the Kitchen or Family Room

If the Powder Room is attached to the Kitchen or a Family Room do NOT paint a bright color or use distinctive wallpaper because you will draw everyone's eyes right to the toilet! Paint the Bathroom the same color as the other room so that it visually disappears.

Down the Hall Out of Sight

If the Powder Room is tucked away and out of direct line of sight from other rooms then this is a space where you can have some fun with wallpaper or a bold, dramatic color. This is a small space so it's a good place to experiment with a color that you may be afraid to try in a larger room. If you have a window, then try a dark color like teal, navy, charcoal gray or even black!

If you have a white pedestal sink and a white or wood floor, then you may be at a loss for an idea for a color. Refer to the **Color Seasons** palettes for ideas.

If the wall behind the sink is hidden from view in the Hallway try an accent wall of a fun color, wallpaper, shiplap or tile to give the room a little pizazz.

Kids' Bathrooms

I always believe that kids' spaces should be fun. When kids are young, I encourage parents to use fun colors. Then when the kids become teenagers, you can use a serious, grown up neutral color. Boys and girls both tend to like blue and green, or bluish green so it's a good choice if you have both boys and girls. These colors also look good with most tile. Yellow is OK, but kids aren't always that neat and I have seen a lot of toothpaste splattered on walls, so blues and greens hide that better than yellow. Speaking of splatter, if there is no tile behind the sink and you think the kids will splatter onto the walls then you may want to use an eggshell finish. That goes for little boys with bad aim too. (wink).

If you have white tile, you can use clear bright colors. If the tile is beige, then use muddy and in-between colors. If it's a hall Bath that everyone uses, use a toned down muddy or in-between color. If it's their own private Bath attached to their room, then choose a color that goes well with the Bedroom.

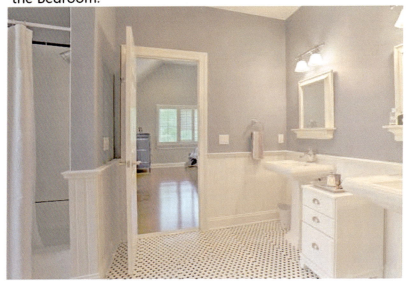

Paint The Sink Vanity

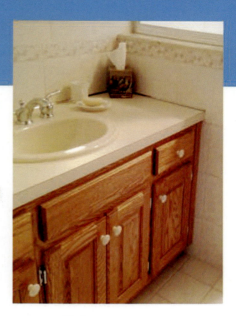

If you have an older Bathroom then painting your sink vanity can give the Bathroom a whole new remodeled look for just the cost of a quart of paint. If your sink vanity has seen better days then replace it, but if it's still in good shape then consider painting it. All you have to do is lightly sand, paint with a coat of primer, and then paint with a satin or semi-gloss finish paint. Ask the paint store which paint they recommend for painting vanities. Refer to page 100 in the **Kitchen** chapter about painting cabinets.

White

Painting the vanity white is great as long as it works with your countertop. If the countertop is a dingy off-white, then it will look worse next to white. Either match the off-white or paint it black or a color. When choosing a white remember to never mix your whites and be sure to match any white tile in the room.

If the countertop is white or has white in it, then you can paint the vanity white.

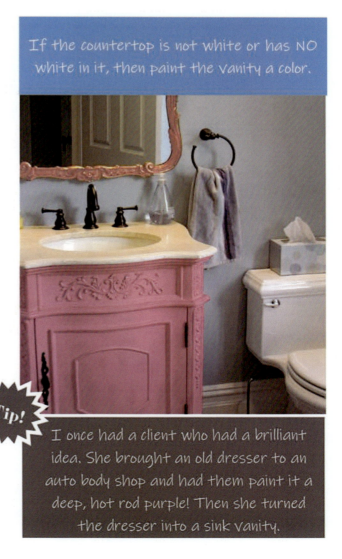

If the countertop is not white or has NO white in it, then paint the vanity a color.

Tip! I once had a client who had a brilliant idea. She brought an old dresser to an auto body shop and had them paint it a deep, hot rod purple! Then she turned the dresser into a sink vanity.

Green Top

If there is white veining then you can paint the vanity white. Other options would be black, gray, or a gray green. For the walls, paint them a silver gray, blue/green/gray, or a soft sage green.

Blue Top

White looks great with blue. Sometimes it works and sometimes it doesn't. If all the tile in the Bathroom is beige, then white will stick out like a sore thumb, so paint it cream or gray. If the tub and toilet are white though, white will work. Be sure to paint the trim the same white.

Pink or Peach Top

If there are specks of white in the countertop, or if the sink is white, then you can do a white vanity. If the top is granite, then it probably has beige and gray in it, so you can paint the vanity either gray or taupe. Take a look at the floor to decide what would look best. You could also create the illusion of a dark stained wood by painting it a very dark black/brown.

Cream or Yellow Top

If your countertop is cream or pale yellow, then white will make it look dirty. Either match the cream or choose a color. If it's dingy yellow then it's muddy, so paint it a stronger muddy yellow, khaki or olive green. A warm gray/beige also works well as long as it looks good with your tile.

Gray Vanity

Look for any sign of gray in your floor, tile or countertop and try to match it. If nothing is gray then you may be forcing it to work, so it may not be the right choice. A taupe, black or navy may be a better choice. If you have beige tile then use a warm, beigey gray.

Black Vanity

Black goes with almost anything and tones down tile you don't like, so it's always a good choice.

Blue, Navy, or Green Vanity

These colors look great with almost any countertop that is cream, beige, gray, taupe, or white, and also look great with almost any tile. If you hate your floor tile you should paint the vanity a great color and paint the walls a lighter version of that color. Then the vanity will become the star of the show and take attention away from the floor tile.

Before

Other Colors

Most people are conservative and want the neutrals mentioned above. But don't be afraid to have a little fun, especially in a Powder Room or a kid's Bathroom. Just make sure the color works with the countertop and the floor tile. In a girls' Bath you can use a hot pink or in a Powder Room you could paint the vanity and mirror a fun color like yellow, turquoise or red. Remember it's only paint. When you get tired of it you can change it.

After

Which Type of Paint to Use

I have seen too many Bathrooms with black mold and mildew stains on the walls and ceiling. Even in newly remodeled Bathrooms sometimes the exhaust fans don't work as well as they're supposed to and the Bathrooms get moldy or the paint peels off of the ceiling.

Years ago, I recommended an Eggshell finish because the sheen helped to repel moisture. (Flat paint just soaked in the moisture) and I suggested adding "mildecide" to the paint. Just as "insecticide" kills insects, "mildecide" kills mold. It's a powder or a paste that was added into the can of paint when it was mixed and killed mold in hot, steamy Bathrooms.

Most paint brands carry Bathroom paint, or "Kitchen and Bath" paint which comes in a Satin finish. It's even shinier than an Eggshell finish and it has mildecide in the paint. But the first problem is that it's too shiny and in my opinion that looks terrible. The second problem is that after a hot steamy shower the moisture literally drips down the walls and I have heard many people complain about the dripping and they thought something was wrong with the paint.

A few years ago, Benjamin Moore created "Aura Bath and Spa". Aura is their top-of-the-line, self-priming paint and has mildecide in it. Aura Bath and Spa was made for steamy hot saunas, steam rooms and bathrooms and it comes in a **Matte finish**. For the first time ever we don't have to have shiny Bathroom walls! To be honest I was skeptical about the paint at first and was afraid that when wet hands splattered water on the walls it would leave water marks on the walls, but it didn't. This stuff works like magic and now it's what I always recommend for Bathrooms.

Also available by Sherwin Williams is their SuperPaint. It has zero VOC's, prevents mold and mildew and has Air Purifying Technology. Use either their Flat or Satin finish.

Don't forget about the ceiling! Most of that hot steam from the shower hits the ceiling the most, so I always tell clients to paint the Bathroom ceiling white in the Aura Bath and Spa or Bathroom paint too.

Checklist

- ✓ Type of Furniture
- ✓ Fabric and Rugs
- ✓ Carpet
- ✓ Keep it Calm

One time a woman came into the paint store and asked "Does anyone ever paint their Bedroom red? Because my husband said he wants me to paint the room a color that will make me more in the mood". TMI.

Most of the time "Calming, Restful, Spa-like" are the words I hear repeatedly when clients describe the feeling desired for a Master/Primary Bedroom. My goal for the Bedroom is to create a space that feels like a resort. The way to get that calming, restful feeling is to use soft, calming colors.

Type of Furniture

Traditional Furniture

Following the same school of thought as for Dining Rooms, if you have a traditional wood Bedroom set that is a sea of wood, wood, wood, then the last color I will use is beige or brown. It just does nothing for the room. Because the wood is dark, and the room is usually dark, many people go the easy route and use an off-white thinking it will make the room feel brighter, or bigger. It does neither. All it does is make the room look BORING! If, however, you have an architecturally amazing room with crown molding and beautiful fabrics, then beige is just fine. But I have found that soft blues and greens compliment wood and make it look much prettier, and they keep the look bright, light, and airy. Even a cool silver gray can do the trick. You can look at bedding, pillows, or rugs for color ideas.

Beige only works in this room because it has crown molding and color in the area rug and fabrics.

Stock colors like Linen White and Navajo White are beautiful colors if they contrast against white molding. But these colors are also "builder specials" and found in every condo and apartment. So, if there is no crown molding then these colors are just too bland. Try soft blues, grays, greens, and golds.

Tip! My favorite Bedroom color is a soft blue-green-gray called "Quiet Moments".

New Furniture

If you have gray, dark wood, or contemporary furniture, or a beautiful tufted, fabric covered headboard, then neutral colors will work well. Take clues from the fabrics and especially the headboard to decide whether you want to use gray, taupe, or beige. Variations of gray work too, like lavender gray, or blue gray. You don't want a bright, stimulating color in the place you want to rest, so if you want color then use colorful pillows and maybe add an accent chair.

Fabric Headboard

A beautiful headboard is the star of the show in the Bedroom so you don't want it to disappear. First lay paint chips on the headboard to see what colors match it. Then go slightly lighter or darker on the walls. Another trick is to add an accent wall. For color ideas, look at the fabrics, art, area rug, or refer to the **Color Seasons** palettes.

In the top left photo the headboard disappears. In all the other photos it stands out.

Color Inspiration

Fabrics

These days people tend to use all white bedding so look at your pillows and window treatments for ideas for a wall color. If you have pretty neutral fabrics in the room then try to match a color that you see in them for a nice calming, restful feel to the room.

Tip! You can repeat a deeper color found in your area rug as an accent wall.

Area Rugs

Area rugs are always a good source of inspiration for color ideas in any room.

Artwork

Sometimes there is nowhere else to turn for ideas. If you have a favorite piece of art then try to find a color in there for inspiration.

Light or Dark?

Keeping it Light

Many Master/Primary Bedrooms seem to be on the dark side of the house and don't get a lot of natural sunlight, so most of the time I will do a soft, light color that doesn't make the room feel too dark. I find most people repeatedly tell me they don't want a room or color to be too dark, so I am programmed to always make sure a room does not feel dark. If there is not a lot of natural light then the colors may look dull and washed out, so follow the sampling guidelines to find a color that looks pleasing.

Calming, Restful, Spa-Like

This may sound like Goldilocks and the Three Bears, but I don't want the color to be too bright, or too dark, I want it just right. I never use a bright, sunny yellow unless the homeowner is a bright, cheery morning person who loves to wake up to bright sunlight and they specifically request yellow. I think in all of my years choosing paint colors I have done 2 bright yellow Bedrooms and one of the clients came back a year later saying, "What was I thinking? It's too bright and I can't fall asleep!" Gray blues, gray greens, and cool silver grays are all calming, restful colors that work really well in Bedrooms.

Medium to Dark

Some Bedrooms are actually too bright. So the way to make it feel more calm and relaxing is to use a darker color on the walls. Darker colors are fine because it's a room to fall asleep and they will make you feel warm and cozy and wrapped up in a blanket of deep color. If you have an exceptionally large Master/Primary Bedroom or tall ceilings then a medium to dark color will help the room feel cozier and you won't feel like you have large, empty walls. When people worry that the room will become too dark and cave-like I tell them to make sure the ceiling and trim are white, and to use white curtains and bed linens. It's a great balance.

Other Things to Consider

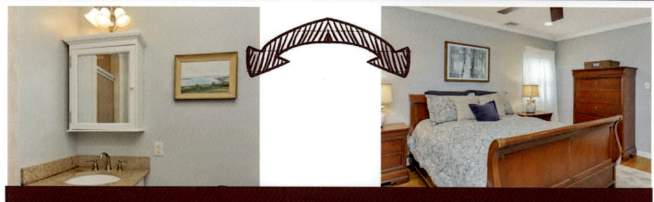

Both of these Master/Primary Bedroom and Bathrooms are the same color.

Coordinating the Bathroom with the Bedroom.

Most Master/Primary Bedrooms have an attached Bath, and if so, it's nice to create a "Master/Primary Suite" by coordinating the two rooms together.

When trying to choose a color for the Master/Primary Bedroom you can try matching a color in the bedding. But I have found that most people prefer all white bedding to recreate that hotel/spa look. That doesn't help much in trying to decide upon a color.

When I'm not sure which direction to go in for color in the bedroom, I will start by choosing a color for the Bathroom and then either use the same color in the bedroom, or a shade lighter or darker. Sometimes I will coordinate both rooms. For instance, there may be taupe tile in the Bathroom and I'll do a blue/green on the walls. Then in the bedroom I'll do taupe walls, but the bedding and window treatments are that same blue/green color. If you're one to change the bedding often, then it's better to stay neutral. It's okay to do beige in one room and gray or taupe in the other.

The blue bedding color was repeated in the Master/Primary Bath.

Tray Ceilings

If you are fortunate enough to have a tray ceiling in the Bedroom, read Tray Ceiling guidelines in the *Ceilings* chapter.

Wall-to-Wall Carpet

If you have neutral wall-to-wall carpet, and want to paint the walls neutral, then it's best to match the walls to the carpet to make sure it doesn't look dirty. It can be a lighter version of the color, but in the same family. If you want to paint a color, use a muddy color that doesn't clash with the carpet color. As we have learned in earlier chapters, if the carpet is a little pink and the color you choose is a little green, they will clash. If the carpet is a strong color like blue or green, then use a neutral. Use a cool color if the carpet is a cool color, and if it's a warm color choose a warm neutral.

Walk-In Closets

The typical thing to do in closets is to paint them a plain, flat white. But tossing shoes against the walls can make the walls pretty scuffed up, so I tend to paint them a neutral color. The easy thing to do is just to paint it the same color as the Bedroom. You can paint it a coordinating color with the room, or you can even have some fun with a bold color or wallpaper. It all depends on your personality and what you like. Nobody is going to see the closet except you, so do whatever you want. If you're the type who likes to keep things simple then just go white, but if you like leopard prints and bling, then go wild. I tend to reuse a neutral color used somewhere else in the house inside closets.

Checklist

- ✓ Fabric and Rugs
- ✓ Who Will Be Your Guests?
- ✓ How Else Will the Room Be Used?

Once a client told me her Mother-In-Law was planning to come for a few days, and she showed me a black and white wallpaper that she planned to use as an accent wall in her guest room. The pattern was so busy it made my eyes go wonky when I looked at it. I said I didn't know how long her Mother-In-Law would be able to look at the paper and she may not want to stay in that room for too long. She glared at me and said "Exactly!". We had a good laugh! So it depends on what your goal is for the room.

Some people do not want their guests to feel too comfortable and over extend their stay, but most want their guest room to feel warm and inviting so their guests feel welcome. If you fit into the latter category, then you'll want to mostly follow the same rules as for a Master/Primary Bedroom and make the room feel **calming, restful and spa-like,** like a hotel room.

How Will the Room be Used?

Spare Bedrooms can be used in different ways. I have seen them used as an Office, Playroom, Workout Room, Craft Room, Sewing Room, Den, you name it. When choosing colors for this room the first question I ask is, **How will this room be used?"**

In this room red would be great for an Office but not very relaxing for a Bedroom.

True Guest Bedroom

It's much easier to choose a paint color to match bedding than to choose bedding to match a paint color! **So choose the bedding first**. Choose bedding that you really like and then pull a color from there. As with every room, take a look at the fabrics in the room, and the flooring for ideas for color. If the fabrics are very vibrant colors, then choose a more muted, muddy version of the color, or do a neutral.

If you like to rotate bedding however, then you may want to choose a neutral. If you have wall-to-wall neutral carpet, then match the carpet.

Catch All Room

If you're choosing colors for the whole house and there are no design plans for the guest room, no bedding chosen, and it's just an extra space that needs to get painted, then simply use a color from another room. Very often this room is one of the least important rooms and will probably just be the "catch all" room. If so, then there is no sense in buying more cans of paint in another color. If there is paint left over from the Living Room or Family Room, just repeat it in the guest room. **This is not a room to stress over**. If it will eventually become a nursery then figure out a new color when the time comes. For now, just get it painted and move on. For more on ideas for Bedrooms see the chapter on **Master/Primary Bedrooms**.

This color was left over paint from the Hallway.

Fabrics and Carpet

Headboard

If you have a fabric headboard then it's the star of the show in the room. You can make it pop by doing a lighter or darker color on the walls. If it's neutral then try to match it and then do a lighter or darker version of that neutral color on the walls. For more on this see the **Master/Primary Bedrooms** chapter.

Look at the Fabrics

If you have colorful bedding then choose a neutral for the walls. If you have plain white bedding then you may want to choose a color. Look at pillows or area rugs for more ideas.

Wall-to-Wall Carpet

If you want the walls to be neutral, then it's usually best to match the wall color to the neutral carpet. If not, the color you choose may make the carpet look dirty. If the carpet is a cool color like green or blue, choose a cool neutral color. If it's a warm color, use a warm neutral. You can also paint the walls a color. Just use a muddy color to make sure the carpet doesn't look dirty.

Multi Purpose

Personal Space

If you're using this room as a Craft Room, Workout Room or an Office space, then you can have fun with color if you want. If you're the only one that will really ever see it, then choose a color that makes you happy. If there is no furniture yet then this is a room where I will ask clients, "What's your favorite color?" I will "allow" colors that may be considered dated (like peach or mauve) or too wild (like purple), because it's not part of the main living area of the house and really the only one who will see it is you.

Tip!
An area rug or pillow is always a good source of inspiration.

Bedroom Office Combo

If the room doubles as a Bedroom and an Office then choose a color that compliments the bedding. If you do Zoom calls in this room, use a color that you look good in! For more ideas see the **Offices** chapter.

Who Will be Your Guests?

If the room is truly being used as a guest room, then the second question I ask is, **"Who will be staying here?"** Sometimes the Grandparents will stay there when they come to visit the kids. Some people have relatives that come from other countries and stay for extended periods of time, sometimes six months at a time. If so, then I like to choose a color that will appeal to those guests. Other times, nobody in particular stays there. If so, then go crazy and have fun! Create a pretty space that makes you happy!

Grandparents

If it's a room for the Grandparents I will ask the homeowner what color their mother likes, but sometimes their reply is, "But it's MY house." It's funny how the family dynamics begin to be revealed as we choose paint colors for different family members.

Interestingly, when I have chosen paint colors for my mother's generation, they seem to all hate neutral colors, and especially hate gray. They all use the same word and say that gray reminds them of a "Battleship". The last color they want is "Battleship Gray." So if you have Grandparents from that generation staying in that room and you want to make them happy, give them a happy color, not gray. This is usually about the only room that I will paint a soft yellow. Blue and green work too. If you want to paint the room neutral, then try using colorful bedding to cheer up the space.

Grandkids

If you are a grandparent and want a color that will appeal to the grandkids, then refer to the **Kids' Bedrooms** chapter. If you have numerous grandchildren, a mix of boys and girls, then I have found that most boys and girls both like blue. Green works too. Many Grandmothers tend to like yellow, and that's fine, but I always point out that yellow shows all the dirt and fingerprints. If it's too bright it will be too stimulating, so the kids may have a hard time going to sleep. If you do use yellow, use a muddy, softer shade of yellow. Refer to the chapter on **Toning Down and Fixing Colors** .

Checklist

 Boy or Girl?

 Age

 Personality

 Bedding

After working with thousands of families I have noticed some patterns when working with children. Different age groups tend to like certain things. For instance, a four-year old-girl is not going to like the same thing that her tween sister is going to like. So when choosing colors for kids' rooms the first two questions I ask are, "Are they boys or girls?" and "How old are they?"

In this chapter we will discuss choosing colors for boys and girls in different age categories.

Kids Love Color!

The first room you will decorate for your children is their nursery, and you the parents will be the ones in control and will choose whatever paint colors you want. But within a few very short years your kids, girls especially, will develop a definite opinion about the color of their room. This usually strikes a note of fear in their parents because they have learned by now that kids are not afraid of color! Grown-ups however are very afraid of color!

Many times I act as the mediator between moms and their kids because a lot of moms just want a beige or off-white room, (and want it to be spotless too!) and really do not want to allow their kids to choose their own color. But my philosophy is that **kids should love their rooms**. So I always take sides with the kids. Now I'm not saying to allow them to have colors that are too bright, but if the girl wants pink, then let her have pink. As a mom of four who has watched my own kids grow up way too fast, I remind parents that before you know it your kids will be off to college and you will wish they were back in their crazy colored room! When that day comes then you can paint their room whatever boring, neutral color you want. Kids will have their whole adult life to be serious. For now, let the kids have some fun!

I took this picture in the paint store one day of a girl trying to decide which color she wanted for her room. She couldn't decide!

Basically, the thing parents need to do when choosing colors for a child's room is to simply get in touch with their inner child. Remember what it was like being a kid, and then just let go and have some fun!

215

"The System" for Kids

If you bring your child to the paint store to choose a color for their room, you will immediately find yourselves in the middle of a battle of wills with your child. Almost always they will choose the brightest color they can find, and they will have a hard time choosing which color they want because they love ALL of them. Meanwhile, you as the parent will spend the entire time in the store trying to convince your child to pick a lighter, softer, or more neutral color. It doesn't work. This is why I came up with **"The System"**

By following these simple rules your child will feel that they get to have a say in choosing the color for their room, but YOU are ultimately still the one in charge. (You are the one paying the bills after all). I have used this system thousands of times and it works like a charm.

The System

1. Do NOT take the kids to the paint store. They will automatically choose the brightest colors they can find!

2. Pick THREE COLORS for their room that you can live with.

3. Take those three colors HOME and show them to your child and let them choose out of the three.

Nurseries

While Mommy is pregnant and "nesting" she will probably be on Pinterest for nine months pinning ideas for her dream nursery. Most expecting parents learn the sex of the baby before it's born and begin to plan accordingly, but some do not. Sometimes they decorate nurseries in pink for girls, and blue for boys and usually these colors are soft pastels. Occasionally parents get a little more bold and daring and paint a color like a lime green, or do an accent wall in wallpaper. But most of the time they tend to paint the room in a neutral.

Years ago, I used to tell parents to "Buy the bedding first and then match the paint to the bedding." However, mothers today don't use bumper pads, dust ruffles or blankets anymore! So you'll have to find something else to use for inspiration!

Gray

Beige was popular for a while but now gray reigns supreme. I recently shopped for a baby shower and pretty much all of the nursery accessories in the stores are gray. In order to find a shade of gray you like, try to find something gray you like and then try to match it. If you have chosen something for the room that is gray, like an area rug, a blanket, or a chair for instance, then simply match that gray. You may even find a pillow or a gray shirt that you like. Take it to the paint store and try to match it. Then sample it on the wall following the instructions in the chapter on sampling colors.

Pink, Blue, and Other Colors

Sometimes if parents don't know the sex of the baby, I will suggest that they paint the room neutral for now, and then later add an accent wall painted in pink or blue, or of wallpaper.

If you want to paint a color that is soft and not too bright or intense then read the chapter on **Toning Down and Fixing Colors**. But if you want the color to last for a few years without having to repaint the walls then you may want to think forward. Read about choosing colors for kids around age five.

The neutral walls in this room match the carpet.

Boys' Bedrooms

Don't Call it "Pretty"!

Choosing colors for boys' rooms is usually easy, because to be honest, most of the time they just don't care. In my experience, most boys do not want to be involved in decorating their room, picking out their bedding, curtains or paint color and coming up with a "decorating scheme." Sometimes they do, but most of the time they do not.

When you ask a boy what color they want you will typically get the answer *"I don't know"*. If you press them for an answer, it will probably be *"I don't care. Whatever. Blue, I guess."* They just let their moms choose for them. However, letting moms choose a color for a boy's room can be tricky because moms tend to choose "pretty" colors! Think about that moms, boys don't want a "pretty" room! Try to think more about what a "guy" would like instead.

> **Tip!** Blue is the color of the sky so visually it pushes the walls back and makes the room look bigger. Boys many times get the smallest Bedroom, so blue will help to make the room appear a little larger. If there is a toss-up between blue and another color, and the room is small, go with the blue.

0-4 Years

The softest pastel colors work in a nursery. As they grow into a big boy bed you may want to repaint the room. Look at the bedding for color ideas. Light blue says, "Baby Boy Blue". As boys get older, this color will become too "babyish". A Grayish blue will look soft yet won't look as babyish so you will probably be able to get a few more years out of it. Green is another option but 95% of the time boys' rooms end up blue.

5-10 Year Old Boys

If you start out with a stronger blue in the nursery, then you probably won't have to paint again until they are around 10 years old. Little boys' bedding usually has trains, trucks and cars and comes in primary colors of red, denim blue, navy blue, and green. To find a color for the room lay paint chips on the bedding and try to match one of the colors. If you choose a grayish blue like a denim blue then it will be neutral enough to make Mom happy and blue enough to make the son happy. If you like a color in the bedding but feel it's too dark for the walls, then you can use it on just one wall, or go a shade lighter than the actual color in the bedding. Just make sure you choose a color in the same color family.

Other boys bedding will have brightly colored Superheroes or cartoon characters, and this bedding comes in brighter versions of blues, red and lime green. Occasionally boys will prefer to go with green, and I can count on one hand the times that boys have chosen red. If the color they choose scares you, make a compromise by painting just one accent wall or accent stripes.

Tip!

The ceiling is always another place to put color. A calming night sky is a great place to put glow in the dark stars.

11-14 Year Old Boys

As boys get older their personalities take shape and they usually choose colors based on the things they like, like their favorite sports team. Some paint companies have the colors already matched like Benjamin Moore's "New York Yankees Blue". Your boy may want the addition of a bright color like gold or orange based on their favorite team. If so, you will have to get creative with how to use the bright color in small doses. A dark colored accent wall is a great option and looks great with life sized stickers and framed jerseys on the wall.

Some boys are more artistic and get creative, and some are into music and want to hang music posters and guitars on the wall. The ceiling can be a 5th wall, and closet doors can also be a place to play with color. But many boys still just don't care and let their mom choose the color. If so, remember moms, they want a "guy space" not a "pretty room". Army green, olive green, khaki beiges, and gray colors look great with bedding in navy blue and red.

Boys 15 and Up

The older boys get, the darker they like their room to be, because they usually want a "Man Cave". Think about it. What do teenagers do? They want to play video games and sleep until noon. (I'm not saying that's the best thing to let them do, but it's what they would LIKE to do.) So a dark brown, charcoal gray, navy blue or hunter green is perfect for them. Again, Moms, if you are freaking out about the color then do an accent wall.

As boys approach their late teens and twenties the reality is that they will hopefully be leaving home soon. I know it's hard for moms to let go. I have been to homes of parents in their 60's and their sons haven't lived home in 20 years, but yet they still call the room "Johnny's Bedroom". As they get older it's better to choose a neutral, more "grown up" color like a neutral beige, slate blue, or gray for their room. They are no longer little boys and baby blue is just no longer appropriate for them. Look at their bedding, pillows, or an area rug for color ideas.

Girls' Bedrooms

Choosing colors for girls is a whole different story than choosing colors for boys. When you ask a girl what color she wants to paint her room she will usually have a very strong opinion about what color she wants. It usually becomes a battle of wills by around the age of four or five and sometimes even earlier. For girls' rooms think in terms of a 5-year plan. Every five years you will need to change her room because biologically girls change as they get older and they will want their rooms to change too as I will explain in this chapter. When that little girl hits pre-school age she will begin to have little opinions of her own and will start to tell her parents how she REALLY feels about the yucky color on her walls! I have asked parents to leave the room then sat little girls down and asked them what they really thought of the beige color on their walls and their response is usually something like, "It looks like poop!" Kids say the darndest things.

Age 2-6 Think Pink!

Girls this age love pink, and by pink, I mean PINK! The pinkest, Pepto pink that you can find! Now, the funny thing is that the girls that want the REALLY pink rooms are usually the ones that have a mom that HATES pink. Ha ha. Hence the mom tries to convince her daughter to love beige, to no avail and that mom will shop for the palest shade of blush pink available. If you really want to make your daughter happy however, buy her that pretty, pink princess bedding and then match the pink color in the bedding. If you're afraid of the color being too bright, then you can use a lighter version of the color in the bedding. You may think that I am stereotyping with these colors, but truthfully, I'm basing this on experience with thousands of customers.

I personally loved purple as a girl, and thought for sure, that girls would be split down the middle with 50% loving pink and the other 50% loving purple. But when I went to work in a paint store, I was very surprised to find out that almost all little girls wanted pink! If I were to create a pie chart, it would show that 95% of the time boys wanted blue and 95% of little girls wanted pink!

Pink Alternatives

Pale Blush Pink

If you just don't like pink but your daughter loves it you can try the softest version of pink which is a soft blushy pink. (Refer to the **Toning Down and Fixing Colors** chapter.) If there is no pink in the bedding to match then look at the girls' clothes and try to match a dress or shirt.

Another way to compromise is to do a pink accent wall.

Other Colors

If you have one of the 5% of girls who wants a different color then consider their age. If she's only two years old then you can do a soft pastel or a neutral. But if she's almost seven then you may want to plan ahead knowing what is coming next as a pre-teen. To avoid having to repaint in another year refer to the next page for color ideas.

The easiest way to choose the right color is to buy the bedding first, then match a color in the bedding.

This "not a girly-girl" prefers primary colors and her mom got creative with a woodland theme. The olive green wall color is in the bedding.

Girls 7-9

Ten years ago, I used to see girls flip from pink to a new color at around the age of 9 or 10. But over the past few years I have seen the flip happen as early as seven years old. I'm assuming it's probably because they may have older siblings or cousins that they like and younger girls want to be cool like the older girls. I'm not sure. But what I do know is that it is about this age when they start to prefer blue over pink. So this age group I consider to be part of the "pre-teen" stage.

Pre-Teens

When girls enter the pre-teen stage they begin to rebel against their pink rooms and their love for color only intensifies. It's like they are saying,*"I'm not a baby anymore and I don't want my little girl , pink room anymore."* I think it's probably due to the biological changes that their bodies are starting to go through.

When girls get to Middle School, they all become clones of each other and they all want what their friends have. They all have the same hair style, the same clothes, and they also want the same color room. If their friends all have tropical blue colored walls, then that's what they will want too. Their lives become more dramatic, and they will also want a more dramatic room color. They are changing. They are growing up and they will want their room to change too! Moms, the trick to working with pre-teen girls is simply to remember when you were their age. Try to put yourself in their place and think about how they feel and what they want. Because after all, pre-teen and teenage girls are very emotional and it's always about their selves, or should I say, their selfies! But don't worry, this stage doesn't last long. My advice is this: These next few years will fly by, so let them be happy. Before you know it they'll go off to college and go out on their own, and when that day comes, then you can paint their room a boring neutral.

If your furniture is off-white then use a muddy color and off-white trim. If it's truly white, then you can use a clear bright color.

Pre-Teen Girls

At this age girls want color, and that means BRIGHT color. This is the stage when you'll look at clear bright colors, not muddy, soft pastel colors. Typically, they will like cool colors like blue, turquoise or purple. Occasionally they may choose citrus colors like lime green, orange or yellow. As long as it's bright and it's different than what they had when they were "little" they'll be happy. If they still like pink, then they will usually prefer a more intense shade of pink like raspberry or hot pink. Preferably they would like ALL of these colors! If they could tie-dye their room, they would be happy! (Every time I say that to parents in front of their daughter the girl breaks out into a huge, mischievous grin! :) I once had a girl that got her parents to paint a different color on each wall AND the ceiling too!

Occasionally they may want to be more creative and want something like a navy accent wall and then bright colored bedding. But no matter what, they will want strong, bright color. So if you decided to do a very pale pink when they were younger, I'm just warning you, they will probably start bugging you for stronger colors. It's only a matter of time. If they don't know what they want, then I usually direct girls to look at websites like **PB Teen** for room ideas. Again, it's always much easier to choose the bedding first, then match one of the colors to use on the walls.

Tip! *With these colors be sure to use white trim. My favorite is "Super White" by Benjamin Moore. But if your furniture looks more like White Dove, then choose a muddy color instead.*

Teenage Girls

When it comes to choosing colors for their rooms, teen girls are all over the place. It depends on how long it's been since their room has changed. If they were able to switch over to a non-pink room when they were a pre-teen then they may still be happy with their room. But if the room hasn't changed since they were six then they will want a new older, more mature room.

Choose Bedding First

What kind of bedding will they choose? It really all depends on their personality and what they're into at this age. Some girls are really into decorating their rooms and some are not. But by choosing the bedding first it will help to determine which direction to go with color. Simply match a color that you find in the bedding, or something that complements it.

Neutrals for Teen Girls

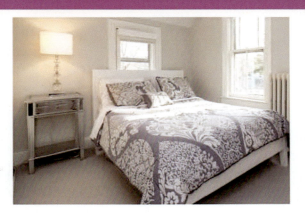

Teens that are into fashion, art or design will probably want to decorate their whole room. They will search online for ideas and tell you exactly what they want. They may want a sophisticated neutral, or they may want a creative color on the walls. If there is wall-to-wall carpet on the floor be sure to take it into consideration. Refer to the **Guest Bedroom** chapter for more on this. Some girls are not really into decorating, and some don't want their room to change. If so, then to be honest, just leave it alone until she moves out. If it's been a long time since the room has been painted and it just needs to be repainted, then it's probably smart to just paint it a neutral color. This way you can change up the bedding as time goes on and not have to worry about matching the walls.

Other times girls don't want to match the bedding at all and may choose an accent wall of a dark blue, deep purple or charcoal gray and add pops of color with artwork or accent pillows. These are their last few years of being a kid so let them have fun.

Black and White

Some moms secretly fear that they will have "that" daughter that wants to paint her room black. (Which really isn't so bad!) To be honest, in all my years as a color consultant I've only had one girl want her room black. So don't worry.

Some teens simply want a room that's **all white**. If so, make sure the white you choose looks okay with her furniture. If the furniture is **off-white** it will look dingy and dirty next to walls that are pure white, so you'll need to do an off-white on the walls instead.

Gender Neutral

For keeping a room gender neutral the key word is "neutral". Look at the bedding or carpet to choose the right neutral color. Also refer to the **Guest Bedroom** chapter for more ideas.

Kids on the Spectrum

Kids with autism typically have trouble sleeping so be sure to use a calming color in their room. Avoid red, orange, and bright yellow. Do not use clear brights. Navy, blue, gray, or an earthy green is a better choice.

Trim Choices

White Trim

If the furniture is white, stained wood or a color like navy or black, then you can use a bright white trim. You can use any color for the walls including clear bright colors.

Off-White Trim

If the furniture is off-white then the trim should be off-white too. Try to match the color of the furniture as closely as you can and make it your trim color. If the furniture is creamy or off-white then you should choose a muddy or in-between color for the walls so that the trim doesn't look dirty. Do not choose clear bright colors for the walls because then the trim will look dingy and dirty. I have found that Pottery Barn furniture tends to match White Dove by Benjamin Moore.

Colored Trim

I'm not a fan of colored trim, however in kids' rooms sometimes you will need to get creative with the colors that they choose so you may opt for painting the windows, doors or trim in a color. If your kid is an LSU fan and insists on purple and gold, you may end up painting the walls purple and the trim gold. It's fine in a kids' room, just don't do it in your Living Room please.

* For ceiling colors, see the **Ceilings** chapter.

Siblings Sharing a Bedroom

Boy and a Girl

The trick to choosing a color for a bedroom for a boy and a girl is to find a color they both like. Most boys and girls both like blue and green, so one of these colors will be your best bet. Blue is almost always the winner. Although your daughter may prefer pink walls, you can choose other pink things to make her happy like a pink comforter or give her a pink accent wall by her bed.

Twins

As a mother of twin girls, I understand this dilemma. It's important that each child maintains their own identity and they're not constantly referred to as "The Twins". So if they share a room I think it's important to somehow divide up the room so that they each have their own space. This can be done by painting accent walls or getting creative. See below.

Choose Bedding First

Ideally try to find bedding for each child with a common color. So when you choose bedding for the room keep this in mind. Most boys bedding has blue in it, and even girls princess bedding has touches of blue in it, so a soft sky blue will probably work best with boys and girls bedding.

Colors to Avoid

White and yellow walls get really dirty very fast so if the kids are going to spend time playing in their bedroom then these colors are probably not a great idea. Kids hate neutrals! The whole rest of your house can be neutral, but let kids be kids and give them some color. If you really want a neutral then choose colorful bedding and think about painting accent walls for color.

Accent Walls

Sometimes each kid is completely different and you just need to compromise. You can always give each child an accent wall of a color of their choice, but you'll run the risk of the room becoming too stimulating rather than a place for them to rest. So try to avoid really bright, contrasting colors. Another option is to paint stripes, polka dots, or tape off a large square or rectangle at the head of each bed like a faux, colorful headboard.

Checklist

✓ Is the Room for Boys, Girls, or Both?

✓ Where is the Room Located in the House?

✓ Have Some Fun!

Most moms love their neutrals, so it's hard to convince them sometimes to choose playful colors. But Playrooms are exactly that, rooms to play!

When choosing colors for a Playroom take a few things into consideration. Is the room for boys, girls, or both? Is it part of a space that the whole family will use too? Is the room tucked away in the Basement, or upstairs on the second or third floor? Or is it on the first floor where all your guests will see the room? We will take all of this into consideration.

Is the Room for Boys, Girls, or Both?

For color ideas that will appeal to boys or girls refer to the **Kids' Bedrooms** chapter. If it's a space that boys and girls will share then choose a color that they will all like. Both tend to like blue. Green, aqua, and soft yellow are fun yet still calm. Colors like bright yellow, yellow/green, orange, and red are stimulating. If your kids are already stimulated enough, then using a calmer color may be a good idea. If it's a space like a Basement where boys and girls, grownups and kids all use the space, then consider a color that will make everyone happy. If you're going to put it up to a vote then refer to the **Kids' Bedroom** chapter and use "The System".

Neutral

Of course moms love neutral colors and will always try to make every room in the house neutral if they can, but they will probably get complaints from the kids! So consider using a colorful accent wall to make it more fun. When choosing a neutral consider a color with a touch of gray in it to hide fingerprints and remember that yellow shows all the dirt. So if you choose a neutral color, choose a gray or taupe, rather than a yellowy beige. If the room has wall-to-wall carpet it may be a good idea to match the color of the carpet.

Where is the Room Located?

Basement

If the Playroom is in the Basement and there are tiny Basement windows, then one goal may be to brighten up the space. Blue, light green and yellow makes the space brighter. Fingerprints and scuff marks are gray so yellow usually shows all the dirt. So if you think the kids will be touching the walls a lot, then consider using blue, green, or aqua blue. If the ceilings are low then refer to the chapter on **Ceilings**.

Upstairs

If the Playroom is up on the second or third floor and not part of the main living space then you can have more fun with color because nobody will really see it except your kids. Think about adding stripes, wall decals, a wallpaper accent wall, or even a mural. Have some fun.

This Dining Room was converted into a Playroom on the first floor.

First Floor

Some homes convert a typical Living Room or Dining Room space into a Playroom. Some use a Sunroom or another room off of the Kitchen that can be seen from the main living space as the Playroom. In this case you may want to balance having a fun color with being a color that works with the rest of the house. Since this room will probably be messy most of the time you won't want to use a clear bright color that will draw attention to the room. It can be a fun color, but not TOO much fun, so use a muddy color.

Choosing a Finish

Which Finish to Use on the Walls?

Sometimes it's a toss-up which finish to use. You will have to think about what could possibly go wrong, and then choose between the lesser of two evils.

Flat, NO!

You won't be able to wash the walls well.

Matte

Matte looks flat but is washable and hides imperfections, such as nail heads popping out and bad spackling jobs. It's also better for paint touch ups. So if you have little boys that like to crash toy cars into the walls, or knock holes in the walls with hockey sticks and you can foresee the walls needing to be patched up and frequent paint touch ups, then use matte.

Eggshell

If your darling daughter is a budding artist and likes to draw pictures on the walls, or your toddler forever has sticky fingers and likes to touch the walls leaving greasy fingerprints everywhere, then you may want to use an eggshell finish. It's more scrubbable and the slight sheen will camouflage the shiny fingerprints.

* Any other finish besides these is too shiny and unnecessary.

Tip! Boys & girls seem to both like blue, so it's usually a winner. Moms & Dads can usually live with this color, too.

The Writing is on the Wall!

Fun Paint Ideas For Playrooms and Other Creative Spaces.

As a solution to kids drawing on the walls or putting holes in the walls from hanging artwork with thumbtacks or tape, try these ideas to save your newly painted walls.

Whiteboard Paint: You can create your own whiteboard wall and use dry-erase markers to draw pictures, write reminders, create a calendar, you name it. I have a friend who is a business coach with a home Office who did an entire wall as a white board. You can do a whole wall, or tape off a section. The drawback to this paint is that it has a strong odor when applied, so you will want the room to be well ventilated and stay out of the house until it dries.

Magnet Paint: Magnet paint has actual metal shavings in it to make magnets stick. It's black, but can be painted over, so you can paint an area with magnet paint and then paint the wall color right over it. The more coats you apply, the better the magnets stick. I have found that with three coats a magnet will stick, but if you put a piece of paper behind it, they will fall off. But five coats will hold the paper and the magnet. If you're going to paint over it, you may want to add one more coat.

The paint is not cheap and is sold by the quart so you'll probably want to do a small area. Think about using it on a closet door, or taping off an area, like the size of a bulletin board. You can get really creative and tape off a racing stripe around the room, or giant circles, and then paint it a fun color. You can paint a border of circles around their room, and then cut out pictures and stick them into each circle like a frame. If your kids want to hang posters magnet paint will allow them to use magnets instead of tape. The only drawback is there is a very slight bumpy texture due to the metal shavings.

Chalkboard Paint: Once only available in black, now chalkboard paint comes in a variety of colors. Several coats need to be applied. Think about taping off an area to paint with chalkboard paint, and then you can paint a fun frame around it. You can paint it on a door or a cabinet, or just about anywhere you can think of. Use it in the Kitchen for calendars, recipes, and grocery lists. The only drawback to this is the chalk dust on the floor.

Checklist

- Tile Floor Color
- Will the Mud Room get Muddy?
- Is it Seen from the Kitchen?
- Is the Laundry Tucked Away out of Sight?

Mud Rooms have become the "must have" thing for new construction and are usually added as part of Kitchen remodels. They are usually right near the garage or the back door to the house so that when the family enters the house, they can dump all their stuff into the cubbies. This back entrance ends up becoming the main entrance to the house and the first thing that people see when they enter. Sometimes the first room you see is the Laundry Room.

When choosing colors for these spaces you'll take into consideration the floor tile and cabinetry colors just like the Kitchen. You will also want to think about whether you want to have some fun with color or if you want to be more conservative. This will depend on where the room is located in the home.

Mud Rooms

When choosing color for a Mud Room the first thing that enters my mind is "Mud!" I imagine the kids coming home from soccer, baseball or lacrosse covered in dirt and grass stains, and the dog coming in from playing in the wet back yard with muddy paw prints. So foremost in my mind is choosing a color that will hide dirt.

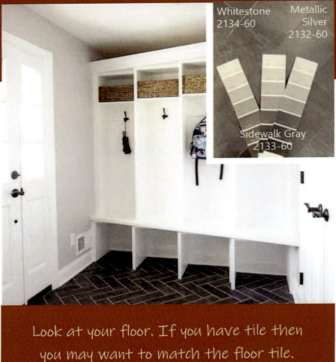

Look at your floor. If you have tile then you may want to match the floor tile.

If the floor is dark, match the overall color and then choose a lighter version of that color on the paint strip. If you have hardwood floors then you can use any color. Gray or greige colors are the best at hiding scuff marks. You can also paint the walls a color but use a muddy color simply for the dirt factor.

If there is white beadboard you can be more daring with color because the actual wall space is up high above "dirt level". You can use a dark color without worrying that the room will become dark because the white beadboard will keep the room light and bright.

Take into consideration how much a part of the Kitchen the Mud Room is. If it's right off of the Kitchen and it's almost part of the Kitchen, then you should probably paint the walls in the Kitchen wall color. Since the Mud Room is an area that can get cluttered and messy you don't want your eye to be drawn into that room every time you're in the Kitchen. So don't paint it a bright color that will draw your eye in there. You'll want the space to visually disappear and blend in with the Kitchen.

Colored Cubbies

If you can see the cubbies from the Kitchen, then you may want to match them to the Kitchen cabinets. If you think white will get too dirty then you may want to choose a color. If there is a slate or tile floor then you can match a color in the floor. Other color options could be a warm gray, muddy green, or navy blue. Red is a fun pop of color too, but use a muddy brick red. Whichever color you choose it should be a muddy version, not a clear bright that will show dirt. Refer to the **Color Seasons** palettes for color ideas.

Colored Beadboard

Beadboard should either match your trim color (a shade of white) or it should be the same color as the cubbies. It could also be or a lighter or darker version of the cubby color.

Tip! Another way to add a pop of color in the Laundry Room is the paint the cabinets or door a fun color!

238

Laundry Rooms

First Floor Laundry Rooms

If the Laundry Room is on the first floor right off the Kitchen, follow the same rules as for the Mud Room. Sometimes it's the main entrance to the house. Many times, if there is a slop sink in the room then the walls get splattered and scuffed, so choose a good dirt hiding color like gray, greige or a color with gray undertones. If it has the same cabinets and flooring as the Kitchen then paint the Laundry Room the same color as the Kitchen.

Keeping it Simple

If you're on the conservative side with color, then simply use a neutral. You can pull a color from the tile floor or use a color you've already used somewhere else. You can use a color from one of the Bathrooms for two reasons. One, because hopefully you've used a paint specifically used for hot, steamy Bathrooms and some Laundry Rooms get a little humid. Secondly, just to save money. Since the Laundry and Bathroom are usually not that big, you should have paint left over from the Bathroom, so use the leftover paint in the Laundry. Many times, both rooms have the same tile floor too so the color just works in both rooms.

Tip! Hate doing laundry? Paint the Laundry Room a pretty color that just makes you happy!

Hidden Laundry Rooms

Sometimes the Laundry Room is a separate room behind a closed door and not really seen from the other rooms. You can either paint a color that works with the floor tile, have fun with color, or just keep it simple and use the paint from the Hallway or Kitchen.

Basement or Second Floor Laundry

If the laundry is not visible from the main living area, then you can have fun with color. Try something like tropical aqua blue, orange, lime green, yellow, purple, or whatever color makes you happy! Why? Because nobody wants to do laundry and be stuck in the Laundry Room! So why not make it a fun place to be? If it's in the Basement then it's probably creepy and scary down there, so make it a bright fun space. If it's on the second floor, the kids probably have bright pink, purple and blue rooms, so what's another colorful room going to matter? If you have white cabinets, you can do any color you wish. If you have colored cabinets, then refer to the **Kitchens** chapter for color suggestions. If you have a beige floor then use a muddy color so the floor doesn't look dirty. If you have a white floor or hardwood floor and white cabinets then you can use a clear bright color. If you have old, stained wood cabinets you can paint them white to brighten up the room.

Tip! If the Basement laundry has a low ceiling then use a light color. The contrast of a dark color will make it very noticeable that the ceiling is low.

Checklist

- ✓ Who will use the Space?
- ✓ Where is the Room Located?
- ✓ Does it Double as a Bedroom?

An Office is usually a pretty boring space with a desk, maybe some bookcases, a printer, computers, and piles of paperwork. Often it has furniture that's stained wood, or possibly gray or white. Sometimes it's very formal with walls of cherry wood wainscoting and bookcases and looks like a library in a mansion. But most of the time it's just an eclectic mix of leftover furniture that gets thrown into a spare bedroom or a small room off of the Kitchen. The Office is a workspace, so you don't want a calming, restful color, unless it doubles as a bedroom.

Where is the Office Located?

First Floor Office

In some homes, especially Center Hall Colonials and newer construction, the Office is right off of the Foyer and one of the first rooms you see. If so, then you'll want to pick a sophisticated color that flows with the rest of the house. These Offices many times are taken pretty seriously and are formal spaces. They usually have a massive desk and may have an entire wall of bookcases. It's a pretty masculine space too if it has tons of stained wood. To narrow down a color then take into consideration who will use the space.

When the Office can be seen from the rest of the house make sure it's a color that compliments the other rooms. This Office got the inspiration from the painting in the other room.

Bedroom Office

If you're using a Bedroom as an Office, as opposed to in the Basement, then you probably have windows to create light, so the goal is not necessarily to brighten the space. If the room doubles as a Guest Bedroom, then choose colors that go with the bedding, and you may want a calming, restful color. If you don't use it as a Bedroom and it's your own private space that no one will see but you, then have a little fun and paint your favorite color that makes you happy! If you love peach or purple, then go for it! It does not have to go with the rest of the house if there's a door that closes it off from the rest of the house. For more on this, refer to **Guest Bedrooms** chapter.

> *Tip!* Do you do Zoom calls? Think about creating a colorful backdrop! Read more on page 248.

Basement Office

Sometimes an Office is tucked away in a Basement and they are usually spaces for someone who runs their own business and needs an Office in the house. Usually, people just paint this room a boring beige because they don't care about color in this room. But then it runs the risk of becoming a space that's depressing to be in. Think about going for something bright and cheerful to make the space more inviting. What's your favorite color? Use it here.

If there are no windows or just tiny Basement windows then choose colors to brighten the space. Sometimes just painting three walls a nice bright white with one accent color of a bright color will do the trick. You can use a clear bright color to keep you awake and stimulated to get your work done. Hanging artwork on the walls will visually create "windows" on the wall. If the ceiling is low then refer to the **Ceilings** chapter.

Who Uses the Office?

Women and Kids

If a woman uses the Office, then she may want a softer look. Women typically prefer everything to be light and bright and want white trim, not stained wood. With white trim and hardwood floors you can pretty much do whatever color makes you happy.

This is a space where the kids may do homework and you need to stay awake to get some work done, so you don't want a "calming, restful" space that will put you to sleep. If the room is tucked in the back of the house, you could use clear bright colors like yellow, red, orange, green, blue, or aqua blue. If it's in the front of the house and will be seen a lot, then use a calmer, muddier version of these colors. Of course you can always use basic, boring beige, but the whole rest of the house is probably neutral, so why not live a little? Maybe try an accent wall for a pop of color.

Men and Women

Many times men prefer colors that are a little darker and they like more contrast. But women prefer rooms to be light and bright. If a couple shares the space then there needs to be some compromise. Choose a color that goes with the furniture and if it's a room on the first floor that everyone sees then stay conservative. Men love stained wood and if the trim is stained, the man will almost always insist that it remain stained. So, if he wins that argument, then the woman should choose the color. An accent wall is another way to compromise. If he insists on having royal blue because it's the color of his favorite sports team, then let him have it on one wall and let him hang his jerseys on that wall. Then the woman can get her softer neutral on the other walls.

Man's Office

1990's Office

In the 80's and '90's a man's Office would have had stained wood on the desk, walls and bookcases, been painted a dark hunter green, and there would be lots of golf pictures hanging on the walls. Today these spaces are usually not quite so formal, but it's still a pretty masculine space. Men typically love stained wood and leather furniture. If there is cherry wood, then red and orange paint colors are too much like the color of the wood, and light cream and beige are just too boring. Great color choices are deep slate blue, navy, charcoal gray, or a deep khaki beige. If the man of the house likes green, try to stay away from the '90's green and instead do a more olive, earthy green. All of these colors look great with stained wood.

Red is a power color so it's quite a statement in an Office. Orange is vibrant and fun. Dark grays and blues are like the colors of slate and stone and are good masculine choices for a man's Office.

Conference Call Wall

Today many people work from home and talk to people via Skype or they're on Zoom calls. Others create videos from their laptop. This means people will be looking at you in your Office. It's like they're looking at you as a moving, talking photograph, so you may want to think about creating a good looking backdrop. Think about painting an accent wall behind you of a color that will make you stand out and look great. Consider a "power" color like red to make a statement.

Look at your wardrobe for ideas. What's your favorite outfit? What color do you look best in? If you're not sure, ask your family and friends what color they think looks best on you.

I look at clients' eyes to see what color they are and then we go into the Bathroom to look in the mirror. I hold up paint chips next to their face to see which colors compliment their eyes, hair, and skin tone. Choose a color that makes you look good! If you own your own business consider using your branding colors.

Bringing the Outdoors In

Sunrooms and Porches

Checklist

- ☑ Furniture
- ☑ Flooring
- ☑ Bring the Outside in
- ☑ Does it Need to Flow with Other Rooms?

Sunrooms and Three Season Porches are like little bonus areas to the house where you can sit and pretend you are outdoors, without actually being outdoors. They have tons of windows and not much wall space so you can take in as much of the view as possible. In every other room of the house you will choose colors based on the furniture and things in the room, but in a Sunroom you will also take into consideration the view outdoors. When choosing a color for this space you'll want to make sure the color you choose doesn't distract you from the view.

About 10 years ago I had a client with a small Sunroom off of her Living Room with a slate floor. She had a sample of a beige color up on the walls, and my first thought was that the beige did absolutely nothing for the room. I needed to come up with something better. First, I looked outside the windows for clues from nature. The green shrubs, trees, grass, and a blue sky were all so vibrant. But yet as I was standing in the Sunroom, I did not feel part of that outdoor landscape. Instead, I felt enclosed inside a white box and the beige color she had sampled would not have helped. I knew that what I needed to do was to make the walls disappear.

Before

After

Green would have been an obvious choice, but none of the other colors we were choosing for the house were green. So instead, I matched the deep gray-blue color of the slate floor. By darkening the walls, they seemed to slide into the outdoors. The outside was now brighter than the inside and the view outdoors became the dominant feature. She loved the color and so did her friends, so I got several referrals from that job just because of that color. But more importantly, I learned a lesson about using color which I am now passing on to you.

Natural Colors

Typically, people choose bright, sunny colors for sunrooms, like bright yellow and mint green, but that doesn't make you feel like you're outdoors. It just feels like you're sitting inside in a bright yellow or mint green box. The trick is to keep the color very natural. Look at the color of the bark on the trees, and the colors of slate, moss, and stone. You'll want to use a muddy color, not a clear bright. If you're choosing a color to match your furniture, then choose one of the natural colors. If you have a red accent pillow for instance, and painted the walls red, then the wall color would be the center or attention rather than the view outdoors.

Don't be Afraid to Go Dark

Sunrooms do not have much wall space to begin with, so a darker color on the walls will not make the room feel dark. Because there are so many windows, the view out of the windows will be the real "color" in the room. A darker color makes the walls disappear and the leaves of the trees and flowers outside will be brighter than your wall colors, so your eye will be drawn to the brighter colors outdoors.

This pale yellow is "fine", but it's kind of boring and safe. It also feels like you're just sitting in a yellow box, rather than part of the outdoors.

This green color matches the curtains and is similar to the color of the greenery outside. It's really fun! But it competes with the outdoors. You see the wall color first, then look outdoors later. That's all fine. You just have to decide what you want.

This dark, smokey greige color is similar to the color of the bark of the trees. The outdoor colors are brighter than indoors so your eye is drawn past the walls to the outdoors.

Matching the Floor and Furniture

When looking for color ideas take a look at the flooring and the furniture. If you have a tile floor, then you may want to pull out a color that's in the tile. You can choose a color that compliments the furniture but remember that in a Sunroom the furniture is not the important accessory of the room, nature is.

The color above is pretty, but it steals the show. The muddy color below fades into nature better.

Going With the Flow

Many times the Sunroom is seen from the Living Room or the Dining Room. You can either think of the Sunroom as a pretty color that is framed out by the Living Room doorway, or you may want to choose a color that compliments the Living Room. Sometimes by simply adding accent pillows in the Living Room it can tie in the color of the Sunroom and then they will flow together.

Porches

Porch walls should be painted to match the exterior of the house. But you can always have some fun with color on the ceiling!

254

Checklist

- ✓ Who Uses the Space?
- ✓ How is the Space Used?
- ✓ Are There Any Windows?
- ✓ Are There Low Ceilings?

As I descend the stairs with clients to the Basement I begin asking "Who uses the space? How is the space used?". This helps to know which direction to go with colors. Is there a bar, a Billiard table, a Workout Room, a kids' Playroom, a TV area? Knowing who uses the space and how it will be used will help with color selection.

The first thing to consider is how the space will be used and who will be using it. If older kids and adults will be hanging out down there to watch TV and play some games then use clear bright colors for fun, or deep dark colors, as long as the ceilings are not too low. But if you have young kids who will be touching the walls and banging toys into the walls, then you'll want to consider using a color that will hide the dirt and fingerprints.

Little or No Windows

Other than white, the two colors that brighten up a space the best are yellow and blue. They seem to bring an element of sunlight into the room. If you only have those tiny Basement windows and bad lighting, then consider these colors. If you want yellow and have kids that are going to be bouncing balls or hockey pucks off the walls, then use a muddy, beigey yellow, not a soft yellow or a clear bright lemon yellow because it will show all the dirt. If you want a warm color then choose a gold or an orangey color with a bit of brown in it to hide the dirt.

Colors for Everyone

Blue and green are colors that boys and girls, adults and kids usually can all live with. Cool blues and greens go well with a gray floor or couch. A smokey blue, denim blue, or a slate blue work well in this space. A greenish blue has a drop of yellow in it so it will brighten up the space well. These colors and Khaki and olive greens go well with beige and brown, so they will look fine with beige carpet, beige tile and with a beige or brown leather couch.

Neutral Walls

As much as gray may look great upstairs, in the Basement it may look too much like gray cinderblocks in the Basement. Stay away from cinderblock gray unless it's a nicely finished Basement with plenty of recessed lighting and new furniture. A silver gray that looks blue is a better choice. A beige, greige or taupe may be even better because they are warmer. Choose the neutral that works the best with the couch, carpet, or flooring.

Gray only works here because they have crown molding and daylight in this space.

Play with Some Color!

The Basement is different than your main living space upstairs. Upstairs you can play it safe and keep it all neutral. But in the Basement, you can go down there and have some fun!

Extra Large Basements

Some Basements are very large but have several different uses. If it's all open you don't have to choose different colors for each space, but you may want to do one accent wall. Choose the overall color based on the flooring. Most Basements don't have real hardwood, but they may have a laminate that looks like wood, in which case any color will go with the floor. If there is carpet or tile, then pull a color from there.

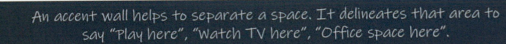

An accent wall helps to separate a space. It delineates that area to say "Play here", "Watch TV here", "Office space here".

Basement Bedroom

In Basement Bedrooms keep the color light and bright, especially if there is no window. To make the space feel larger or taller, match the color of the floor or carpet. To create a sense of daylight, use a soft blue or yellow. Beige may make the space feel like you're in a cardboard box, so try a soft gray blue or gray green as an alternative.

Bar and Pool Table Room

This is man cave space. Dark colors look great, but if you have a low ceiling don't go too dark, except for maybe just the wall behind the bar. (See "Low Ceilings"). Wives, the same rule applies here as when choosing colors for your son's room, don't pick a "pretty" color. Let your husband have what he wants here. Let him hang his sports jerseys and neon signs. If you have kids, and they have taken over every room in the entire upstairs, then this is the only space he has left anymore! Ha ha.

Soffit

Many Basements have soffits to hide the pipes and these are usually the Basements with low ceilings. Usually, painters will paint the horizontal side, (the underneath side) in white. But that visually lowers the ceiling. Instead, I like to only paint the highest part of the ceiling white, and paint the entire soffit in the wall color. If you stand back and take a look, then you'll notice that if you paint the entire soffit in the wall color it will visually disappear and blend in with the wall, and your eyes will only see the actual ceiling as the ceiling. (For more, see the **Ceilings** chapter).

260

Low Ceilings

Many Basements have low ceilings. The trick to working with a low ceiling is to make sure there is not too much contrast between the walls and the ceiling. Use a lighter color on the walls or put the same color on the ceiling to blur the lines between wall and ceiling. Another trick is to match the floor. Match the color of the carpet or tile and blend the walls with the floor. A dark accent wall isn't the best idea because a dark color will exaggerate the low ceiling. A bright color accent wall is fine though like a lemon yellow, light blue, or a neutral. Many Basements have beige carpet or tile. Beige and gray look great together so you can match the floor and do beige on three walls and gray as an accent wall.

The room above blended the walls with the carpet on the floor. The room to the left blended the walls with the ceiling. Either trick helps to make a room feel taller.

If you want to use a dark color then paint the ceiling dark too. It will blur the lines between the walls and ceiling and create a pub-like feeling.

Rooms with low, white ceilings need a lighter color. A dark color will contrast with a white ceiling and exaggerate how short the walls are.

Workout Room

If you're going to do yoga then use a calming, restful color, like something soft and pastel. But if this is a room with a treadmill, Elliptical machine, and weights, then you may want something more stimulating and exciting. To keep the room light and bright, you can do the walls in a white or a light neutral. You can always add an accent wall or even just paint the whole room in a clear bright color of a stimulating red, orange, yellow-green, purple, or cobalt blue. Whatever color gets your juices flowing and gets you excited, go for it because it will raise your heart rate and you'll burn more calories. A mirrored wall is always a good idea to check your form plus it makes the room look much larger and brighter. If you tend to bang the wall with equipment, then gray will hide the scuff marks. If the room is small with a low ceiling, then blend the walls in with the color of the floor.

Garages

Many Garages are just white, but they get all scuffed up by bicycles, sports equipment, shovels, rakes and whatever else gets thrown into the Garage. Since scuff marks are gray, then it's just a commonsense decision to paint the walls in the Garage gray to help hide the dirt.

Another choice is to match the exterior color of the house, as long as it's not yellow because yellow shows all the dirt. If the exterior is a dark color, then you may want to use a lighter version of that color, or the trim color. But gray goes with pretty much anything, and many Garage floors are gray, so that's why it's usually the winner.

Bonus Rooms

Library

Some extra-large homes have additional rooms like a Theater, Library or a Billiard Room. These are the rooms where you can go dark and moody, and even play with color on the ceiling and trim. In a Library, if it has a fireplace, you may want to keep it dark and masculine. But if it's a room you'll use all the time, you may want to lighten it up. Don't be afraid to paint over the stained wood. If you don't like dark rooms, then paint it white. If you want to have some fun, then paint it a color like navy or teal.

If there were no gadgets on the ceiling they could have also painted the ceiling dark blue, too.

Before

Theater Room

In a Theater Room, you can paint the walls dark. Think about using navy, dark plum, burgundy, or even black. You can also paint the ceiling the same color as the walls. Refer to the **Color Seasons** palettes for color ideas.

Wine Cellar

Wine cellars can stay neutral. Once it's filled with wine bottles you won't see much wall space.

After

When a woman took over this Library she wanted it light and bright, so she painting the shelves white.

This Billiard Room went for full on drama with high gloss, deep blue everywhere!

Before

This Library said "Goodbye" to the Sea of Wood, and said "Hello" to a more modern look!

After

Part 3

Now that you have chosen colors for the walls in each room, we will discuss choosing colors for your ceiling and trim, how to sample paint, which paint to buy, and do some problem solving.

Choosing Trim Colors

Where to Start.

The whole main living area (Living Room, Dining Room, Kitchen, Family Room, Foyer) should have the same trim color if possible. If you are painting every one of these rooms, then in order to figure out exactly which trim color to use, start in the Kitchen. If the cabinets are white, then try to match the white, and then that will become the trim color for these spaces. Lay chips on the cabinets and try to match the color. I'm talking about a simple match here, don't go crazy trying to mix some custom color. Just try to find the closest color you can. If it's a nice, clean white, then it will be easy and you'll simply use that white everywhere. Next choose color for the other rooms. See if the Kitchen trim color will work in the Living Room, Dining Room, Family Room and Foyer. If not then choose a white for the other rooms and let the Kitchen stand alone.

Guidelines for Choosing Trim Colors:

1: Choose the Trim Colors After the Wall Colors.
Choose all your room colors first, then choose a white based on the overall room undertones.

2: Don't Mix Trim Colors!
Use the same trim color throughout the entire first floor of the house. (If it's a one-story house like a ranch, then I'm talking about the main living area, not the Bedrooms or Bathrooms.) You may need to break this rule in the Kitchen to match the cabinets, however.

3: Don't Mix Your Whites!
One will look dirty; one will look clean. For instance, if you have off-white Kitchen cabinets and you paint the window over the sink in a pure white, then your cabinets will look dirty, or like they are stained by tobacco. If you have a pure white ceiling and you paint your trim a creamy off-white, then the trim will look like you painted them with oil-based paint that has turned yellow over the years. Find whatever is white in the room and match the white. It can be slightly lighter, but it should be in the same family.

4: Stick to the Basics.
In other words, stick to the colors meant for trim. There are classic white and off-white colors that are typically used for trim. We will discuss these colors later in this chapter.

Keep it Simple

One of my jobs when I worked in a paint store was "The Color Matcher". Very often customers would come into the store to buy paint because they had to touch up an area, but they threw out the old can of paint, and couldn't remember which color they used. So they would bring in a teeny, tiny chip of paint to the store to match it. Most of the time, the Spectrophotometer couldn't match the color. The guys working behind the counter couldn't match the color themselves either, so they would send the customers over to me to match the color.

Since people like me are pretty hard to find, I suggest that you keep it simple. When you choose a color for the trim, stick to the basics. This way if you ever have to go back and touch it up some day, it will be easy to figure out which color you used. Trust me, I am trying to make your life easier. The problem with trying to match trim colors is that paint chips are FLAT and trim is usually SEMI-GLOSS, and when a color has a sheen, it looks lighter, which makes it hard to match the color. That's why I always recommend keeping good records and keeping it simple.

Now if you want to play with a color on your trim, by all means have some fun. But I would suggest doing it in only one or two rooms and make sure you keep a record of what the color is in case you ever need to go back and touch up the trim.

Don't

This is one of my pet peeves. Muddy, yellowy trim looks dingy and dirty next to a soft color on the walls and against a white ceiling. This trim should have been a nice, clean white.

Transitioning into Other Rooms.

If you're painting the trim in the Kitchen a beigey or yellowy type of color, then jumping to a bright white trim in the next room may be too much of a stark transition. A creamy white like White Dove will be an easier, less noticeable transition in the next room. If White Dove doesn't work in the next room, then consider lightening the Kitchen trim up a bit by cutting the formula in half (see page 303.) It's OK if the color is lighter than the cabinets as long as it's in the same family. This is really only a concern if the rooms are open to each other. If there is a door into the other room, then don't concern yourself about whether or not the trim colors look good next to each other or not.

Common Trim Colors

When choosing which white to use it depends on the colors you choose for the rooms. If you're following my guidelines, you should have chosen colors that all flow from one room to the other, and each room has similar undertones. Pick up a brochure at your local paint store on "Whites" and you'll find the most common white and off-white colors in your brand. Here is a list of popular trim color choices from Benjamin Moore and Sherwin Williams, starting with pure whites.

White

This color is just that. It's white, and it works with anything. *Ceiling White* is also this color, so if you're painting the ceilings in Ceiling White, then use this trim color. The paint can was always labeled **"01 White"** which is probably what your painter will call it. Also known as **PM-2** and **OC-151**.

Super White

This white really is super! It has become my "go to" color for ceilings and trim throughout the entire house. I describe it as a "clean, warm white". Use Super White especially with all clear bright colors and with all grays. If your trim is Super White, then I prefer Super White on the ceiling because it's just a bit brighter than Ceiling White. The paint can will read **"02 Super White"** and it's also known as **PM-1** and **OC-152**.

High Reflective White SHERWIN-WILLIAMS

SW 7757

This is the whitest white you'll find. It's so white that it seems to reflect back to you, hence it's name.

Pure White SHERWIN-WILLIAMS

SW 7005

This white has a little bit of warm gray undertones to it making it a good trim color to use with... you guessed it, warm gray colors.

White OC-151

Super White OC-152

Cool Whites

Decorator's White

I assume people use this color because of the name and think it's what "Decorators" must use, but I rarely use it because it's a very cold, stark, blue white. Use it with blue and in a room that is depressingly dark that needs to desperately be brightened up. Known as **PM-3** or **OC-149**.

Chantilly Lace

Also a cool white, but not as blue as Decorator's white. Known as **OC-65** and **2121-70**.

Extra White   Sherwin-Williams

SW 7006

This color is said to be a pure white but it's slightly on the cool, blue side. If you use Sherwin Williams' **Ceiling Bright White (SW 7007)** on the ceiling, then use Extra White as your trim color because they go together very well.

Decorator's White OC-149

Warm Off-Whites

Atrium White

This color has just a hint of pink in it, but when it's next to red or a strong color with red in it like burgundy, orange or purple, you'll never see the pink. Atrium white will just look like a creamy white with no yellow in it. DO NOT use this color with colors that have yellow or green undertones because those colors will make your trim look pink. Also known as **PM-13** and **OC-145**.

Ibis White   and   **Arcade White**

SW 7000   **SW 7100**   Sherwin-Williams

These colors have a hint of pink in them and are similar to Benjamin Moore's Atrium White. Read above.

Atrium White OC-145

White Dove

This used to be my "go-to" trim color when beige was all the rage. It has a drop of gray and a drop of yellow. Of course it doesn't look gray or yellow, it just looks like a creamy off-white. It works with most muddy colors, like gold, beige, green, and greenish blues because they all have a drop of yellow in them. It works with warm grays with some beige in them because they also have a drop of yellow.

DO NOT use white dove with cool blues or lavenders because there is no yellow in these colors, and your trim will look yellow. Also DO NOT use it with any clear brights because it will look dingy and dirty. However, if the majority of all your colors have beige undertones, then White Dove will look great. Also known as **PM-19** and **OC-17**.

Steam

A color from the Affinity Collection known as **AF-15**, Steam is slightly whiter than White Dove and tends to match some Kitchen cabinets. It's a good choice if you're looking for a color that's not as bright as white, and yet not quite as muddy as White Dove.

Alabaster   and   Greek Villa
SW 7008   **SW 7551** SHERWIN-WILLIAMS

These colors look very much like White Dove. Read above.

Snowbound   SHERWIN-WILLIAMS
SW 7004

This color has just a hint of warm gray without any yellow, making it a good choice to go with taupe and gray colors.

Cotton White   SHERWIN-WILLIAMS
SW 7104

This color has warm peachy-yellow undertones and works well with any color with warm, peachy beiges and colors with warm yellow undertones.

White Dove OC-17

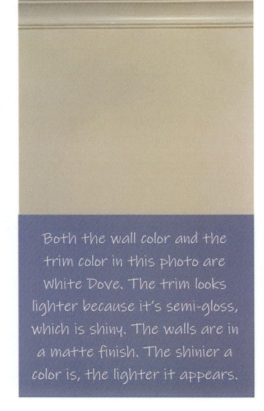

Both the wall color and the trim color in this photo are White Dove. The trim looks lighter because it's semi-gloss, which is shiny. The walls are in a matte finish. The shinier a color is, the lighter it appears.

Linen White and **Navajo White**

These colors are slightly beigey, yellowy, creamy colors and go very well with warm beiges and colors with yellow undertones. They are muddy so only use them with muddy colors. If there is absolutely nothing white in the room, and white trim would just stick out being too stark white, then use these colors for trim. Linen White is known as **912, PM–28** and **OC-146**. Navajo White is known as **PM-29, 947** and **OC-95**.

Marshmallow Sherwin-Williams

SW 7001

This color does NOT contain yellow. It reads slightly gray and pink, making it warm without looking yellow. It goes well with taupes and beiges.

Simply White

Simply White is NOT simply white! It has a hint of a yellowy green undertone to it so it goes well with yellow and green. It's whiter than White Dove and it's not really muddy. It is a warmer alternative to using White and can be used with clear brights as well as muddy colors. It's known as **OC-117** and **2143-70**.

Mayonnaise

Interior Designers loved to use this color in the 90's because it's warm, slightly peachy-yellow undertones went really well with golds, reds and warm beiges. If you use these deep warm colors and white is too stark then try this color for your trim. Known as **OC-85** and **2152-70**.

Whitetail and Dover White

SW 7103   **SW 6385**   Sherwin-Williams

These colors are slightly yellow making them good choices to use with any warm colors with yellow undertones.

Linen White OC-146

Simply White OC-117

Colored Trim

I pretty much never paint the trim a color. Back in the '80s some people painted their trim in colors like blue, green, red or gold to match the wallpaper. It's also a very Colonial style look and in the 90's when people were hanging wicker baskets from the ceiling and decorating with ducks and ivy, some people painted colored trim. If you have an Historical house and want to stay true to the period, then choose a muddy color from either the Historical Colors or the Colonial Williamsburg Collection. Sometimes people want to paint the trim fun, bright colors in kids' Playrooms. I think the reason some people paint color on the trim is because they are actually afraid to put color on the walls. But personally, I just really dislike color on the trim. (By color I mean colors like blue, yellow and red). It looks too dated to me. I would prefer the walls to be a fun color with white trim. Occasionally I have painted the trim and wainscot in a neutral color to give a traditional house a more contemporary feel. I will paint the trim either the same color as the walls, but in a semi-gloss finish, or I will paint them with a tone-on-tone look, with one slightly lighter and the other slightly darker. Beige, taupe, gray and black are colors that can look great on trim because they're neutral.

Using Black

The Farmhouse style has made black windows, doors and trim popular over the past few years. The same rule with whites applies to using black. Use a warm black with warm colors, and a cool black with cool colors. A warm black is slightly brownish, like '**Night Horizon**" by BM, or '**Black Fox**" by SW. Use it with warm off-whites and warmer neutrals from the **Spring** palette. A cooler black like '**Black**" by BM or '**Tricorn Black**" by SW works well with cooler whites and grays from the **Winter** palette. See also page 137 for more on using black trim.

Beyond Basic White Trim

Tip! Try a Board and Batten accent wall in a dark, mossy green or navy blue in a Satin finish for a "Wow Factor"!

After / Before

An exception to the "no colored trim" is when you match the trim to the wall color in a room where you're going for some drama! Try wrapping the entire room in the same dark color in a Library, Study, Billiard Room, Office, or Dining Room. Decide on your color and your sheen. The top two photos are low sheen. In the bottom photos the walls are matte and the cabinets and trim are semi-gloss.

Wainscoting

The idea behind wainscot is to create the look of all wood that is carved out, and it's usually painted all white. The cheap knock-off version is to create picture frame molding by adding pieces of trim on the wall in box shapes. 20 years ago, it was a popular idea to paint the walls inside the boxes in one color and the molding the trim color. That's fine if you have a really large space and you're trying to break it up. But I personally don't care for the look. It reminds me of a freight train.

Most people have wainscoting in their Foyer and Dining Room. If you have picture frame molding which is a cheaper version of wainscoting, and you paint inside the boxes the wall color, then you're only exaggerating the fact that you just added cheap pieces of trim on the wall. The way to paint it to look like real wainscoting is to paint all semi-gloss from the chair rail down to the floor to create the illusion that it's all wood, not trim and drywall. You can paint it white, or paint it a color, but paint it all the same color and paint it in either satin or semi-gloss. Typically, I paint it in the same paint as the trim.

Board and Batten Wainscoting

Picture Frame Molding

Wainscoting

Dark Wood Trim

When it comes to dark wood trim, some people love it and some people hate it. (In the chapter on **Communication and Mediation** we will discuss this further.) In my experience, every time I work for a client who has dark wood trim, they complain that the rooms are too dark. The best way to brighten the room is to paint the trim. However, sometimes people don't want to do that. The best colors to brighten a room are blue, yellow, and white. A cousin to blue is a silver gray, and a cousin to yellow would be a cream. But the truth is the room will never look truly bright unless you paint the trim.

My clients were contemplating buying this house. The husband loved the dark trim, but the wife hated it. I showed them a photo of a similar house with gray trim and they both liked it, so that was the compromise. Gray trim brightens up the space yet still keeps the character of the Tudor style home.

Another compromise would be painting some of the trim and leaving the rest natural. In this space, we left the beams stained but painted the rest of the trim white. However, in my opinion the beams still feel heavy. Another idea would be to paint them gray to match the couch to lighten them up.

Color Options

Original

White

Gray

Blue

Cream

Here we tried all of the colors that would potentially brighten up the space. They look a little bit better. But it will never look truly bright unless they paint all the trim white like they did in this other house!

Choosing a Sheen

Matte and Flat

Matte looks flat but it's washable, and it's the preferred finish for walls in most rooms. It's typically never used for trim. Flat is typically the cheapest grade of paint and is not really washable. Its best use is on ceilings and in rooms that don't get much use.

Eggshell

If you really dislike shiny trim then this is an option but it's rarely used for trim. Eggshell is used more for walls when you really want the walls to be washable.

Satin and Pearl

In brand new Kitchens and Baths, the painted cabinets are not quite as shiny as Semi-Gloss. They look more like a Satin or Pearl finish. If you want your trim to match the look of the cabinets, or if you just prefer a less shiny trim, then use a Satin or Pearl finish. This is a personal preference thing. Shiny finishes just don't seem to be that popular these days. Nobody wants shiny walls or shiny floors. Many clients choose a Matte finish for their walls and for their floors and I have been noticing a movement toward a finish on the trim that is also less shiny.

Semi-Gloss

The standard finish for trim is Semi-Gloss and almost everyone uses it. The purpose for the shine on the trim is simply a practical one. Shinier finishes are easy to clean on windows and doors. It also helps crown molding to pop out a bit and stand out visually.

High Gloss

Occasionally, an Interior Designer may want to use a High Gloss finish but it really shows brush strokes and imperfections, so if you use a High Gloss make sure you have really perfect trim work. The best way to get a nice, smooth finish, and the only paint that used to be available in a High Gloss finish, was oil-based paint, called "Alkyd". The nice thing about it was that the paint

"floats out" and the brush strokes disappear. However, it's pretty old school now because Alkyd is not great for the environment and most paint stores don't carry them much anymore. There are other products on the market that have replaced oil-based paints. Ask your paint store which paint they have now that is available in a High Gloss finish, like Benjamin Moore's "Advance", and Sherwin Williams' "Emerald Urethane Trim Enamel". Another way to get a smooth finish is the spray the trim with a latex paint.

Bookcases

Many people ask if they should paint an accent color behind the bookshelves. If the shelves are thin and cheaply made, then painting the back wall a different color will only highlight the fact that they are cheap shelves attached to the wall. But when it's all painted the same color, it looks more like a nice expensive piece of built-in furniture. So I usually recommend to paint bookcases all the same color, usually white. (The same white as your trim color.) Every once in a while, I will do an accent color on the back of the bookcase, but only if they are nice, thick, solidly built shelves.

You can paint the whole bookcase a color, like a sophisticated black or neutral, or a fun pop of color. When you choose a color think about what you will put on the shelves. Don't paint them red and then put a bunch of brown and red leather books on the shelves because they will disappear. Likewise, don't put a bunch of white items on white shelves.

Skimpy shelves don't look great with color behind them. Only do this if you have thick, sturdy shelves.

This room is so much brighter now!

Ceilings

1) First Choose Your Wall Colors.
2) Next Choose Your Trim Color.
3) Choose Your Ceiling Color Last.

Back in the '90's and early 2000's Interior Designers liked to get fancy with ceiling and trim colors. When choosing wallpaper for a room they would use a custom color to match the paper, and they liked to use color on the ceiling as a "5th wall". During the "Tuscan Era" when I was painting faux finishes, I myself used to glaze trim and wainscoting, and also got very fancy on the ceilings painting faux finishes, metallic finishes, medallions, scrolls, ivy, flowers, lattice, and even heavenly cherubs in the "sky". Even when I stopped painting, I still enjoyed some color on the ceiling to make crown molding pop.

Avoiding "Spaceships" on the Ceiling

I have gotten away from using color on ceilings over the years. The main reason is because most of the colors I choose for the walls are soft off-whites and gray, and they just look better against white trim and white ceilings. Another reason is that when we remodel homes, we use recessed lighting in the ceiling. If there were color on the ceiling, then all of the little round, circle shaped lights stand out and look like little spaceships on the ceiling. The third reason is because most people's number one fear is their house being too dark, and my goal is always to make sure the house feels light and bright. The best way to achieve that is having a nice white ceiling and white trim.

Occasional Color

Occasionally I may do color on the ceiling if there are no recessed lights. A Dining Room is the perfect place for this because it draws your eye up to the chandelier. Another place to play with color is the Powder Room. If it has crown molding and a cool chandelier or light fixture, color is fun on the ceiling. Of course if you want to go for a dramatic effect in a room then go for color. If I do color on the ceiling these days it's usually the same color as the walls and trim for a moody look like on page 264 and 275. But as a general rule, in most rooms I keep the ceilings and trim all the same shade of white.

Which Sheen?

In all rooms except the Bathroom, almost 100% of the time you will paint the ceilings in FLAT. There is absolutely no need to have a shiny ceiling. Fingers don't usually touch the ceiling on a regular basis so there is no need to have a washable paint on the ceiling. Unless of course you are going for a highly dramatic effect, or you have a coffered ceiling which we will discuss later in this chapter. You can buy **"Flat Paint"** or **"Ceiling Paint"** which can be tinted to a color.

Which White Should You Use?

Keeping in mind Rule #6 on page 71, **DON'T MIX YOUR WHITES**. I prefer to match the ceiling to the trim color. Colors do however tend to look a little darker on the ceiling than they do on the walls, so sometimes I will create a lighter version of a color. (See the Foldover Test on page 286). As I just mentioned earlier, there really is a paint called "Ceiling White". Most brands sell paint made for ceilings. It's a cheaper grade of paint because you don't need fancy, scrubbable paint on the ceiling. Usually, painters buy it in large five gallon pails and this is their "go to" for ceilings. If you want to make your life simple, then just use Ceiling White. Basically, it's just plain ol' white, and goes with all whites.

Ceiling White

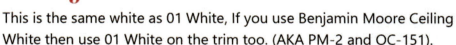

This is the same white as 01 White, If you use Benjamin Moore Ceiling White then use 01 White on the trim too. (AKA PM-2 and OC-151).

Super White

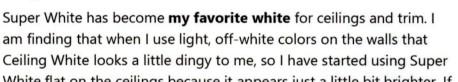

Super White has become **my favorite white** for ceilings and trim. I am finding that when I use light, off-white colors on the walls that Ceiling White looks a little dingy to me, so I have started using Super White flat on the ceilings because it appears just a little bit brighter. If you use Super White on the trim, then you can use Super White on the ceiling too. (AKA PM-1, OC-152).

Ceiling Bright White SW 2007   SHERWIN-WILLIAMS.

This is a very cool, blue white. If you use this paint I would recommend using it only with cool colors on the walls and use Extra White 2006 on the trim to avoid blue looking trim.

Extra White SW 7006   SHERWIN-WILLIAMS.

This color is cool and whiter than Ceiling Bright White. I prefer Extra White instead of Ceiling Bright White.

Off-Whites and Colors

One thing I really dislike is yellowy trim with a white ceiling because the trim looks old and dirty. This is why I recommend when using off-white colors on the trim like Bone White, Navajo White, Linen White and White Dove, then use the same color as the trim on the ceiling. If you think the color may be too dark you can cut the formula in half to create a lighter version of the color.

Cut the Formula by 50%

Usually colors look a touch darker on the ceiling than they do on the walls. If you want to create a lighter version of the color for the ceiling and there's no lighter version of the color available, then ask the paint store to cut the formula in half to create a lighter version of the color. Refer to page 303 for cutting color formulas. **When I use White Dove on the trim I usually use White Dove 50% on the ceiling.**

Matching the Ceiling and the Trim

When you paint the ceiling and trim the SAME COLOR there are 2 things to know:

1) You'll use two different cans of paint. Even though they are the same COLOR, they are different SHEENS. The trim will probably be semi-gloss and the ceiling will be flat. You will either buy "flat paint" or "ceiling paint". If you choose Super White then you'll use Super White semi-gloss on the trim and Super White flat on the ceiling.

2) Your trim will appear lighter. When you add a sheen to a color, like semi-gloss, light will reflect off of it and the color will appear slightly lighter than the walls, and lighter than the color you see on the paper paint chip which is flat. So this means your trim color will look lighter and that's OK. It's fine for one to look lighter or darker, as long as it's in the same color family.

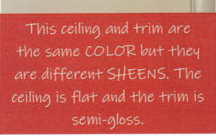

This ceiling and trim are the same COLOR but they are different SHEENS. The ceiling is flat and the trim is semi-gloss.

1) This ceiling color matches the creamy cabinets and trim. If the ceiling and trim were white then all the cabinets and trim would look yellow.

2) If your room is not well lit then you may want to cut the formula for the color 50% to make it lighter. Try the "Foldover Test" on page 286.

Color on the Ceiling

Painting color on a ceiling can make the crown molding pop and can show off architectural interest like a tray ceiling. However, if the ceiling is loaded` with recessed lighting and air vents, then these "gadgets" will stick out like a sore thumb against a dark color. Either choose a light color or paint over the gadgets.

The ceiling to the left has the spaceship effect. The ceiling below painted the gadgets to help them disappear.

Different Angles

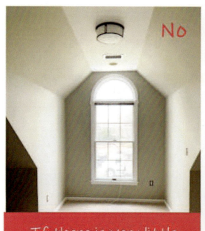

If there is very little ceiling then it will look odd being white with a strong color on the walls. Keep the color really light on the walls, or paint the ceiling the same color as the walls and dormer.

Painting the slanted dormered walls white makes the ceiling feel too low.

What if your ceiling isn't flat? Here's how to tackle different situations.

Dormered Ceilings

In order to keep the ceiling from feeling like it's coming down onto your head paint the slanted part of the ceiling in the wall color. Only paint the highest part of the ceiling in white, so that visually your mind will perceive that the ceiling is up higher. See page 232 for an example.

Another trick is to blur the lines between wall and ceiling. Either paint the walls a very light color or paint the entire room all one color including the ceiling. Sometimes the dormer and ceiling look too dark due to shadows and lighting. If so, you can paint the dormer and ceiling a lighter version of the wall color.

Try to make small, angled pieces of wall and ceiling disappear. By painting it the wall color it will go away. But if you paint the wall a dark color and paint the ceiling white, it will stick out too much, so paint the walls a light color. If there is a recessed light on the angled section then either paint over it or make sure to paint the walls a lighter color.

Tip!

If the ceiling is curved, you'll have to use painter's tape to create your own dividing line.

284

Soffit

You will find soffits typically in the Basement where there is a lower ceiling and the soffits hide the pipes. The goal here is to make the ceiling feel higher. The ceiling area underneath the soffit is even lower, so I want to fool the eye in the room to make that section go away. It's done by painting the entire soffit area the wall color. This way your eye will think that you're still looking at the wall, and the taller area with a white ceiling will feel like only THAT area is the ceiling.

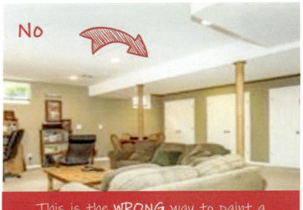

This is the **WRONG** way to paint a soffit. The white ceiling area underneath visually lowers the ceiling.

IF you hire a painter, place post-it notes to give them specific instructions on how to paint this area.

Tip!

Do **NOT** use shiny paint on the ceiling section of the soffit. Ceilings should be painted in a Flat finish. But if you're concerned hands will be touching a low ceiling then the best sheen would be matte finish on the walls and this section of the ceiling. It's washable but it doesn't look shiny.

This is the **RIGHT** way to paint a soffit. Paint both the horizontal and vertical areas of the soffit in the wall color so that visually your eyes will blend the soffit in with the walls, and you'll only see the highest point of the ceiling in white.

Problem Solving

Open Floor Plans

For an open floor plan there is really nowhere to start and stop a new color on the ceiling, so you'll need to choose one color for all ceilings. This is why you will want to choose colors that flow together and one trim color for the entire space because your ceiling will touch all of that trim. If you really don't want to have to make a decision about it and want to make life easy for you and for your painter, then just use the default, Ceiling White.

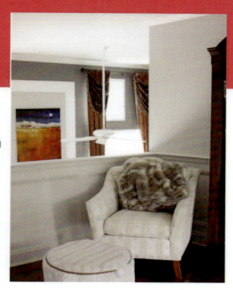

Awkward Angles

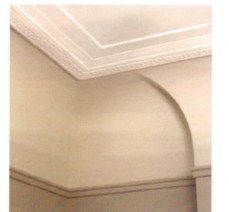

This ceiling had so many different shapes and angles that the best way to make it all look cohesive was to paint the walls and the ceilings all the same color.

Wall Space Above the Crown Molding

Sometimes in older homes there are a few inches of wall space above the crown molding. I once had a customer in the paint store that had this in every room on her first floor. We talked about doing different options.

A) Doing a tone-on-tone look with a lighter version of each color above. The top space would be a different color in each room.

B) Doing a different color in each room but keep the top space the same neutral beige in every room.

C) Painting the space above white in each room. Any are OK.

The Fold Over Test

If you want a little color on the ceiling then keep in mind that ceilings tend to look a little darker than the walls in the daytime. If you want to make sure the color won't look too dark, then fold the chip over and hold up the chip to look at the color horizontally like the ceiling instead of vertically like the walls. This way you'll get a better idea of how it will look on the ceiling.

Tray Ceilings

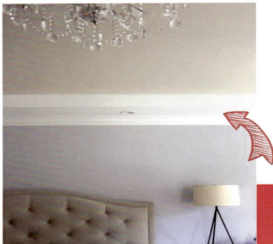

If the highest point of the tray ceiling is free of gadgets then you can paint the ceiling a color to show off the architecture. If it does have gadgets, either paint it a light color, or paint over the gadgets so you don't have spaceships on the ceiling. Decide by looking to see which area has the gadgets, and which does not.

Look at the room for clues as to what color to use. For instance, if the carpet is beige you could match the carpet and paint the tray in that beige. You can take clues from the bedding and choose the color palette from there. I DO NOT paint the ceiling blue. Maybe it's from my days of painting murals when I painted many ceilings with clouds, rainbows and cherubs, so now I feel like it's just too cutesy to have a blue ceiling. I would rather have a room look sophisticated. I prefer to use neutrals, and I DO like to mix beige and gray, so I may paint the walls gray and the ceiling light beige, or vice versa.

This tray ceiling is painted a taupe color to coordinate with the headboard.

This house has a completely open layout. To define the Living Room space they created a tray ceiling and wanted it to stand out. The darker ceiling created a warm, cozy, casual atmosphere. To avoid the "spaceships" they simply painted the lighting trim to match the ceiling.

If a room has architectural interest, then you may want to show it off and put some color in the top of a tray ceiling. The problem that may arise however is that when builders put these ceilings in, they add heat vents, sprinkler systems and recessed lighting. If you paint the tray a dark color, then all the white gadgets will stick out like a sore thumb and you'll see a bunch of spaceships on the ceiling. The only time a dark color works is if the ceiling is clean of gadgets. A nice light neutral would work, but not a dark color.

There are too many gadgets on this ceiling to do a color.

To choose a color look at fabric and rugs in the room for ideas. Tone on tone neutrals will give you the most sophisticated look. The ceiling on the left is painted a light greige that is a lighter version of the color of the headboard.

Tray with a Soffit

Painting the vertical portion the wall color, and then painting the horizontal section white will create a white racing stripe effect. Paint the whole soffit area the same color. If there are gadgets then paint the whole soffit area white. If it's free of gadgets then you can paint it the wall color or the tray ceiling color.

Avoid "Racing Stripes"

Angle Options

The question that arises with painting an angled tray ceiling is whether or not to paint the angled side, or just the flat, horizontal portion at the very top. If the angle is free of vents, then paint it a color. If the contractor framed it out in crown molding, then you could paint the whole area all the way to the crown to make it look like the tray is the "artwork" and the crown is the "frame".

This entire tray ceiling is free of gadgets, so any of these options will work. It's just a matter of personal preference. My preference is option B.

Sometimes builders get really fancy and there are several tiered levels. Back in the Tuscan Era these ceilings were fauxed to death. Try not to go too crazy with color because of my "Rule of 3's" and "Less is More". Too much just gets to be too much. Keep it more neutral and toned down for a cleaner look. You could do the lower levels in a lighter or darker version of the wall color. Then the top ceiling can be darker or lighter than the soffits but keep it all neutral and tone-on-tone. Keep the color light and neutral to avoid creating racing stripes.

When there is crown molding framing out sections it just seems to cry out to be painted a color, rather than just remaining white. This room could have used a lighter version of the wall color to prevent the racing stipes.

Thinking Inside the Box

If you have picture frame molding do NOT paint the wall color inside the boxes or it will look like a freight train on your ceiling! You can either paint it all flat, or flat with semi-gloss on the trim. Or, if the room is particularly dark you can paint it all in a sheen so that light will reflect off the ceiling for more light. Paint it all white like wainscoting, or a complimentary neutral.

Coffered Ceilings

Coffered ceilings have large box shapes on the ceiling. There are several ways to treat this ceiling.

1) **Paint two different colors.** This is a more casual look that works well in a room with a stone fireplace and a leather couch. If you paint a color inside the boxes, just be sure to avoid spaceships".

2) **Paint the boxed area to look like beams by painting them a neutral color.** If your trim is a neutral color, then you may want to paint them the same color as the trim.

3) **Paint the ceiling flat white with white semi-gloss on the wood beams.** This is the most typical way to paint a coffered ceiling. Remember, don't mix your whites. This ceiling color should match your trim color.

4) **Paint the whole ceiling all semi-gloss.** This follows the same idea we discussed for wainscoting on the walls. It creates the look of the ceiling being all wood, rather than pieces of wood stuck on the drywall ceiling. A ceiling painted in all semi-gloss is formal and very classy. As for the color, typically this will be painted in the trim color. If the fireplace has a white mantel and there is a lot of white trim in the room, then keep the ceiling white.

Sampling Paint Colors

So, you've read the chapters on all of the rooms that you're going to paint.

You've taken notes, and you've narrowed it down to the colors you think that you want to try out.

Now what!?!? The next step is to purchase paint samples.

"You're not going to paint it THAT color, are you?"

One day a woman ran into the paint store in a panic because the painters were getting ready to begin painting the exterior of her house and they had put up the samples of the colors that I had helped her pick. One of her neighbors came over and said the infamous, "You're not going to paint your house that color, are you?" That simple comment sent this woman into a total panic. She begged me to leave the store and come to her house immediately to check on the color.

I arrived at the house and asked her which house belonged to the neighbor who had made the comment. She pointed to a house with one of the worst paint jobs I had ever seen. "That one?!" I asked. "You're worried about THEIR opinion? Do you like the color of THEIR house?" She thought for a moment and suddenly realized how silly the whole thing was, and said sheepishly, "Oh yeah, you're right". The moral of the story is, **do NOT ask your friends and family for their opinion!**

How to Sample Colors.

How do you know what a color will look like once it's up on the walls? The best way to figure it out is to sample it and find out how it will look in your lighting. Sampling is simply buying a small sample jar or sample pint of paint and applying it in the space you intend to paint. At this point of the book you have hopefully narrowed your choices down to only two to three colors for each room. It's time to go to the paint store and purchase paint samples.

There is however a **right way** and a **wrong way** to sample colors. I can't tell you how many times I have heard "The sample doesn't look right" and then I'll ask questions like, "Did you paint two coats?" The answer is "No". Not only that, they painted one coat over an old color that is bleeding through, and the old color is making the new color look terrible. If they bought a bunch of samples and put them all next to each other, then usually they don't like any of them! Let's talk about the right way to paint samples.

No

These gray samples look blue against the gold wall.

Make sure the old color doesn't bleed through.

Step 1: Paint Samples on Something White.

After you find the chip that looks good, then buy a paint sample. You don't want your old color to bleed through and affect how the sample color looks, so you need to paint over white. In a perfect world, you'll have a nice white wall to sample on, but that almost never happens. If you're remodeling or building a new house, sometimes you can have the contractor put up a coat of primer first. Many people prefer to not paint on the wall and paint onto a sample board made for sampling paint colors, which is fine. Another option is to buy white poster board. Paint in the middle of the board leaving a white edge and tape it on the wall using painter's tape.

Step 2: Visually Block Out the Old Color.

I have found that most people have trouble visualizing a new color, so I'm trying to help you block out the old color and only visualize the new color. If you can, paint a section of your walls with primer first, especially if it's a very dark or bright color. Prime a 3 ft. square section of the wall, and then paint a 2 ft. square section inside that area with the sample color leaving a white border around the edges. If you paint onto a sample board, leave a white edge around the paint. Then when you look at the sample, try to only focus on the new color. If you have trouble visualizing, then try taping up some newspaper or white paper on the wall with some painter's tape.

If you paint on the wall try blocking out the old color with sheets of white paper.

Step 3: Don't Put Samples Next to Each Other.

Colors affect each other and make them look different. If you line up 10 different shades of gray, one will look blue, one beige, one purple, one green, one pink etc. and you won't like any of them! If you're going to sample a bunch of colors then paint them each onto a separate sample board and then look at each of them individually. Look at how each color looks with your furniture and flooring, rather than looking at how different paint colors look next to each other. It's OK to put lighter and darker versions of the same color together though to help you decide if you like the lighter one or the darker one.

Step 4: Paint 2 Coats.

You don't want the old color to bleed through. Sample paint is NOT self-priming paint so it won't cover as well. Another option is to purchase peel and stick samples online. Many of my clients have ordered through a company called "Samplize".

Put samples right next to the cabinets or trim.

Peel and stick samples from "Samplize".

Step 5: Look at Your Samples for a Couple Days.

Observe them during the day and at night, on a sunny day and a cloudy day. You'll see that the colors look different each time. But don't get hung up on this. If you are matching the other stuff in your room it's fine. You are doing this step only to make sure the color doesn't turn into something you **hate**. For example, if your gray color is turning too purple at night in the lamp light and you just hate it, then you'll need to tweak it following the guidelines in the chapter on **Toning Down and Fixing Colors** . (Or you may need to change your light bulbs!)

Note: Different Paint Types Change the Color.

I have found that sometimes the colors turn out a little differently in the different grades of paint. Self-priming paints sometimes come out a little lighter. Also, if you decide to use a paint that has some shine to it, the color will be slightly lighter. Sometimes paint sample pints come in an eggshell finish but people plan to use matte, so the sample will be a bit lighter than what your walls will look like once they're painted. If you're being very particular about your color being absolutely perfect, then the smart thing to do is to buy an actual quart of paint in the correct paint type and sheen that you'll be painting in to make sure it's more accurate.

Paint Basics

Ordering Paint at the Paint Store.

Now that you have chosen your colors, if you're painting yourself, you'll need to go to the paint store to buy your paint. You can't just go up to the counter and say, "Can I have a can of Navajo White please?" They're going to ask you for more information. After reading this book, you should be able to go up to the counter and order with confidence.

When you go to order paint at a paint store they will ask these questions:
What color do you want? What finish do you want?
Which TYPE of paint do you want? How much paint do you need?

1. **What Color?** When you order your paint, be sure to order by saying the **NAME and the NUMBER** of the color. If you only order by number, one slip of the hand and you could get a very wrong color. How many times have you tried to text and you were auto corrected because you hit the wrong letter? Or dialed the wrong phone number? Well, when someone mixes your paint, they're typing the name or number of the color into the computer. "Gray Wisp" and "Gray Mist" sound the same. But if you order by name AND number, then you should get the correct color.

2. **What Finish?** When they ask, "Which finish do you want?" what they are really asking is "**Which sheen do you want**?" Many people have no idea what that even means. We will discuss this in this chapter.

3. **Which Type?** When they ask what TYPE of paint, they mean do you want the self-priming paint? Low VOC paint? Or the basic paint? Basically, do you want the cheap stuff or the good stuff? We will discuss this in this chapter. But basically the "Barista" AKA, "The Paint Guy" can recommend the best paint for your project if you're not sure which paint to use.

4. **How Much?** When they ask how much paint you want, that means, "Do you want a quart? Or a gallon? Or several gallons?" A quart is usually enough to paint a door and maybe some trim. But if you're painting a whole room you'll usually need to paint two coats, so you'll need approximately two gallons, one for each coat. It all depends on the size of the room. A gallon typically covers 350-400 square feet. If you can't do the math, then take a basic measurement of the room. Tell them "It's a Living Room that is 15 x 20" and they should be able to figure it out for you. Self-priming paints have better coverage so you'll probably use less paint.

Paint Sheen

The sheen refers to **how shiny the paint is**. Here is a list from no shine to most shiny. When choosing colors keep in mind that the paper paint chips in the paint store have NO SHINE. As soon as you add a sheen the color will appear **slightly lighter**. Today most people prefer no shine on their walls so Flat/Matte is the preferred finish for most rooms. When you have the store mix up paint sample cans, most paint color samples tend to be closer to an Eggshell finish, which means it will appear slightly lighter than matte or flat, so keep that in mind when sampling.

Flat: **Flat has no shine.** This is the most basic "builder grade" finish. Sometimes it's not very washable. Use Flat on ceilings.

Flat/Matte: **Looks almost flat but it's washable.** Use this finish almost everywhere in the home.

Eggshell: **Slight hint of a sheen.** This sheen is much like the shell of an egg, hence the name, "Eggshell finish" and is very washable. Use this in Kitchens and Bathrooms where water, grease or dirt will frequently get splattered on the walls. Most new Kitchens however don't need Eggshell anymore because they have backsplash tile near the sink and stove, so Matte is usually fine in the Kitchen.

Pearl: **A little bit shiny.** This finish is rarely used. When I did faux finishes, I used this finish because I needed the glaze to be able to slide on a slightly shiny wall. Since then, I have not found a need to use this finish except occasionally on trim.

Satin: **Light shine.** Satin is too shiny for the walls but can be used on trim. A lot of new painted Kitchen cabinets seem to look like a Satin finish. If Semi-Gloss is too shiny for your taste on cabinets or trim and you prefer it to be less shiny, then use Satin instead.

Semi-Gloss: **Shiny.** This finish is the most popular for windows, doors, and trim. "Trim" is everything made of wood, including baseboards, crown molding, wainscoting, and the trim around your windows and doors. People prefer shiny trim for its washability.

Gloss: **Very shiny.** Gloss was formerly found in oil-based paint but is now available in water-based paint. Oil was used for its durability and because it floats out eliminating brushstrokes. It gives a smooth, shiny finish. Use a gloss finish on trim, on a front door or on Kitchen cabinets.

Matte or Eggshell Finish?

Walls Do Not Need to be Shiny!

Do NOT use a sheen any shinier than an Eggshell finish on the walls. The walls below are "Before" photos of a home that a client bought and were painted by a previous owner. I have seen this several times and it's not a good look. Walls do NOT need to be this shiny to keep them clean, and the shine shows all of the imperfections. These were done in Semi-Gloss which is a "Don't". Semi-Gloss should only be used on the windows, doors, and trim, never on the walls. Use only Flat, Matte or Eggshell on walls.

These walls have bad spackling jobs done underneath the paint, which has now become even more noticeable due to the shiny paint!

Matte vs. Eggshell - Pros and Cons.

Eggshell: During the years I was painting murals and faux finishes I painted a lot of kid's rooms and restaurants and used an Eggshell finish because of its washability. However, one of the down sides to Eggshell is, because of its slight shine, it will show imperfections on the wall, like poor spackle jobs or nail heads popping out. If you have old, imperfect walls, use matte or flat, which will help hide imperfections.

Matte: Years ago, Eggshell was very popular because of its washability, but Matte has essentially replaced it and has become the preferred finish. Matte is nice and washable without looking shiny, is easy to touch up and will help to hide imperfections.

Touching Up: Matte is easy to touch up and hides imperfections. When you paint over it you won't really see where you have painted. However, with Eggshell you CAN see where you have touched up. You will see every stroke of your roller and a distinction between the old section and the new section. In kids' rooms sometimes it's a difficult call to decide which sheen is better. If your concern is that they will color on the walls, use Eggshell. But if your concern is that they will bang the walls creating little nicks and you'll probably do paint touch-ups, then use Matte.

Which Type Of Paint?

Each paint store will have a bunch of different types of paint to choose from. They will have regular, everyday paint, cheaper grades of paint, self-priming paints, Low VOC paints, Zero VOC paints, and top-of-the-line paints. Remember you get what you pay for. Cheaper paints are probably thin and will need several coats and are not that washable or long lasting. Better quality paints have much better coverage, are washable and last for many years.

So which type of paint should you buy? It basically comes down to these two questions. Do you need primer or not? Do you want less odor and chemical emissions or not? Regular paint is just basic paint, so I won't discuss them. But I will discuss VOC's and self-priming paints to help eliminate confusion.

Self-Priming Paints, and Zero and Low VOC Paints

VOC stands for "**Volatile Organic Compounds**". When you hear the word "Volatile" you probably think of a couple who fight a lot and have a "volatile, explosive relationship", but in the world of science it means "a liquid that evaporates quickly."

As someone with allergies and chemical sensitivity this breakthrough in paint was huge for me. Certain cleaning supplies make me very ill. Ammonia, bleach, and glass cleaners set my head spinning and I get very dizzy and need to lie down. These same solvents can be found in carpet, paint, and furniture. So if you find yourself having these symptoms it may be your carpet or furniture. After paint dried, I was fine. It was the wet paint emitting fumes that made me sick.

When I first went to work in the paint store around 2005, Benjamin Moore invented this paint called "Aura" which was "Low VOC" paint. It was the most expensive, top-of-the-line paint. As far as I knew nobody else offered paint like this. Then they took it a step further and invented "Natura" and "Eco Spec" which are "Zero VOC paints."

Self-Priming

Aura was not only low VOC, meaning low odor and chemical emissions, but it was also SELF-PRIMING. They claimed the paint could cover in almost one coat. I have to admit I was skeptical so I took it home to try it out. I brought home a deep, dark plum color and tried it on a white ceiling in a small space. I was pretty shocked at how well it covered. Normally a color that dark would have taken 3 coats, but this paint almost covered in one coat. I only had to do a quick second coat.

The next test was painting over a mural I had done of the ocean, palm trees, sailboats and surfboards. It had lots of strong colors like red and navy blue which normally would definitely need a good coat of primer if not two coats to cover it. I painted a coat of gray blue and could still see some mural coming through. Then I took a lunch break. When I returned, I was shocked to find the paint had floated out and covered the mural! I could see the darkest colors bleeding through a bit, so it needed a normal second coat, but the coverage was amazing. It was done in two coats instead of the normal 3-4 coats it would have taken with a cheaper paint. I then became a believer in self-priming paint.

So the lesson I learned was that not only was Aura amazing paint, it's not as expensive as you think if you add up the cost of 2 coats versus 4.

Benjamin Moore Gennex® Color Technology

When I was painting murals and faux finishes, I used to also paint the base coat of paint, so essentially I was a painter too. Sometimes when I was in a tight space like a small Bathroom, I would feel nauseated and dizzy and have to leave the room for a while. I noticed that it didn't happen all the time but seemed to depend on which color I was painting. This led to the conclusion that it may have something to do with the tint more than the paint itself.

When Benjamin Moore first introduced Aura paint, it also released a new color line called "Affinity Colors" that you could only get in the Aura paint at that time. They delivered a new paint mixing machine to the paint store to use with the Aura paint. This machine used completely different tints called **"Gennex"** that were water-based Latex. These tints interlocked with the paint like nothing ever seen before and they called it **"Color Lock Technology"**. Not only did it make the paint incredibly durable and scrubbable, but it also truly had no odor.

People began to request the old colors in the Aura paint and I suppose they may have been able to put the old smelly tint in the Aura paint, but that would defeat the whole purpose of Aura. If you truly wanted the paint to be odor-free, you really needed to use the new tint. Since then, they have transferred the color formulas for the rest of the colors over to the Gennex machine and you can pretty much get any color in the Aura and Regal Select paints.

According to their website the color consistency is the precise result of Benjamin Moore paint and Benjamin Moore Gennex colorant, together. This particular pairing is what makes Benjamin Moore products impossible to replicate.

Alkyd vs. Latex

Alkyd = Oil-Based Paint. Years ago, painters loved oil-based paint because as they brushed the paint onto trim or cabinets the paint would "float out" and the brushstrokes disappeared, leaving a beautiful smooth finish. It's also very durable for cabinets and is the best for a high gloss finish. However, it's not good for the environment and it has slowly been disappearing off the shelves. Paint companies have now come up with alternative paints that are mostly water-based, with just a trace of oil, that is durable and "floats". These are the best paints for cabinets.
Latex = Water-Based Paints. Most of your paints today are water-based.

Other Paints and Primers

There are other basic latex paints available in each brand that are not self-priming and are not Low VOC. There are also Primers, Ceiling Paints, and Bathroom Paints. The best thing to do is to talk to your salesperson in the paint store to try and figure out which paints you'll need for your projects.

Do You Need Primer with a Self-Priming Paint?

You would think that because these paints are "Paint and Primer in One" that you would never need primer, right? Wrong. The benefit to these paints is that they cover much better, and if you're painting a dark color, years ago it took 3-4 coats. Or if you were painting over a dark color, you had to prime first before you painted. These paints cover so well that now you can get the job done in 1-2 coats. HOWEVER, if you have just removed wallpaper, you will need to use an oil-based primer before you paint. If you have new drywall or you have just spackled the walls you will need to prime the walls first before you paint. So if that's the case, then do NOT buy paint with primer in it. First paint with a coat of primer, then paint with the regular grade of paint.

Benjamin Moore 0 VOC and Low VOC Paints

Aura: Aura is **LOW VOC** and is **self-priming**. Aura has "Gennex" Color Lock technology which means the paint literally becomes one with the tint making it extremely durable and scrubbable. Aura is the top-of-the-line paint by Benjamin Moore, so of course it's the most expensive. I usually tell people it's organic, which usually always means more expensive. Since then, all other paint companies filed in line and also came out with Low VOC, Zero VOC, and self-priming paints. Some of them have lower price tags, so Benjamin Moore has since released a newer version of their Regal paint called "Regal Select". Aura comes in Matte, Eggshell, Satin, and Semi-Gloss, but does NOT come in Flat.

Regal Select: Regal Select is **LOW VOC, self-priming**, and uses "Gennex" Color Lock technology . It also has a lower price tag than Aura. Regal Select comes in Flat, Matte, Pearl/Satin and Semi-Gloss finishes.

Ben: Ben is "0 VOC, low odor and is self-priming. It's available in Matte, Eggshell, Pearl/Satin, and Semi-Gloss. It does not come in Flat.

Note: It's always a good idea to speak with your local retailer about the best product and sheen to use for your project.

Behr and Sherwin Williams

Behr by Home Depot

Behr Ultra Scuff Defense: This paint sold at Home Depot has **LOW VOC's**, is **"self-priming, but may need primer"** It comes in a Flat, Eggshell, Satin, and Semi-Gloss.

Behr Premium Plus: This paint sold at Home Depot has **0 VOC's**, is **Low Odor** and is **self-priming** and has a Lifetime Limited Warranty. It comes in a Flat/Matte, Eggshell, Satin, Semi-Gloss, and Gloss finishes.

Behr Marquee: This paint sold at Home Depot has **0 VOC's**, is **self-priming**, and guarantees one coat coverage. It comes in Matte, Eggshell, Satin, and Semi-Gloss finishes.

Sherwin Williams   SHERWIN-WILLIAMS.

Duration: This paint is **self-priming** but is NOT a low VOC paint. It has built-in anti-microbial properties that inhibit the growth of mold and mildew. Duration is available in Flat, Matte, Satin, and Semi-Gloss finishes.

Cashmere: This paint is **self-priming** but is NOT a low VOC paint. It has a smooth, silky finish. Duration is available in Flat, Eggshell, Pearl, Low Luster, and Medium Luster finishes.

Super Paint: This paint is 0 VOC and eliminates room odors, but is NOT self-priming. It is available in Flat, Satin, and Semi-Gloss finishes.

Emerald: This paint is **0 VOC** and is **self-priming**. It emits few odors and has built-in antimicrobial properties that inhibit the growth of mold and mildew. This paint is available in Flat, Matte, Satin, and Gloss finishes.

Mixing Custom Colors

Sometimes when people want to lighten a color, they ask, "Can't you just add white?" No. Why? To understand how to lighten colors, you need to understand how paint is mixed. When the "Paint Barista" chooses the paint can off the shelf, depending on which color you choose they will choose different cans for different colors. Primarily there are three types:

White Base

Most colors people choose like beige, gray and light colors go into a white base. In order to lighten a color, you will add less tint into a can of white paint, rather than add white.

Medium Base

When the color is a little darker, it may go into a medium base.

Clear or Deep Base

Dark colors like navy and black, and primary colors like red, yellow and royal blue go into a deep base which is essentially transparent. Why? Because if you put red tint into a can of white paint, what color will you get? Red? No. It will turn pink. But if you put red tint into a clear base, it will remain red. Sometimes you will need to paint three to four coats of these colors to get full coverage. Most paint companies now have self-priming paints that will help with better coverage.

Color Matching.

Contrary to what most people believe, you can't take a sweater or a stuffed animal into the paint store and have them magically match the item to a brand-new paint color. First of all, the color matching machine called a **Spectrophotometer** basically shoots a beam of light onto the object. It needs to hit a solid object that light cannot pass through, like a block of wood. If a beam of light can shoot through it, like a sweater for instance, it won't work.

Secondly, it will only match the object to the closest color already known to the computer. If you want to mix a custom color the computer will need to match your item to an existing paint color first. Then it's up to the person working in

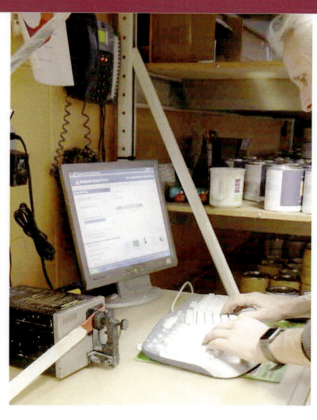

the store to try and tweak it until they can come up with something that looks like the color you're looking for. If you're trying to match an existing paint color that you have in an old paint can the best thing to do is dip a paint stick into the paint, let it dry and then they can shoot it for a match. Then the computer will guess and give them names of about 4-5 existing colors that it could possibly be.

Mixing Paint is Like Baking a Cake.

When you go to the paint store and tell them what color paint you want, they will take a can off the shelf, place it in a paint mixing machine, type in the name of the paint color and then the machine disperses tint into the can. It looks a lot like white cake batter in the can, and the tint looks like squirts of food coloring in primary colors of red, blue, yellow, or brown, black, and orange. The tint colors are very strong and bright, so it only takes a very small amount to tint the whole can of paint. Then they bang on the lid, place the can into a shaker for a few minutes to mix it all up, and then voila!

302

Darkening and Lightening Colors.

Most people don't know that you can create your own color by tweaking the formula for a color. You can either make a color darker by adding extra tint, or you can make a color lighter by not adding as much tint. Let's say you really like a color, but you wish it was just a little lighter. You can create that color. You can do this with colors that don't come on strips where there are lighter and darker versions of the color. Here is how it's done:

Make a Color Lighter.

You can lighten a color by 25% increments. Remember I said it's like adding food coloring to cake batter. Think of it this way. If the formula for a color called for a tablespoon of tint, instead of the full tablespoon, you can add either ¼ tablespoon, ½ tablespoon, or ¾ tablespoon. Or in other words, you can add 25%, 50% or 75% of the original formula. The reason is because paint is sold in quarts and gallons, and a quart is 25% of a gallon. So basically, you're adding the tint for a quart into a gallon of paint. Since there is no way of knowing what the color will look like, I suggest you test it out first. Start with less tint first. Start with 25%, have them dry it with a hair dryer, and if it's too light, then you have to add another 25% to see what 50% looks like. If it's still too light, add another 25%. You can't do this backwards because once you've added the tint, you can't take it back out!

Make a Color Darker.

To create a darker version of your color, you basically do the same thing above but this time you increase the amount of tint by 25% increments. So using the cake batter analogy, it's like using 1 ¼ tablespoons, 1 ½ tablespoons or 1 ¾ tablespoons. This translates to 125%, 150% or 175% of the tint formula. Depending on the color and how much tint is needed to create a color, it's not always possible because by the time you add more tint it will overflow in the can.

Crossing Over Brands.

Most paint companies can mix their competitors colors. For instance, Sherwin Williams can mix Benjamin Moore colors, and Benjamin Moore can mix Sherwin Williams colors. Big stores like Home Depot can mix those colors too. The color may turn out just a hair differently however, so to be on the safe side, make sure you have them mix up a paint sample can first and try it out to make sure it turns out the way you anticipated. If you're very particular about your color though, I don't recommend crossing over. For a list of some comparable colors between Benjamin Moore and Sherwin Williams see page 335.

Problem Solving

In this chapter we will address certain dilemmas that can come up beyond just choosing the right color, like where to start and stop the color in an open layout. These are all little things that come up and questions I am often asked. There are no right or wrong answers, but here are things to think about when making decisions for these spaces.

High Traffic Areas and Heavy Wear.

Fingerprints and scuff marks are gray. So I will always use a muddy color here, especially a gray or a color with gray in it to hide the dirt. Yellow is the WORST color because it shows all the dirt. When choosing colors for rental properties, gray and taupe are good choices because they hide dirt. Decide if you want a matte or an eggshell finish.

Eggshell or Matte Finish?

Eggshell has a slight sheen and is really washable but most people don't like to see the shine and it shows all the imperfections on the wall like nail heads popping out or bad spackling jobs. If the problem is shiny, greasy fingerprints and water splattered on the walls then use eggshell. Matte is also washable but looks flat so it hides imperfections. If you ever nick the walls and need to touch up matte will hide the touch up, whereas with eggshell you will see everywhere your roller has rolled on the wall.

Sloped Ceiling Over Stairs.

When choosing colors for a stairway like this I give it the "Slap Test". I check to see if the ceiling is low enough to touch. I know from having kids that this area is too tempting not to touch on the way down the stairs, especially for teenage boys! If it can't be reached then it can be painted white like in this "before" photo. But if it's low enough to slap, then paint it in the wall color. PS: Choose a color that will help hide the fingerprints.

Very High Ceilings.

If you have very high ceilings then you may need to use a color that is a shade darker than you think because you have a LOT of wall space to fill in! If you only paint an off-white color then you're going to feel like you need to do something with all of that empty wall space. You'll think you need to hang a bunch of artwork or something. It's a simple fix by just adding more color to the walls. In entry Foyers and Family Rooms, if you really want those white walls then think about adding architectural detail like moldings, wainscoting and my favorite look, "board and batten" wainscoting to fill in the space. *(See pages 307 and 309).*

Low Ceilings.

If you paint a dark color on the walls with a white ceiling it will exaggerate the fact that the walls are too low. The way to help this is to avoid having a stark contrast between the walls and the ceiling. Either paint the walls a light color or paint the ceiling in a lighter version of the wall color. This will help to blur the lines. If you have carpet on the floor you can try to match the carpet to make the floor, walls and ceiling all visually blend together.

Accent Walls.

If you're going to paint an accent wall think about WHY you are doing it. What are you accenting? Are you accenting artwork? Adding an accent color to a fireplace wall gives it more of a "Wow factor". TVs look great on a dark wall because it hides all the wiring and the picture really pops off a dark wall. If you have an open layout, an accent wall helps to separate and define a space. Look for a nice, symmetrical, perfect square or rectangular shaped wall. Don't go accent wall crazy though. You don't need an accent wall in every room.

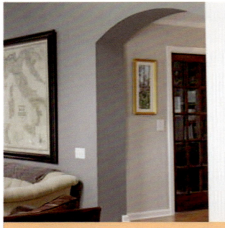

Inside the Door Jam.

Look at your space and decide which space you will see all of the door jams from the most. Is it a central hall that connects all of the rooms? Then paint inside the door jams the hall color. Is it from the Family Room? Then paint it the Family Room color. This is why it's important to choose colors that flow. Try to NOT have all the door jams be a different color.

In this room, the Foyer has trim around all the doorways, but every room connected to the Family Room has an arched doorway. Since the Family Room is the one room that has all arched doorways the door jams were painted in the Family Room color.

Asymmetrical Walls.

You may have one or two walls that are not symmetrical. They may have a slanted ceiling or have more windows on one side than the other. If you paint this wall as an accent wall then you will only exaggerate the fact that it's not even. So if it bothers you then don't use a dark color or an accent wall in that room.

Tip!

Some fireplace walls can appear out of balance because,
A) The fireplace is not centered in the middle.
B) One doorway is larger than the other.
C) There are different sized windows.
D) You have a bookcase on one side and not on the other.
A great way to fix this is to add floor to ceiling Board and Batten trim and paint the whole wall in your white trim paint from floor to ceiling. Now it will appear as one large, symmetrical feature wall!

Open Floor Plans.

When builders build a new construction home with an open floor plan they usually paint the whole house the same color. Then when people move in and want to paint their new home there is suddenly the dilemma of where to stop and start a new color. There is no right or wrong way to paint each area, but after thinking it through with many clients I have found ways to deal with different "problems" or "dilemmas". When looking for a way to begin a new color you can try to follow the floor. When the floor changes from hardwood to tile or to carpet, then it feels more natural for the walls to change color, too.

Look for an area that almost looks like a doorway or a piece of wall that juts out, then you can change the wall color. Many times the Kitchen is the area that can become a different color. Sometimes everything needs to be the same color but you can create an accent wall in the Dining Room or the fireplace wall to break it up.

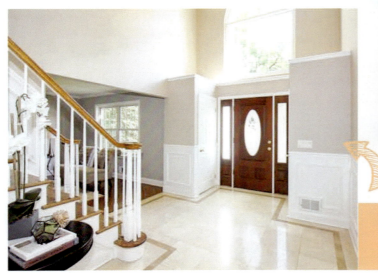

The color changed in the Foyer to match the floor.

308

If the floor is the same throughout the whole home, then look for a place where the wall turns a corner and see if you can change the color there. Remember that the light hits each wall differently. Even if you painted the whole house the same color it will look darker and lighter on walls with different angles. So if you change the color when you turn the corner most people will not really notice. They will simply think that the sunlight is different on each wall.

These days most people tend to prefer one neutral color throughout the whole first floor. If that's you, then base the color off of the Kitchen and use it throughout the first floor.

This house uses the same color throughout the first floor.

If you have chair rails or wainscoting, you can stop a color where the wainscot ends. Sometimes a wall will turn into another room but the wainscot does not extend. You'll have to decide if maybe you want to add wainscot to that section or fake it by painting the wall white on the bottom half.

Another way to decide where to end a color is to follow the molding. Sometimes molding ends but the wall does not. This is another situation where you have to make sure the colors coordinate.

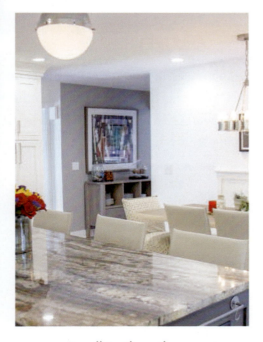

Sometimes a wall will extend into another room. Think of it as an accent wall to the other room. This is a situation where you want to make sure both colors go together and look good in both rooms.

310

Sometimes there seems to be nowhere to start a new color. For instance, a 2-story Foyer wall will connect to the upstairs Hallway and back down the back of the house into a Family Room which is also two stories high. In this case, if you want to change the color then you will just have to settle for 3 walls one color, and the fourth wall will be different because it will flow into a new space. This is the type of situation where you really want the colors to go together and have the same undertones if you want an easy transition, or else just think of the fourth wall as an accent wall. This fourth wall can be in the upstairs Hallway or going up the steps in the Family Room. That 2-story Family Room is also a place where you could do the fireplace wall as an accent color. Try to only do 1-2 accent walls.

The Dining Room could have gotten an accent wall, but they opted to put one in the Family Room instead.

The loft upstairs is the same color as the Family Room, but the fireplace accent wall can be seen from the loft.

In this home the Foyer walls travel up to an open loft that looks over the Family Room in the back of the home. They opted to keep the Foyer, Dining Room, and Family Room all the same color. However, they turned the fireplace wall into an accent wall which can be seen from the loft. The Living Room has a "doorway" and the Kitchen has a partial wall, so these two rooms are different, yet similar colors.

The Living Room has a partition that is almost like a doorway which made it possible to do a new color.

The Kitchen has a small partition which created a way to do a new color.

Myth #1:

"Dark colors make the room feel smaller."

FALSE! From my years of painting murals and faux finishes I know that when I want to push the walls away, I paint them darker. So that means that light walls pull in toward you making you feel closed in, yet darker colors will push walls away. The only time to not use a dark color is if there is a low, white ceiling because you will visually notice that the dark color stops right at eye level and the room is too short.

Myth #2:

"If you paint the room white or off-white the room will look larger."

FALSE! White will just make you feel like you're inside a big white box. I always paint small rooms in some shade of blue, or something similar to blue like silver, turquoise or a lavender because blue is the color of the sky and fools your eyes to think the walls are far away like the sky.

Myth #3:

"A color gets darker when it goes up on the wall."

PARTIALLY TRUE! Well, technically wet paint appears light, almost even white in the can. Then when it dries, it dries darker but it will dry to the color you chose. But I don't think that's what people really mean when they say this. I think what they're really saying is not necessarily that the color gets darker when it goes up, but that it's brighter, deeper, or more intense than they thought it would be. What they need to do is learn how to choose the correct color first before it goes up on the wall. Refer to the chapter on **Toning Down and Fixing Colors** to choose lighter, softer colors.

Communication and Mediation

It turns out that a lot of my job is mediating between husbands and wives, moms and their teenage daughters, and homeowners and their contractors. The job also involves some psychology, and most of all, great listening skills. I don't want to put anyone in a box and say that everyone is the same, but throughout my experience I have come to notice some patterns of behavior. Of course what I'm going to say in this chapter isn't always true, but I'm basing this chapter on my experiences. When you see the

same things happen over and over again, you start to take notice. So these are generalizations, but they ring true with many, many people. The reason I'm writing this chapter is not to start arguments, it's to help you try to avoid them. These are all situations that I have seen over and over again and I want you to know you're not alone! Many people go through this, and in the end just remember, it's only paint!

Men vs. Women.

Ladies, before you get too flustered here are a couple things you need to understand about your man. Some men get really into decorating and want to be involved in the decision-making process when it comes to renovations and painting, but most are not interested. I see some women make sure their husbands are there when I come to do a color consultation and the husbands pay attention for about 5-10 minutes and then they lose interest and trail off to their TV or computer. These sweet women want to include their husbands and ask, "Honey, what do you think of this color for the Kitchen?" A smart husband will say, "Yeah, I like it." It's kind of the same as planning a wedding and the bride-to-be wants to include the poor groom. They're usually fine with most of the choices their wife makes... until the wife says she wants to paint the brick or stained wood trim, and it's then when the battle begins.

Most Men Have a Hard Time Visualizing Things.

I have found that a lot of men have trouble picturing rooms in a different way. They don't want to picture it a different way either because many think, "What's wrong with it? It's fine the way it is." So when we're talking about that fireplace for instance, I like to show them my Pinterest page of "Fireplace Makeovers". As soon as they see pictures of what their fireplace could look like remodeled, suddenly they seem to "get it".

Men vs. Women

Men's Love Affair.

Most Men Seem to Have a Love Affair With Stained Wood, Brick and Stone. Women on the other hand generally like everything to be light and bright and want to paint everything. As soon as a woman suggests painting over stained wood or brick the man's immediate response will be "No! You can't paint over that beautiful wood!" (Or "that beautiful brick!"). I am a woman so of course my first reaction is to paint over that ugly, old, dark, stained brick and brighten up the room. But I am cautious about suggesting painting a fireplace white if there is a husband in the picture because I know what his answer may be. What they don't realize is that old fireplace actually dates the house. Certain brick fireplaces just scream out "I was built in the 1950's!" Many people remodel the Kitchen, the Bathrooms and just about everything in the house except for the fireplace. Men seem to have it in their minds that the old fireplace is still beautiful.

If You Talk "Dollars" to Men, Then it Makes "Cents".

Women want to decorate and make the place look pretty, and men just want to know "How much is this going to cost me?" So when I'm talking to a husband and wife together and he is balking at certain projects, then I'll talk "Real Estate" to them about their biggest investment, their home. By updating the house, it will be worth more money. If they had to sell their house a newer looking, updated house will sell faster. If I go into a home and I see pretty furniture and white trim in every room in the house and then when we go into the Family Room where there is stained wood trim, wood bookcases, a deer head over the brick fireplace and a recliner in front of the huge TV with surround sound, you can tell who decorated the Family Room! This is an argument couples will just have to fight out. Someone is going to have to concede. All I can tell you is if you're having this argument about painting wood or brick, you're not alone. I see it all the time. Sometimes you just have to compromise. As for **choosing paint colors**, I have also noticed that many men seem to be a little color blind (and some women), whether they know it or not. Many times women can see more colors than men. There is a thing called "Tetrachromacy" in which some people's eyes have 4 different cone cells that enable them to see more colors. When I begin to discuss colors and say things like "I see pink in this one, and a little green in this one" some people, mostly men, just get totally lost because they don't see it. So if you're having difficulty discerning colors don't feel bad because many others are in the same boat. And if you're arguing about paint colors but you are the one who can't really see colors, then you need to be the one to jump ship.

Talking To Your Contractor

Things Homeowners Should Know.

Before we talk about this, I want to say that most painters are great and I rarely have problems. But once in a while there are communication issues between painters and their customers and both the painter and the homeowners get upset. I have had customers tell me stories about contractors who don't return phone calls, who don't show up when they say they are going to, and have put so much pressure on customers that **they have brought some of them to tears.** So I would like to address a few things that I have witnessed quite often in hopes of eliminating problems so that everyone can enjoy a happy working relationship.

" Lack of preparation on your part does not constitute an emergency on my part"

Be Prepared Ahead of Time!

I can't tell you how many "**Paint Emergencies**" I have to fix. Way too often I get panicked phone calls from clients who need me to hurry up and come help them because their painter is coming "tomorrow" and they're not ready. Or clients have been working on a renovation for 6 months, but all of a sudden one day their contractor will say "OK we're going to start painting tomorrow so we need your paint colors now." Other times homeowners are waiting to have their interior painted but the painters are busy painting an exterior for someone else, when suddenly the weather report said it's going to rain the next couple of days, so the painter called and said, "We can start tomorrow". Yet again I'll get another panicked phone call.

The moral of this story is, **choose your colors early**. Before you even call a painter to come look at the job and give you an estimate you should have already picked your colors. When you begin a renovation, be thinking about paint colors from the very beginning when you're choosing your cabinets and tile. Be a good little scout and be prepared for the day when they spring it on you.

Painters are Not Movers.

Don't expect your painter to move all of your furniture for you. Some will, and if they do then they are being extra nice. But it's not their job. I had a woman once tell me a painter came to give her an estimate but then she never heard from him again and he wouldn't return her phone calls. When she began to describe her house, I realized she is a hoarder and had so much stuff in the way the poor guy could barely walk through the house. She actually expected him to move all of her stuff before he painted! And she couldn't understand why he never came back.

Things Your Painter Would Want You to Know.

Time Is Money. Painting contractors have a lot of customers that need them and they try to fit everyone in. They also have to pay a crew to work every day. So when you are not prepared with your paint colors and waste their time playing around with samples, you're also wasting money. Do your sampling and decision making before they arrive to start the job.

Some Things Cost Extra. If you're going to paint a dark color it will need paint with primer in it which costs more or need an extra coat. If you're going to paint an accent wall, or a color on the ceiling, they need to know that because it takes more time to paint and will cost extra. A painter doesn't want to have to tell you half the way through the job that what you're requesting is going to cost more, and you're not going to want to hear it either. If you choose your colors ahead of time and tell the painter these things up front when he gives you your estimate then you'll make everyone's life easier.

Things You Should Know Before Your Painter Begins.

Painters Prefer Certain Paints. Some painters prefer working with particular brands of paint. Some prefer Benjamin Moore, some prefer Sherwin Williams, and some prefer other brands. The good thing is that you can usually get the color you want in the other brand. Most paints have the formulas for their competitors colors, so if you really want a Benjamin Moore color and they prefer Sherwin Williams, it should be fine. But you'll make your life easier if you choose colors in the brand they prefer.

Painters Resist Change. They like what they like, and like doing things the way they've always done it. If you ask them to do something they have never done before expect some push back. When Aura first was introduced, it dried very quickly and some painters didn't like it, so now they never use it. Since then, they have changed the paint to extend the drying time to make the painters happy. They need to break out of their box sometimes, whether they like it or not.

Painters Prefer to Paint with Matte or Flat. This is because it's easier for THEM. You don't see the roller strokes in a matte finish, and it hides imperfections like lousy spackling jobs. Years ago, when I wanted an eggshell finish and the painter argued and wanted to use matte because it hid imperfections better, I just told the painter, "Well, if you do a good spackle job then there will be nothing to hide and it won't be a problem!" These days most people prefer matte so it's not a problem. But if you do want eggshell then don't let the painter talk you out of it.

Sometimes Painters make Assumptions. As soon as your painter has finished spackling and sanding, they will probably begin painting all of your ceilings... in Ceiling White... without asking first. They will just ASSUME that you're using ceiling white because "that's what all their other customers do." They may even begin painting the trim right away too, WITHOUT ASKING! This is one of my pet peeves. Who said we were painting ceiling white? Who said we're painting the trim white? So I always coach my clients ahead of time. If we're painting the trim White Dove and the ceilings all White Dove 50%, I tell them to make sure they tell their painter right away before they even start the job. Sometimes they'll complain and say they already bought the paint. Well, white and ceiling white are so common that they can return it or save it for the next job.

Some Painters Stick Their Two Cents in. They may suggest a paint color because "It looked good in their other customer's house." Or worse, they suggest a color they have used in their own house. Thanks for the suggestion buddy, but just because a color looked good in someone else's house that doesn't mean it will go with ANYTHING in your house. They may also say something like, "Are you really sure you want to paint THAT color?" This is the kind of thing that sends clients into a total panic and makes my head spin. They have done it to me and made comments about colors I have chosen for clients and then I have had to go back and put out the fire. I have to calm down my client who is now having a panic attack and justify why I'm choosing the colors I have chosen. Then when the job is done and it looks AMAZING, the painters change their tune. Then guess what? They recommend that color to their next client! They are painters, not Interior Designers. Remember that.

Most Painters are Men. And what did we just learn about men? They are in love with brick, stone and stained wood. As soon as you tell your painter you want him to paint over your stained wood Kitchen cabinets, your wood trim, or your brick fireplace, he will try to talk you out of it. Stick to your guns. Here is what to say to your painter:

> "Thank you for your opinion but it's my house. So, if it's a mistake, I'll be the one to live with it."

Besides, you're paying him to do it so he shouldn't concern himself.

Bottom line- **They** don't want to be accountable for **your** mistakes. So you will have to own your decisions.

Which Painter Should You Hire? Sometimes people say "I want someone who is good but is reasonable" (translation: "cheap"), to which my reply is, "It's either one or the other." I always suggest that clients call three different painters and get three estimates. You'll find each one is very different. If someone is very cheap then they are probably skipping steps. I have seen bad paint jobs where the cheap painter did a lousy job cutting in or didn't sand the exterior well and used cheap paint. Guess what? About two years later they had to pay to have the house painted all over again. A good painter will do proper prep work to make sure the work is done right and use good quality paint. It may cost more, but it will last for years, so in the long run it makes more sense financially. If you want cheap then paint yourself!

A lesson I learned the hard way is this: You know that guy you have to wait for for 6 months because he's so busy? He is the one you want. He is busy for a reason. He's probably very good at what he does, therefore he's worth the wait.

Worksheet

After working in a paint store for many years I learned that people do NOT keep records of their paint colors. Then when they have to do touch ups, they go to the paint store with a teeny, tiny paint chip and ask them to try to figure out what color they painted five years ago. They never wrote it down and threw out the old cans of paint. It was my job to try to match the tiny chip. So I created a worksheet that I do for all of my clients after I choose their paint colors. I'm including it here for you at the end of the book to fill out for all of your colors. You never know what may come up, (like a leaky pipe or tree falling on your roof), and you may need to repaint someday. I know I sound like an insurance commercial, but I've seen everything.

Below is a copy of a filled-out sheet so you can see how to do it. There is a key on the bottom for abbreviations.

Following the key on the bottom of the sheet you'll see that the ceilings are done in Super White Ceiling Paint, and the trim is done in Super White semi-gloss.

Room	Ceiling & Trim	Wall Colors	Finish	Page 1 of 2
Living Room	Ceiling: Sup CP / Trim: Sup S	Cumulus Cloud 1550	m	1550
Foyer	Ceiling: Sup CP / Trim: Sup S	Balboa Mist 1549 (OC-27)	m	1549
Dining Rm	Ceiling: Sup CP / Trim: Sup S	Top: Aegean Teal 2136-40 Bottom: Balboa Mist 1549	m	2136-40 / OC-27
Kitchen	Ceiling: Sup CP / Trim: Sup S	Harbor Haze 2136-60	E	2136-60 harbor haze

Paint Color Key: CW (Ceiling White), L (Linen White), N (Navajo White), SW (Super White), WD (White Dove), W (White 01), A (Atrium white), DW (Decorator's White)
Finish Key: F (Flat) M (Matte/Flat), E (Eggshell) P (Pearl), SA (Satin) S (Semi-gloss) - ABS (Aura Bath and Spa) CP - Ceiling Paint

When you have made all of your final decisions for paint colors in each room, fill out the worksheet. Write the name of the room, the ceiling color, the trim color, the color for the room, and the finish. This way, if you ever have to do touch ups you will have a record of all of the colors you chose. The finish is important because if you paint the walls in eggshell but try to touch up with flat paint, the paint won't match and you'll see everywhere you tried to touch up.

Next, go to the paint store and get all of the paper paint chips for each room and cut and paste them to the sheet. Then take a screen shot of it and save it as a file on your computer in case you lose track of this book. If you go shopping for new furniture, rugs, window treatments etc. bring the sheets with you. You'll find it will make your life much easier to choose things for your home if you know what the paint colors are.

Well, that's it! Hopefully you were able to find colors you love for every room in your house. Be sure to follow me on Facebook and Instagram as **"The Paint Diva"**.

Page _____ of _____

Room:	Ceiling & Trim:	Wall Colors:	Finish:	Add Paint Chips Here:
Special Instructions:	Ceiling:			
	Trim:			
Special Instructions:	Ceiling:			
	Trim:			
Special Instructions:	Ceiling:			
	Trim:			
Special Instructions:	Ceiling:			
	Trim:			

Paint Color Key: **CW** (Ceiling White), **L** (Linen White), **N** (Navajo White), **SUP** (Super White), **WD** (White Dove), **W** (White 01), **A** (Atrium white), **DW** (Decorator's White)
Finish Key: **F** (Flat) **M** (Matte/Flat), **E** (Eggshell) **P** (Pearl), **SAT** (Satin), **SG** (Semi-gloss) , **ABS** (Aura Bath and Spa), **CP** (Ceiling Paint)

Page _____ of _____

Room:	Ceiling & Trim:	Wall Colors:	Finish:	Add Paint Chips Here:
Special Instructions:	Ceiling: Trim:			
Special Instructions:	Ceiling: Trim:			
Special Instructions:	Ceiling: Trim:			
Special Instructions:	Ceiling: Trim:			

Paint Color Key: **CW** (Ceiling White), **L** (Linen White), **N** (Navajo White), **SUP** (Super White), **WD** (White Dove), **W** (White 01), **A** (Atrium white), **DW** (Decorator's White)
Finish Key: **F** (Flat) **M** (Matte/Flat), **E** (Eggshell) **P** (Pearl), **SAT** (Satin), **SG** (Semi-gloss), **ABS** (Aura Bath and Spa), **CP** (Ceiling Paint)

Page _____ of _____

Room:	Ceiling & Trim:	Wall Colors:	Finish:	Add Paint Chips Here:
Special Instructions:	Ceiling:			
	Trim:			
Special Instructions:	Ceiling:			
	Trim:			
Special Instructions:	Ceiling:			
	Trim:			
Special Instructions:	Ceiling:			
	Trim:			

Paint Color Key: **CW** (Ceiling White), **L** (Linen White), **N** (Navajo White), **SUP** (Super White), **WD** (White Dove), **W** (White 01), **A** (Atrium white), **DW** (Decorator's White)
Finish Key: **F** (Flat) **M** (Matte/Flat), **E** (Eggshell) **P** (Pearl), **SAT** (Satin), **SG** (Semi-gloss) , **ABS** (Aura Bath and Spa), **CP** (Ceiling Paint)

Page _____ of _____

Room:	Ceiling & Trim:	Wall Colors:	Finish:	Add Paint Chips Here:
Special Instructions:	Ceiling:			
	Trim:			
Special Instructions:	Ceiling:			
	Trim:			
Special Instructions:	Ceiling:			
	Trim:			
Special Instructions:	Ceiling:			
	Trim:			

Paint Color Key: **CW** (Ceiling White), **L** (Linen White), **N** (Navajo White), **SUP** (Super White), **WD** (White Dove), **W** (White 01), **A** (Atrium white), **DW** (Decorator's White)
Finish Key: **F** (Flat) **M** (Matte/Flat), **E** (Eggshell) **P** (Pearl), **SAT** (Satin), **SG** (Semi-gloss), **ABS** (Aura Bath and Spa), **CP** (Ceiling Paint)

Paint Color Index

When I worked in the paint store customers used to bring in photos from magazines and would ask me to find the chip of the color listed in the magazine. But almost always the actual color never looked like it did in the magazine due to lighting, printing, etc. So, that may happen with this book, but hopefully not. Some of the colors listed below are the actual colors used in the rooms, and others are educated guesses (like the "before" photos). Some photos in the book have been edited in Photoshop, so I list the paint color that looks closest to how it appears on the pages in the book.

Kitchens

75. Storm AF-75 (Cover)
76. Oriole 2169-30
77. Horizon 1478
78. *Left-* Silver Sage 506, *Right-* Muslin 1037
79. *Top left, Right-* Wood Ash 1065, *Bottom-* Kendall Charcoal HC-166
80. *Top, Cabinets-* Smoke Embers 1466, *Walls-* Light Pewter 1464, *Bottom-* Stonington Gray HC-170
81. Cedar Key 982 (Tuscan Era)
82. *Top-* Edgecomb Gray HC-173, *Bottom-* Sweet Spring 1500
83. *Top-* Ionic Column 1016, *Bottom Afters Left-* Kitten Whiskers 1003, Right-Balboa Mist 1549
84. *Left-* Balboa Mist 1549, *Right-* Silver Sage 506
85. *Left-* Shoreline 1471, *Right-* Trout Gray 2124-20
86. Silver Sage 506
87. *Top Left-* Featherstone 1002, *Center Right-* Stonington Gray HC-170, *Bottom Left-* Ionic Column 1016
88. *Top Left-* Sterling 1591, *Center Right-* Whale Gray 2134-40, Bottom left-Shoreline 1471
89. *Left-* Brittany Blue 1633, *Right-* Winds Breath 981
90. *Top Left-* Maritime White 963, *Bottom Left-* Edgecomb Gray HC-173, *Bottom Right-* Cinder AF-705
91. *Top Left-* Whispering Spring 2136-70, *Top Right-* Maritime White 963, *Bottom-* Buttered Yam AF-230
92. *Left-* Classic Gray 1548, *Right-* Iced Slate 2130-70
93. *Top Right-* Firenze AF-225, *Bottom Left-* Stonington Gray HC-170
94. *Top Right-* Incredible White SW 7028, *Bottom Left-* Cumulus Cloud 1550, *Bottom Right-* Wales Gray 1585 (Kitchen-Tina Cole Design)
95. Secret AF-710
96. *Top Right-* Pure White SW 7005 & Loyal Blue SW 6510, *Bottom-* Super White & Cinder AF-705 Island
97. *Wall-* Maritime White 963, *Cabinets-* Nimbus 1465, *Island-* Baltic Gray 1467
98. *Walls-* Nimbus 1465, *Cabinets-* China White PM-20, *Island-* Philipsburg Blue HC-159
99. *Top Walls-* Wickham Gray HC-171, *Cabinets-* Super White, *Island-* Beach Glass 1563, *Bottom Walls-* Stonington Gray HC-170, *Cabinets-* Super White

Family Rooms

101. Nuance SW 7049
102. Montgomery White HC-33
103. *Top Left* -Sail Cloth PM-21,*Top Center*- Stonington Gray HC-170,*Top Right*- Cedar Key 982, *Bottom*- Balboa Mist 1549
104. *Top Walls*- Cumulus Cloud 1550,*Bookcase*- Coventry Gray HC-169,*Center Left*- Weimeraner AF-155,*Bottom Right*- Silver Half Dollar 2121-40
105. *Top Left*- Baltic Gray 1467, (Family Room- Tina Cole Design),*Center Left*- Cinder AF-705,*Center Right*- Davenport Tan HC-76,*Bottom Left*- Blue Heather 1620,*Bottom Right*- Grecian Green 507
106. *Top Left*- Stonington Gray HC-170,*Top Right*- Mayflower Red HC-49,*Center Right Walls*- Nimbus 1465,*Brick*- Cape May Cobblestone 1474,*Bottom Left Walls*- Quiet Moments 1563,*Brick*- Super White,*Bottom Right Walls*- Balboa Mist OC-27,*Fireplace Wall*- Black Bean Soup 2130-10
107. *Top Left*- Winds Breath 981,*Center Right*- Secret AF-710,*Bottom*- Cedar Key 982
108. *Top 3 Photos*- Cedar Key 982,*Bottom Left*- Shelburne Buff HC-28,*Bottom Right*- Shoreline 1471. (Photos courtesy of Cheryl Singer, "My Coastal Chic Life" on Instagram, Limewash by Dave O'Brien, OMC Masonry and Tile)
109. *Top Left*- La Paloma Gray 1551,*Bottom Left*- Shaker Beige HC-45,*Bottom Right*- Cedar Key 982
110. *Top Right*- Natural Wicker OC-1,*Bottom Left*- Tricorn Black SW 6258,*Bottom Right*- Classic Gray 1548 & Kendall Charcoal HC-166
111. *Top Left Top*- Balboa Mist 1549,*Bottom*- La Paloma Gray 1551,*Bottom Left*- Nimbus 1465 & Philipsburg Blue HC-159,*Bottom Right*- Secret AF-710
112. *Center Left & Right-Walls*- Cumulus Cloud 1550,*Bookcase*- Coventry Gray HC-169,*Bottom Left & Right*- Secret AF-710
113. *Top Left*- Concord Ivory HC-12,*Top Right*- Collingwood OC-28,*Center Left*- Edgecomb Gray HC-173,*Center Right*- Smoke Embers 1466,*Bottom Left*- Horizon 1478,*Bottom Right*- Stonington Gray HC-170
114. Accessible Beige SW 7036

Living Rooms

115. Sail Cloth PM-21
116. Spring Valley 438
117. *Top Left*- Richmond Gray HC-96, *Top Right*- Secret AF-710, *Bottom Left*- Polite White SW 6056
118. *Top Right*- Cedar Key 983, *Center Right*- Stonington Gray HC-170, *Bottom Right*- Winds Breath 981
119. *Top Right*- Gray Owl 2137-60, *Center Right*- Harbor Town 493, *Bottom Left*- Cedar Key 982, *Bottom Right*- Pale Smoke 1584
120. *Top Right*- Shoreline 1471, *Top Left*- Reliable White SW 6084, *Center Left*- Nuance SW 7049, *Bottom Right*- Everlasting 1038
121. *Top Right*- Stonington Gray HC-170, *Bottom Left*- Balboa Mist 1549, *Bottom Right*- Oxford Gray 2128-40
122. *Bottom Left & Right*- Collingwood OC-28

Dining Rooms

123. Gray Wisp 1570
124. Engagement 1277
125. *Top Left-* Silvery Blue 1647,*Center Left-* Linen White PM-28,*Center Right-* Vale Mist 1494,*Bottom Left-* Huntington Beige HC-21,*Bottom Right-* Waterbury Green HC-136
126. *Top Right-* Stonington Gray HC-170,*Center Left-* Warm Springs 682,*Center Right-* Collingwood OC-28,*Bottom Left-* Shoreline 1471,*Bottom Right-* Light Pewter 1464
127. *Top Left-* Silvery Blue 1647,*Top Right-* Silver Chain 1472,*Bottom Left-* Nimbus 1465,*Bottom Center-* Blue 2066-10,*Bottom Right Top-* Harbor Haze 2136-60,*Bottom-* Classic Gray OC-23
128. *Top Left-* Schooner AF-520,*Bottom Left-* New York State of Mind 805
129. *Top Center-* Everlasting 1038,*Top Right-* Stonington Gray HC-170,*Center Left-* Stone Harbor 2111-50,*Bottom Center-* Raccoon Fur 2126-20,*Bottom Right-* Witching Hour 2120-30
130. *Top Left-* Vale Mist 1494,*Center Left-* Salisbury Green HC-139,*Center Right-* Horizon Gray 2141-50,*Bottom Left-* Prescott Green HC-140,*Bottom Center Right-* Winter Lake 2129-50,*Bottom Right-*Hale Navy HC-154
131. *Top Left-* Silver Mink 1586,*Top Right-* Azores AF-495,*Bottom Left-* Warm Springs 682,*Bottom Right-* Lucerne AF-530
132. *Top Left-* Dinner Party AF-300,*Top Right-* Bedford Blue 1679,*Center Left-* Dolphin AF-715,*Bottom Left-* Butterscotch SW 6377 & Mindful Gray SW 7016
133. *Top Center Top-* Vellum 207,*Bottom-* Marblehead Gold HC-11,*Top Right Top-* Vellum 207 & *Bottom-* Linen White PM-28,*Center Left Top-* Light Pewter 1464,*Bottom-* Navajo White PM-29,*Bottom Right-* Wood Violet 1428
134. *Top Right-* Light Pewter 1464,*Center Right-* Sail Cloth PM-21,*Bottom Left-* Balboa Mist 1549,*Bottom Right-* Nimbus 1465 & New Hope Gray 2130-50
135. *Top Left & Right Top-* Mocha Cream 995,*Bottom-* Baja Dunes 997,*Bottom Left & Right-*Collingwood OC-28
136. *Top Left Top-* Muslin 1037,*Bottom-* Davenport Tan HC-76,*Top Right-* Balboa Mist 1549 & New Hope Gray 2130-50,*Bottom Left & Right Top-* Light Pewter 1464,*Middle-* Nimbus 1464,*Bottom-*Super White
137. *Top Center & Right Top-* Silvery Blue 1647,*Bottom-* White Dove,*Center Left-* Manchester Tan HC-81 & Black PM-9, (Tina Cole Designs),*Bottom Left-* Admiral Blue 2065-10,*Bottom Right-*Shiplap Super White
138. *Top Right-* Putnam Ivory HC-39,*Center Top Right Top-* Smokey Taupe 983,*Bottom-* Creekbed 1006,*Bottom Right-* Alaskan Husky 1479,*Bottom Left Top-* Silver Satin OC-26,*Bottom-* Branchport Brown HC-72
139. *Top Left Top-* Coventry Gray HC-169,*Bottom-* Super White,*Center Left Top-* Silver Gray 2131-50,*Bottom & Next Room-* Balboa Mist OC-27,*Center Right Living Room-* Edgecomb Gray HC-173,*Dining Room-* Top-Revere Pewter HC-172,*Bottom-* Edgecomb Gray HC-173,*Bottom Before-*Yorkshire Tan HC-23 & Audubon Russet HC-51,*After Left & Right Living Room-* Edgecomb Gray HC-173,*Dining Room Top-* Cape May Cobblestone 1474,*Bottom-* Edgecomb Gray HC-173

140. *Top Before-* Dunmore Cream HC-29 & Mars Red 2172-20, *Top After-* Balboa Mist 1549 & Baltic Gray 1467, *Center Before-* Navajo Red 2171-10 & Philadelphia Cream HC-30, *Center After-* La Paloma Gray 1551 & Edgecomb Gray HC-173, *Bottom Before-* Wallpaper, *Bottom After-* Collingwood OC-28
141. *Top Right-* Salisbury Green HC-139, *Bottom Left & Right-* Gray Huskie 1473
142. *Kitchen & Butler's Pantry-* Balboa Mist OC-27, *Dining Room-* New York State of Mind 805

Foyers & Hallways

143. Montgomery White HC-33, Putnam Ivory HC-39, Beach Glass 1564
144. Golden Lab 178
145. *Top Left-* Waterbury Green HC-136, *Top Right-* Wickham Gray HC-171, *Bottom Left-* Edgecomb Gray HC-173 & Palladian Blue HC-144, *Bottom Right-* La Paloma Gray 1551 & Edgecomb Gray HC-173
146. *Top Left-* Maritime White OC-5 & Alaskan Husky 1479, *Bottom Left-* Nimbus 1465, *Bottom Right-* Revere Pewter HC-172
147. *Top Right-* Smokey Taupe 983, *Center Right-* Winds Breath 981, *Center Left-* Collingwood OC-28, *Bottom Left-* Philadelphia Cream HC-30, *Bottom Right-* Horizon 1478
148. *Top Right-* Truffle AF-130, *Center Left-* Wickham Gray HC-171, *Bottom Left-* Wickham Gray HC-171, *Bottom Center-* Shaker Beige HC-45, *Bottom Right-* Sleigh Bells 1480
149. *Top Right-* Horizon 1478 & Super White, *Center Left-* Edgecomb Gray HC-173, *Center Right-* Fusion AF-675, *Bottom Right-* Lenox Tan HC-44
150. *Top Left-* Stonington Gray HC-170, *Top Right-* Stonington Gray HC-170, *Top Center Left-* Hepplewhite Ivory HC-36, *Lower Center Left-* Horizon 1478, *Center Right-* Incredible White SW 7028 & Loch Blue SW 6502, *Bottom Left-* London Fog 1541
151. *Top Right-* Blue Nile SW6776, *Top Center Right Walls-* Accessible Beige SW7036, *Bookcase-* Blue Nile SW6776, *Lower Center Right Walls-* Silver Satin OC-26, *Door-* Yarmouth Blue HC-150, *Bottom Left After Walls-* Nimbus 1465, *Door-* Black 2132-10, *Bottom Center-* Super White, *Door-* Baltic Gray 1467, *Bottom Right Walls-* Silver Satin OC-26, *Door-* Suntan Yellow 2155-50
152. *Top Foyer & Dining Room Bottom-* Classic Gray OC-23, *Dining Room Top-* Silvery Blue 1647, *Bottom Left-* Thunder AF-685, *Bottom Right-* Muslin 1037
153. *Center Left Before-* Pale Oak OC-20, *Center Right After-* Truffle AF-130, *Bottom Left Before-* 01 White, *Bottom Right After-* Winds Breath 981
154. *Top Left-* Cedar Key 982, *Center Left-* Stonington Gray HC-170, *Center Middle-* Super White, *Center Right-* Silver Satin OC-26, *Bottom Left-* Abington Putty HC-99, *Bottom Right Foyer-* Cedar Key 982, *Living Room-* Stonington Gray HC-170
155. *Top Left-* Sleigh Bells 1480, *Bottom Left Living Room-* Cedar Key 982, *Foyer & Dining Room-* Nimbus 1465, *Bottom Right Family Room-* Pashmina AF-100, *Foyer-* Manchester Tan HC-81, *Living Room-* Richmond Gray HC-96
156. Shoreline 1471 & Lucerne AF-530

Bathrooms

157. Nimbus 1465
158. Charcoal Slate HC-178
159. Smoke Embers 1466
160. *Top Left-* Super White,*Top Right-* Classic Gray 1548,*Bottom Left-* Super White & La Paloma Gray 1551, *Bottom Right-* Richmond Green 553
161. *Top Right-* Bleeker Beige HC-80,*Bottom Left-* Graytint 1611,*Bottom Right-* Arctic Gray 1577
162. *Top Left-* California Blue 2060-20,*Top Right-* Hawthorne Yellow HC-4,*Bottom Left-* Cinder AF-705, *Bottom Right-* Tropical Turquoise 2052-30
163. *Top Left-* Paper White 1590,*Top Right-* Silver Crest 1583
164. *Top Left-* Pelican Gray 1612,*Top Right-* Gray Wisp 1570,*Bottom Right-* Silvery Blue 1647
165. *Top Left-* Van Deusen Blue HC-156,*Top Right-* Coventry Gray HC-169 & Super White,*Bottom Left-* Oxford Gray 2128-40,*Bottom Right-* Winds Breath 981 & Smokey Taupe 983
166. *Top Left-* Boca Raton Blue 711,*Top Right-* Smoke Embers 1466,*Bottom Left-* Decorator White, *Bottom Left Center-* Limon 334,*Bottom Right Center-* Wedgewood Gray HC-146,*Bottom Right-* Storm AF-700
167. *Top Right-* Balboa Mist 1549,*Center Left-* Gossamer Blue 2123-40,*Bottom Right-* Ashen Tan 996
168. *Top Left-* Light Pewter 1464,*Top Center-* Wickham Gray HC-171,*Top Right-* Horizon 1478,*Bottom-* Light Pewter 1464
169. *Top Left-* Classic Gray 1548,*Top Right-* Alphano Beige 989,*Bottom Right-* Balboa Mist 1549
170. *Top Center & Right-* Cedar Key 982,*Bottom Right-* Smoke Embers 1466
171. *Top Left-* Pelican Gray 1612,*Top Right-* Coastal Fog 976,*Bottom Left-* Catalina Blue 703, B*ottom Right-* Agreeable Gray SW 7029
172. *Bottom Left-* Limon 334,*Bottom Center-* Graytint 1611,*Bottom Right-* Revere Pewter HC-172
173. *Top Left-* Silver Lake 1598,*Top Center-* Smokey Taupe 983,*Top Right-* Stingray 1529,*Bottom Left-* Kensington Green 710
174. *Top Left-* Bar Harbor Beige 1032,*Top Right Sample-* Creamy Custard 1145,*Center Middle-* Pittsfield Buff HC-24,*Center Right-* Lambskin 1051,*Bottom Left-* Frappe AF-85
175. *Top Left-* Cedar Key 982,*Top Right-* Barely Beige 1066,*Bottom Right-* Everlasting 1038
176. *Top Right-* Wickham Gray HC-171,*Bottom Left-* Montgomery White PM-26,*Bottom Right-* Arctic Gray 1577
177. *Top Left-* Cumulus Cloud 1550,*Bottom Left-* Ionic Column 1016,*Bottom Right-* Cedar Key 982
178. *Top Right-* Light Pewter 1464, Bottom Left- Storm AF-700, Bottom Right- Ionic Column 1016
179. *Bottom Left-* Aztec Brick 2175-10,*Bottom Center-* Maple Sugar 2160-30,*Bottom Right-* Yosemite Yellow 215

180. *Top Left-* Bermuda Turquoise 728, *Top Center-* Coastal Plain SW 6192, *Top Right-* Blue Heather 1620, *Bottom Left-* Drizzle SW 6479, *Bottom Center-* Tranquil Aqua SW 7611, *Bottom Right-* Chesapeake Blue CW 595
181. *Top Left-* Quiet Moments 1563, *Top Right-* Healing Aloe 1562, *Bottom Center-* Pale Smoke 1584, *Bottom Right-* Silver Mink 1586
182. *Top Left-* Palest Pistachio 2122-60, *Top Right-* Cedar Key 982, *Bottom-* Bird's Egg 2051-60
183. *Top Left-* Coventry Gray HC-169, *Top Right-* Dusty Road 1017, *Bottom Left-* Ashen Tan 996, *Bottom Right-* Cedar Key 982
184. *Top-* Arctic Gray 1577, *Bottom Left-* Ice Cap 1576, *Bottom Right-* Alaskan Husky 1479
185. 1960's and 1970's Tile
186. *Top Right-* Tissue Pink 1163
187. *Center Left-* Sea Foam 2123-60, *Center Right-* Fantasy Blue 716, *Bottom Left-* Feather Green 625, *Bottom Right-* Storm AF-700
188. *Top Left-* Shoreline 1471, *Top Right-* Ocean Air 2123-50, *Bottom Center-* Balboa Mist 1549 185.
189. *Top Right-* Metropolitan AF-690, *Bottom Left-* Everlasting 1038, *Bottom Right-* Nimbus 1465
190. *Top Left-* Seduction 1399, *Top Right-* New York State of Mind 805, *Bottom Left-* Alaskan Husky 1479, *Bottom Center-* Silver Satin OC-26, *Bottom Right-* Caribbean Blue Water 2055-30
191. *Top Left-* Blue Heather 1620, *Top Right-* Apple Green 2026-40, *Bottom Left-* Mellow Pink 2094-70, *Bottom Right-* Blue Seafoam 2056—60
192. *Bottom Left-* Soft Chamois 969, *Bottom Right Walls-* Gray Timber Wolf 2126-50, *Vanity-* Pink Taffy 2075-50
193. *Top Left-* Muslin 1037, *Bottom Left-* Malton 1073, *Bottom Right-* Light Pewter 1464
194. *Center Left Vanity-* Navajo White, *Center Middle Walls-* Coastal Fog 976, *Vanity-* Sag Harbor Gray HC-95, *Top Right Walls-* White Sand 964, *Vanity-* La Paloma Gray 1551, *Center Right Walls-* Winds Breath 981, *Vanity-* Cape May Cobblestone 1474, *Bottom Left Vanity-* Smoke Gray 2120-40, *Bottom Right Walls-* Classic Gray 1548, *Vanity-* Black PM-9
195. *Top Right Walls-* Coventry Gray HC-169, *Vanity-* Hale Navy HC-154, *Center Left Walls-* Sea Foam 2123-60, *Vanity-* Blue Rapids 745, *Bottom Right Before Walls-* White PM-2, *Vanity-* Witching Hour 2120-30, *After Walls-* Silver Satin OC-26, *Vanity-* Richmond Green 553

Master/Primary Bedrooms

197. Pashmina AF-100
198. Smokey Taupe 983
199. *Top Right-* Smokey Taupe 983, *Center Right-* Mineral Alloy 1622, *Center Left-* Everlasting 1038, *Bottom Right-* Quiet Moments 1563
200. *Top Right-* Eider White SW 7014, *Center Left-* Maritime White 963, *Center Right-* Pelican Gray 1612, *Bottom Left Accent-* Delray Gray 1614, *Bottom Right Accent-* Bella Blue 720
201. *Top Right-* Arctic Gray 1577, *Center Left-* Coventry Gray HC-169, *Center Right-* Agreeable Gray SW7029 & Roycroft Bottle Green SW2847, *Bottom Left-*Arctic Gray 1577
202. *Top Left & Bottom Right-* Crystalline AF-485, *Top Center & Right-* Quiet Moments 1563
203. *Top Left-* Amherst Gray HC-167, *Top Right & Bottom-* Van Deusen Blue HC-156
204. *Top Left & Center-* Beach Glass 1564, *Top Right-* Stonington Gray HC-170 & Hale Navy HC-154, *Center Left & Middle-* Stonington Gray HC-170
205. *Top Left-* Shoreline 1471 (50% lighter), *Top Right-* Crystalline AF-485, *Bottom Left-* Shoreline 1471
206. Eider White SW 7014. Photo courtesy of Patti Roberts Design Co.

Guest Bedrooms

207. Paper White 1590
208. Clover Green 2048-60
209. *Top Left-* Beach Glass 1564, *Bottom Right-* Paper White 1590
210. *Top Left-* Stonington Gray HC-170, *Center Left-*Montgomery White HC-33, *Center Middle & Right-* Cumulus Cloud 1550, *Bottom Left-* Shoreline 1471, *Bottom Right-* Stone Hearth 984
211. *Top Right-* Green Belt SW 6927, *Center Left-* Iced Marble 1578, *Center Right-* Winter's Eve CC-844, *Bottom Left-* Quiet Moments 1563
212. *Top Right-* Winds Breath 981, *Bottom Left-* November Skies 2128-50, B*ottom Middle-* Filtered Sunlight 2154-60

Kids' Bedrooms

213. Tropicana Cabana 2048-50
214. Jamaican Aqua 2048-60
215. Photos courtesy of Christen Holly Photography
216. The System
217. *Top Right-* Heaven on Earth 1661, *Center Left-* Eider White SW 7014, *Bottom Right-* Philipsburg Blue HC-159 & Classic Gray 1548. Photo courtesy of Patti Roberts Design Co.
218. *Center Right-* Ocean Breeze 2058-60, *Bottom Right-* Caribbean Mist 2061-70
219. *Center Left-* Sapphire Ice 808 & Blue Dragon 810, *Center Middle-* Edgecomb Gray HC-173 & Newburyport Blue HC-155, *Center Right-* Stonington Gray HC-170 & Hale Navy HC-154, *Bottom Left-* Bluebelle 2064-60, *Bottom Middle-* Pale Sea Mist 2147-50, *Bottom Right-* Pottery Red 2085-20 & Blue Heather 1620

220. *Center Left-* Newburyport Blue HC-155 & Smokey Taupe 983,*Center Middle-* White PM-2, Admiral Blue 2065-10, Pumpkin Cream 2168-20, *Top Right-* Worldly Gray SW 7043 & Rosemary SW 6187, *Bottom Left-* Grant Beige HC-83,*Bottom Middle-* Old Glory 811,*Bottom Right-* Stonington Gray HC-170 & NY Yankees Blue SC-51
221. *Top Left-* Modern Gray SW 7632 & Naval SW 6244,*Top Right-* Newburyport Blue HC-155,*Center Right-* Artichoke SW 6179, *Bottom Left-*Ashley Gray HC-87,*Bottom Right-* Graytint 1611
222. *Bottom Right-* Ballerina Pink 2082-70
223. *Top Right-* Hint of Pink 884,*Center Left-* Classic Gray OC-23 & Pink Innocence 2082-60,*Bottom Left-* Flowering Herbs 514,*Bottom Middle-* Windham Cream HC-6,*Bottom Right-* Soft Sky 807
224. *Bottom Left-* Peach Parfait 2175-70,*Bottom Right-* Serenity 2055-60
225. *Top Left-* Royal Fuchsia 2078-30,*Top Right-* Sausalito Sunset 074,*Bottom Left-* California Lilac 2068-40,*Bottom Middle-* Early Spring Green 2-32-50,*Bottom Right-* Big Country Blue 2066-30
226. *Top Middle-* Seafoam 2123-60,*Top Right-* Lavender Mist 2070-60 & Darkest Grape 2069-30,*Bottom Right-* Silver Bells 1458
227. Flint AF-560
228. *Top Left-* Denim Wash 838,*Top Right-* Bahamian Sea Blue 2055-40,*Top Right-* Rose Rococo 1275 & Easter Ribbon 1381

Playrooms

229. Lake Placid 827
230. Fiesta Orange 084
231. *Top Right-* Fruit Punch 140 & Cloud Cover 855, *Bottom-* Light Pewter 1464 & Florida Keys Blue 2050-40 (Photos from The Toy Tamer)
232. *Top Left-* White Winged Dove (photo from The Toy Tamer), *Center Right-* Big Country Blue 2066-30, *Bottom Left-* Weston Flax HC-5
233. *Bottom-* Incredible White SW 7028 & Adriatic Sea SW 6790 (Designer)
234. Pashmina AF-100 & Blackboard Paint

Mudrooms and Laundry Rooms

235. Cedar Kay 982
236. Happily Ever After 173
237. *Top Right-* Stonington Gray HC-170,*Center Left-* Downpour Blue 2063-20,*Bottom Right-* Hush AF-95
238. *Top Right Walls-* Drift of Mist SW 9166,*Cubbies-* Rosemary SW 6187,*Center Left Walls-* Edgecomb Gray HC-173,*Cubbies-* Copley Gray HC-104 in stain,*Center Middle Walls-* Shoreline 1471,*Cubbies-*Jet Black 2120-10,*Bottom Right Walls-* High Reflective White,*Cubbies-* Indigo Batik SW 7602-(Photo courtesy of Kendyl York, @the_york_style on Instagram),*Bottom Center Walls-* Silver Satin OC-26, *Door-* Downpour Blue 2063-20,*Bottom Left-Cubbies-* Slate Blue 1648
239. *Top Right-* Nimbus 1465,*Center Right-* Horizon 1478 & Boothbay Gray HC-165,*Bottom Left-*Marlboro Blue HC-153,*Bottom Middle-* Raindrop SW 6485
240. *Top Left-* Banan-Appeal 332,*Bottom Left-* Bahaman Sea Blue 2055-40,*Bottom Right-* August Morning 2156-40

Office

241. Bedford Blue 1679
242. Old Glory 811
243. *Top Left-* Cork 2153-40, *Top Right-* Weimaraner AF-155, *Center Left-* Bone Black CW-715, *Bottom Right-* Horizon 1478 & Kensington Green 710
244. *Top Right-* Summer Nights 777 & Muslin 1037, *Bottom Right-* Classic Burgundy PM-17 & White Dove PM-19
245. *Top Left-* Simply Irresistible 205, *Top Middle-* Kensington Green 710, *Top Right-* Classic Gray 1548, *Bottom Right-* Sterling 1591
246. *Top Right-* Steamed Spinach 643, *Bottom Left-* Philipsburg Blue HC-159, *Center Right-* Cypress Green 509, *Bottom Right-* Rockport Gray HC-105
247. *Top Left-* Fall Harvest 2168-10, *Top Right-* Merlot Red 2006-10, *Bottom Left-* Oxford Gray 2128-40, *Bottom Right-* Sweatshirt Gray 2126-40
248. *Top Right-* Sail Cloth PM-21 & Americana 770, *Bottom Right-* Super White PM-1 & Smokestack Gray 2131-40

Sunrooms and Porches

249. Colorado Gray 2136-50
250. Birds Egg 2051-60
251. *Top Right-* Black Pepper 2130-40, *Bottom Right-* Louisburg Green HC-113
252. *Top Left-* Hawthorne Yellow HC-4, *Top Right-* Van Deusen Blue HC-156, *Top Center Left-* Navajo White PM-29, *Center Left-* Avocado 2145-10, *Bottom Left-* Sparrow AF-720
253. *Top Left-* Peacock Feathers 724, *Top Right-* Weimeraner AF-155, *Bottom Left-* Colorado Gray 2136-50, *Bottom Right-* Pashmina AF-100
254. *Top Right-* Pashmina AF-100, *Top Left-* Colorado Gray 2136-50, *Bottom Left-* Manchester Tan HC-81 & China Blue 2052-60, *Bottom Right-* Ceiling- Glass Slipper 1632 50%, Walls- White Dove 50%, Floor- Shaker Gray 1594. Photo courtesy of Judy Tillman, Tillman Long Interiors

Basements, Garages, & Bonus Rooms

255. Copper Harbor SW 6634 (Interior Designer)
256. Habanero 1306
257. *Center-* Suntan Yellow 2155-50, *Bottom-* Brittany Blue 1633
258. *Top Right-* Lenox Tan HC-44, *Center Left-* Shoreline 1471, *Bottom Left-* Incredible White SW 7028 & Copper Harbor SW 6634, *Bottom Right-* Adriatic Sea SW 6790
259. *Top Left-* Sail Cloth PM-21 & Cabot Trail 998, *Top Right-* Manchester Tan HC-81 & Admiral Blue 2065-10, *Center-* Subtle AF-310 & Caldwell Green HC-124, *Bottom-* Spa AF-435
260. *Top Left-* Nantucket Gray HC-111, *Top Right-* Philipsburg Blue HC-159, *Center Right-* Secret AF-710, *Bottom Right-* Salsa Dancing AF-280
261. *Top Left-* Webster Green HC-130 & Linen White PM-28, *Top Right-* Shoreline 1471, *Center Left-* Black PM-9 & Super White PM-1, *Bottom Left-* Silver Crest 1583, *Bottom Right-* Silver Satin OC-26

262. *Top Left-* Decorator's White PM-3 & Margarita 2026-20, *Top Middle-* Mayonnaise 2152-70 & Sunbeam 328, *Top Right-* Silver Song 1557, *Bottom-* Stonington Gray HC-170 & Coventry Gray HC-169
263. *Top Right-* Newburyport Blue HC-155, *Center Left-* Philipsburg Blue HC-159, *Bottom Left-* Silver Satin OC-26 & Super White PM-1
264. *Top Left and Right-* Fine Paints of Europe, photos by Jimmy Canabe Painting, *Bottom Left & Right-* Newburg Green HC-158

Choosing Trim Colors

268. *Walls-* Lily White 2128-70, *Trim-* Navajo White PM-29, *Ceiling-* Ceiling White
269. *Top Right-* La Paloma Gray 1551, Cumulus Cloud 1550, Stonington Gray HC-170, *Bottom-* Balboa Mist 1549, Bone White PM-30, Classic Gray 1548
270. *Top & Bottom Right-* Beach Glass 1564
271. *Top Left-* Cosmos SW 6528, *Bottom Left-* Spanish Red 1301
272. *Top Right-* Revere Pewter HC-172, *Bottom Right-* White Dove PM-19
273. *Top Left-* Pensive AF-140, *Bottom Left-* Hawthorne Yellow HC-4
274. *Top Right-* Super White PM-1 & Black PM-9, *Center Left Windows-* Tricorn Black SW 6258, *Bottom Left Walls-* Repose Gray SW 7015, *Trim-* Gauntlet Gray SW 7019
275. *Top Left-* La Paloma Gray 1551 (Pearl Finish), *Top Right-* Vermont Slate 1673 (Satin Finish), *Bottom Left-* Dark Teal 2053-20 (Semi-Gloss), *Bottom Right After-* Evening Sky 833, *Before Walls-* Corlsbad Canyon 076, *Ceiling-* Golden Delicious 390, *Trim-* Golden Honey 297
276. *Top Left-* Nimbus 1465, *Bottom Left-* Jet Black 2120-10 & White Dove PM-19, *Bottom Center-* Abyss 2128-20 & Super White PM-1, *Bottom Right-* Atmospheric AF-500 & Super White PM-1
277. *Top Left-* Navajo White PM-29, *Top Right-* White Dove PM-19 & La Paloma Gray 1551, *Bottom Left & Right-* Wickham Gray HC-171
278. *Top Left-* Homespun Charm 1249, *Top Right-* White PM-2, *Center Left-* Silver Satin OC-26, *Center Right-* Harbor Fog 2062-70, *Bottom Left-* Navajo White PM-29, *Bottom Right-* Summer Nights 777
279. Sheens
280. *Top Left-* Pacific Ocean Blue 2055-20 and White Dove PM-19, *Top Right Walls-* Silver Lake 1598, *Bookcase-* Black 2132-10, *Bottom Left Foyer Walls-* Blue Nile SW6776, *Living Room Walls-* Accessible Beige SW7036, *Bookcase-* Blue Nile SW6776, *Bottom Right Walls-* Nimbus 1465, *Bookcase-* Super White PM-1

Ceilings

283. *Top Right-* White Dove, *Center Left Walls-* Agreeable Gray SW 7029, *Trim-* Dover White SW 6385, *Bottom Middle-* Alexandria Beige HC-77, *Bottom Right-* Davenport Tan HC-76
284. *Top Left-* Coastal Fog 976, *Top Right-* Wales Gray 1585, *Center Middle-* November Skies 2128-50, *Bottom Left-* Stone Hearth 984, *Bottom Right-* Smokey Taupe 983
285. *Top Left-* Sag Harbor Gray HC-95, *Top Right-* Sleigh Bells 1480, *Bottom Left-* Wickham Gray HC-171, *Bottom Right-* Woodlawn Blue HC-147

286. *Top Right-* Stonington Gray HC-170 & Puritan Gray HC-164,*Top Left-* Secret AF-710,*Center Left Top-* Cedar Key 982,*Bottom-* Grege Avenue 991,*Bottom Left-* Puritan Gray HC-164
287. *Top Left-* Pashmina AF-100,*Center Left Walls-* Feather Gray 2127-60,*Ceiling-* Winds Breath 981, *Bottom Walls-* Stonington Gray HC-170,*Ceiling-* Fusion AF-675
288. *Top Left Walls-* Cedar Key 982,*Ceiling-* Weimeraner AF-155,*Center Right-* Coventry Gray HC-169, *Center Left Walls-* Chelsea Gray HC-168,*Ceiling-* Edgecomb Gray HC-173,*Bottom Middle & Right-* Dunmore Cream HC-29
289. *A. B. C. D. Walls-* Linen White PM-28,*Ceiling-* La Paloma Gray 1551,*Bottom Right-* Cape May Cobblestone 1474
290. *Top Left Walls-* Half Moon Crest 1481,*Ceiling-* White Dove PM-19,*Top Center Left-* Duxbury Gray HC-163,*Trim-* Decorator's White PM-3,*Bottom Center Left Walls-* Repose Gray SW 7015,*Trim-* Gauntlet Gray SW 7019,*Bottom Left-* Super White PM-1,*Bottom Right-* White Dove PM-19

Sampling Paint Colors

292. *Top Left-* Roxbury Caramel HC-42
293. *Top Right-* Philipsburg Blue HC-159

Paint Basics

296. *Top Left-* Gypsy Love 2085-30 (Semi-Gloss), *Top Right-* Shelburne Buff HC-28 (Semi-Gloss)

Problem Solving

305. *Top Left-* Lighthouse Landing 1044,*Center Left-* Navajo White PM-29,*Bottom Left-* White OC-151
306. *Top Left Walls-* Revere Pewter HC-172,*Trim-* White Dove PM19,*Center Left-* Simply White OC-117, *Bottom Right-* Wickham Gray HC-171 & Normandy 2129-40
307. *Top Left-* Winter Lake 2129-50 & Edgecomb Gray HC-172,*Center Left-* Province Blue 2135-40 & Wickham Gray HC-171, *Bottom Left-* Super White PM-1
308. *Center Right-* Horizon 1478, *Center Left-* Storm AF-700,*Bottom Left-* Smokey Taupe 983 & Coventry Gray HC-169
309. *Center Right-* Super White PM-1, *Center Left-* Silver Chain 1472,*Bottom Left-* Coventry Gray HC-169
310. *Top Right-* Stonington Gray HC-170,*Top Left-* Azores AF-495,*Bottom Left-* Cape May Cobblestone 1474 & Edgecomb Gray HC-173
311. *Top Left-* Silver Chain 1472, *Top Center & Top Right-* Silver Chain 1472 & Cape May Cobblestone 1474,*Bottom Left-* Silver Chain 1472 & Horizon 1478,*Bottom Right-* Gray Huskie 1473 & Silver Chain 1472
312. *Top Right-* California Blue 2060-20,*Bottom Left-* Lily White 2128-70

Comparable Colors

The following is a list of crossover colors between Benjamin Moore and Sherwin Williams. Obviously, it does not include all of the available colors. Consider it a list of "If you like this color by this company, then try this color.

Benjamin Moore	Sherwin Williams
Abalone 2108-60	Popular Choice SW 6071
Antique White OC-83	Choice Cream SW 6357
Atrium White OC-145	White Flour SW 7102
Balboa Mist 1549, OC-27	Natural Tan SW 7567
Bleeker Beige HC-80	Downing Sand SW 2822
Breath of Fresh Air 806	Balmy SW 6512
Cameo White 915	Vanillin SW 6371
Cedar Key 982	Rivers Edge SW 7517
Chantilly Lace 2121-70, OC-65	Extra White SW 7006
Classic Gray 1548, OC-23	Aesthetic White SW 7035
Collingwood 859, OC-28	Accessible Beige SW 7036
Decorator's White OC-149	Snowbound SW 7004
Dune White 968	Alabaster SW 7008
Edgecomb Gray HC-171	Urban Putty SW 7532
Everlasting 1038	Tres Naturale SW 9101
Gray Cloud 2126-60	Icicle SW 6238
Gray Mist 962, OC-30	Natural Choice SW 7011
Gray Owl 2137-60	Silverpointe SW 7653
Hale Navy HC-154	Charcoal Blue SW 2739
Horizon 1478, OC-53	Reserved White SW 7056
Kensington Blue 840	Denim SW 6523
Linen White 912, OC-146	Summer White 7557
Manchester Tan HC-81	Softer Tan SW 6141

Benjamin Moore	Sherwin Williams
Midnight Dream 2129-10	Tricorn Black SW 6258
Mountain Mist 868	Mountain Air SW 6224
Muslin 1037	Bisquit SW 6112
Nantucket Gray HC-111	Herbal Wash SW 7739
Natural Linen 966	Natural Tan SW 7567
Nimbus 1465	Agreeable Gray SW 7029
Natural Wicker 947, OC-1	Antique White SW 6119
Navajo White 947	Crisp Linen SW 6378
Pale Oak OC-20	Egret White SW 7570
Palladian Blue HC-144	Rainwashed SW 6211
Pewter 2121-30	Network Gray SW 7073
Putnam Ivory HC-39	Sundew SW 7688
Quiet Moments 1563	Sea Salt SW 6204
Revere Pewter HC-172	Sandbar SW 7547
Seattle Mist 1535	Worldly Gray SW 7043
Shoreline 1471	Big Chill SW 7648
Silver Chain 1472	Repose Gray SW 7015
Silver Gray 2131-60	Lullaby SW 9136
Silver Satin OC-26	Incredible White SW 7028
Smokey Taupe 983	Accessible Beige SW 7036
Stonington Gray HC-170	Colonnade Gray SW 7641
White Dove OC-17	Greek Villa SW 7551
Winds Breath 981, OC-24	Natural Linen SW 9109